DATE DUE

NOV 2 '07			

TILLIE OLSEN

A Study of the Short Fiction

A Selection of Titles from Twayne's Studies in Short Fiction Series

Twayne publishes studies of all major short-story writers worldwide. For a complete list contact the Publisher directly.

Twayne's Studies in Short Fiction

Gordon Weaver, General Editor
Oklahoma State University

Tillie Olsen
Photo by Leonda Finke © 1981

TILLIE OLSEN

A Study of the Short Fiction

Joanne S. Frye
The College of Wooster

TWAYNE PUBLISHERS
An Imprint of Simon & Schuster Macmillan
New York

Prentice Hall International
London   Mexico City   New Delhi   Singapore   Sydney   Toronto

Twayne's Studies in Short Fiction, No. 60

Copyright © 1995 by Twayne Publishers

Twayne Publishers
An Imprint of Simon & Schuster Macmillan
866 Third Avenue
New York, NY 10022

Library of Congress Cataloging-in-Publication Data
Frye, Joanne S., 1944–
    Tillie Olsen : a study of the short fiction / Joanne Frye.
        p.   cm.—(Twayne's studies in short fiction ; no. 60)
    Includes bibliographical references and index.
    ISBN 0-8057-0863-4 (alk. paper)
    1. Olsen, Tillie—Criticism and interpretation.   2. Women and literature—United States—History—20th century.   3. Short story.   I. Title.   II. Series.
PS3565.L82Z65   1995
813'.54—dc20   94-49320
                                                                                      CIP

10 9 8 7 6 5 4 3 2 1

Printed in the United States of America

For Ron

Contents

Preface

"Sometimes the young—discouraged, overwhelmed—ask me incredulously: 'You mean you still have hope?' And I hear myself saying, yes, I still have hope: beleaguered, starved, battered, *based* hope. Through horrors, blood, betrayals, apathy, callousness, retreats, defeats—in every decade of my now 82-year-old life that hope has been tested, reaffirmed. And more than hope: an exhaustless store of certainty, vision, belief . . ."[1] I begin in Tillie Olsen's own words, taken from the piece she wrote for *Newsweek*'s series of brief essays on decades of the twentieth century. Not surprisingly, Olsen was asked to speak for the 1930s. Also not surprisingly, she spoke, beyond the one decade, of her irrepressible hope and belief: formed in the 1930s, carried through the 1950s, reaffirmed in the 1990s.

Olsen's voice is very much integral both to her convictions and to history, the historical forces that have shaped her life and this century. So too with her fiction. Although most of her short fiction was written in the 1950s—that collected in *Tell Me a Riddle*—each piece opens out from that decade into the history of this century and the convictions of a writer who retains a powerful vision of human capabilities. Through those convictions she has found a language and a narrative form that speak to us still and that speak well beyond the particularities of any specific historical moment, even as they articulate the intertwining of history with language.

From my own moment in history, my own convictions, I have pursued this inquiry into Olsen's short fiction. My approach, too, is intertwined with history. I read and respond to her stories through perceptions shaped, for example, by my childhood in the 1950s—memories of assumptions about family and gender roles, of bomb drills in school, of increasingly widespread cultural consciousness of racism, of anticommunist rhetoric. I respond through my own personal feminism, my experiences of mothering two daughters, of sharing within my adult family life a strong working-class and union consciousness, of talking with my mother about her experiences of earlier decades in the century. I respond as a teacher and critic, working in a small liberal arts college, joining with numerous teachers and critics elsewhere in commitments to both textual and feminist analysis, to interdisciplinary work, to assessments of the intersections of language and culture, to the acts of teaching and writing. I respond as well through my ongoing commitments to feminist and social change, commitments I have in common with Olsen.

In each of these self-definitions, I respond as a personal reader, sensing commonalities with Olsen, despite our differences. But I respond, as well, as a member of a public audience, placed within history and culture. I participate in a community of readers, all of whom, despite personal and historical differences, respond to Olsen's language and to her complex human awarenesses. Together with one another and with Olsen we participate in an interactive partnership that is essential to the reading process.

The interactive partnership—of reader, writer, and narrative form—also helps to define the structure of this book. Part 1 is my own expression of this partnership: close readings of the five stories, centering on narrative form and developing from my awareness of Olsen as writer and myself as reader. The readings present an "argument" for the interaction between life experiences and narrative form but do not pretend to provide definitive interpretations, precisely because my understanding of literary form precludes the possibility of definitive answers and because Olsen's fiction similarly resists such answers.

Part 2 of the book offers another approach to the question of what nourishes the "life comprehensions"[2] that develop in the fiction. It asks, what are the "roots, sources, and circumstances" of the fiction? The response is a series of "conversations," distilled from discussions Olsen and I had in 1988 and 1990 about the circumstances that have shaped her life and her fiction. Finally, part 3 is an investigation of the critical response to Olsen's fiction over time and of the ways in which readers—especially "common readers"—are an essential and integral part of the way in which Olsen writes.

The book as a whole is premised on an understanding of literature that seems particularly appropriate to the short fiction of Tillie Olsen: that writer and reader are coparticipants in any insight that emerges from the narrative and that neither writer nor reader can be seen as an isolated individual separate from historical, cultural, linguistic, or literary context. Within this understanding of literature, textual analysis makes an important contribution, but it cannot be undertaken without drawing from linguistic, cultural, and biographical considerations as well. The aim is not only to enrich the reading of the fiction but also to develop a fuller understanding of how language and narrative form work: for the writer, the reader, and the culture.

Notes to Preface

1. Tillie Olsen, "The '30s: A Vision of Fear and Hope," *Newsweek*, 3 January 1994, 26–27.
2. Tillie Olsen, *Silences* (1978; New York: Delta/Seymour Lawrence, 1979); see, for example, 27.

Acknowledgments

I owe my deepest gratitude to Tillie Olsen herself, for her openness in conversation, her generosity of spirit, her love of language. I am extraordinarily grateful for the many hours she contributed to the development of this project, especially part 2. I am also grateful to my students at the College of Wooster, especially those in English 120: Language, Literature, and Culture, and in a number of women's studies classes. Through them I have been able to expand my understanding of the reader's contribution to the interactive partnership I make central to this book.

To the College of Wooster, I am particularly grateful for a research grant during the summer of 1988 and for a one-year research leave in 1989–90. I am also grateful to the Henry Luce III Fund for Scholarship at the College of Wooster for financial assistance with project expenses, as I am to the Beatrice M. Bain Research Group at the University of California-Berkeley for fruitful discussions and assistance during the 1989–90 leave year. I wish as well to express my appreciation to India Koopman, editor at Twayne, for her attentive reading and careful editing of the manuscript.

Finally, I am grateful to colleagues, friends, and family for their patience, support, and shared insights throughout the writing process. The value of these personal interactions is incalculable.

Acknowledgments

Press/Seymour Lawrence, a division of Bantam Doubleday Dell Publishing Group, Inc.

Excerpts from *Silences* by Tillie Olsen. Copyright © 1965, 1972, 1978 by Tillie Olsen. Used by permission of Delacorte Press/Seymour Lawrence, a division of Bantam Doubleday Dell Publishing Group, Inc.

Excerpts from *Silences* published by Delacorte, 1978, copyright by Tillie Olsen 1965, 1972, 1978; *Tell Me A Riddle* published by Delta/Dell, 1989, copyright by Tillie Olsen, 1956, 1957, 1960, 1961; "Requa I" published by Houghton Mifflin, 1971, copyright by Tillie Olsen 1971; "Dream-Vision" copyright 1984; "On the Writing of a Story: Tillie Olsen: Help Her to Believe" published in *Stanford Best Stories, 1956*; "The '30's: A Vision of Fear and Hope" published in *Newsweek*, 3 January 1994, by Tillie Olsen. All rights reserved. Used by permission.

"What's the Riddle . . . " from *The Complete Poems* by Randall Jarrell. Copyright © 1969 by Mrs. Randall Jarrell. Reprinted by permission of Farrar, Straus & Giroux, Inc. Also by permission of Faber and Faber Limited.

Part 1

THE SHORT FICTION

Introduction

British novelist Margaret Drabble has said, "most of us read books with this question in our mind: what does this say about my life?"[1] Though this is hardly the sole reason to read fiction or necessarily the most important one, it is a major one. Readers wonder: how can I better understand my life and the lives of those around me? How can I expand or deepen my awareness of human experience? How can I use the capacities of written language—expressive, communicative, performative—to escape a sense of isolation, of being alone in my own experience?

These questions are deceptively simple as they suggest to us that our reading will somehow "mirror" our experience and simultaneously "free" us from the isolation of unarticulated experience. And yet the urgencies behind them are real. Language, after all, is a social phenomenon, integral to human interaction and responsive to the need for shared perception. However naive it may seem to claim, in the face of contemporary linguistic theory, that language is an agent of human communication and that individual experience is susceptible to linguistic expression, readers do seem to begin with and return to this desire that fiction tell us something about our lives.

To readers of Tillie Olsen's short fiction, this urging has a particularly powerful resonance. For, whatever their own experience, Olsen's readers can scarcely escape the knowledge that these stories are connected with people's lives. Students, for example, have repeatedly told me how "real" the stories seem and how quickly their perceptions of their own lives become intertwined with their reading of the characters' lives. They find immediate connections with their own mothers, siblings, friends, and grandparents, with themselves and their social environments. And Olsen herself has suggested, in lectures and informal comments, that she has a strong commitment to making literature out of "life comprehensions,"[2] a commitment to writing about ordinary human experiences, particularly those of women and of working-class people—men, women, and children. For both Olsen and her readers,

3

these stories—or "pieces," as she prefers to call them[3]—suggest intimate knowledge of people's lives.

Not to feel alone in *her* own experience is apparently one of Olsen's driving motivations as both a reader and a writer. All of her life, she has been what she calls an "insatiable reader" (*Silences*, 118), and she found her own immediate prompting to write in the experience of reading in an old junkshop copy of the *Atlantic Monthly*, at age 15, Rebecca Harding Davis's *Life in the Iron Mills*. In Davis's novella about "slums, kennel-like dwellings, incessant labor" (*Silences*, 49), Olsen saw the message that "Literature can be made out of the lives of despised people." She also claimed the further message: "You, too, must write" (*Silences*, 117). Thus her reading made her aware at an early age that lives and commitments that mattered to her could be promptings to write, and her own writing developed from the wish to express her perceptions about the lives around her, perceptions that were then rarely seen in literature.

Born Tillie Lerner in 1912 or 1913—decisive birth records are unavailable—the second of six children in an immigrant family—working class, Russian, Jewish, atheist, socialist—Olsen's early experiences prepared her to perceive this gap in literature.[4] One of her principle sources of education was the public library. This was all the more crucial as economic necessity prompted her to leave school after eleventh grade. Books, read and pondered on her own, provided access to a world beyond her immediate environment, as they also stimulated her hunger to write about the people she saw around her.

These people, too, were a vital part of her early and continuing education. She speaks with pleasure of the sound of the voices of immigrants, the impassioned speeches of striking workers, the daily conversation of children, the Yiddish of her heritage. She also speaks with pleasure and pride of the roots of her activism: parents who had been active in the 1905 revolution against the czar in Russia, her father who served as state secretary of the Socialist party in Nebraska, the presence in her young life of such eminent socialist leaders as Eugene Debs. The experience of work itself, among other people, and of the effort to organize and empower working people, gave her further access to an understanding of lives rarely given written expression.

From these early roots, Olsen derived her commitment not only to writing but to writing those "life comprehensions" that were missing in much of her extensive reading. Her earliest publications were two poems and two pieces of journalism, all published in 1934, all written in the midst of her involvement in the Young Communist League and expressive of her commitments to class struggle and the articulation of working people's lives.[5] Her first (and only) novel, *Yonnondio*—a chapter of which was also published in 1934[6]—was begun during this same period. It is an active expression of these roots as it portrays the struggles for survival of an impoverished working-class family and the difficult growth of a young girl toward the hope of fruitful adulthood. The novel was not published until 1974, after the manuscript was rediscovered among old papers and prepared for publication by the writer—"that long ago young writer . . . in arduous partnership [with] . . . this older one"—having by then lived through four decades of rich and complex experience.[7]

Still committed to social change—active in union movements and educational and neighborhood issues as well as the political struggles of the American Left—Olsen devoted much of her life during these intervening years to wage-earning labor and to raising four daughters, in partnership with her husband, Jack Olsen. Her activism, too, was often connected with women's concerns, as she, for example, served as president of the CIO's women's auxiliary in the 1940s and worked on educational issues through the PTA. These multiple commitments led her to set aside her fiction writing in the 1930s and 1940s, despite her continuing sense of its importance to her.

Olsen's return to writing fiction in the 1950s, then, reflected the need to create from the midst of these complex circumstances, to seek again a way to express those "life comprehensions." In a lecture given in 1962, she describes this return:

> In the twenty years I bore and reared my children, usually had to work on a paid job as well, the simplest circumstances for creation did not exist. Nevertheless writing, the hope of it, was "the air I breathed, so long as I shall breathe at all." In that hope, there was conscious storing, snatched reading, beginnings of writing, and always "the secret rootlets of reconnaissance."
>
> When the youngest of our four was in school, the beginnings struggled toward endings. This was a time, in Kafka's words, "Like a squirrel in a cage: bliss of movement, desperation about constriction, craziness of endurance."
>
> Bliss of movement. A full extended family life; the world of my job (transcriber in a dairy-equipment company); and the writing, which I was somehow able to carry around within me through work, through home. Time on the bus, even when I had to stand, was

5

enough; the stolen moments at work, enough; the deep night hours for as long as I could stay awake, after the kids were in bed, after the household tasks were done, sometimes during. It is no accident that the first work I considered publishable began: "I stand here ironing, and what you asked me moves tormented back and forth with the iron." (*Silences*, 19)

In another lecture, given in 1971, she emphasizes this gap in her writing life:

As for myself, who did not publish a book until I was fifty, who raised children without household help or the help of the "technological sublime" (the atom bomb was in manufacture before the first automatic washing machine); who worked outside the house on everyday jobs as well (as nearly half of all women do now, though a woman with a paid job, except as a maid or prostitute, is still rarest of any in literature); . . . as distant from the world of literature most of my life as literature is distant (in content too) from my world:
   The years when I should have been writing, my hands and being were at other (inescapable) tasks. . . . (*Silences*, 38)

Like her earlier experiences with political activism and the concerns of the working class, her immersion in specifically female experiences now underscored her sensitivity to the unvoiced, to that life still "distant" from the world of literature.

Not accidentally, Olsen's primary work of nonfiction examines the circumstances that result in such silences as she experienced, circumstances that prevent writers from writing. *Silences* (1978), which begins with the two lectures from which I have just quoted, is an expression of that same "insatiable reader," aroused in childhood. Ranging across literary history and multiple cultures, it is written primarily in the words excerpted from other writers who articulate the multiple circumstances by which they have been silenced themselves. But it is also an expression of that committed writer, immersed in the lives of working people. Its dedication reads:

For our silenced people, century after century their beings consumed in the hard everyday essential work of maintaining human life. Their art, which still they made—as their other contributions—anonymous; refused respect, recognition; lost.

For those of us (few yet in number, for the way is punishing), their kind and descendants, who begin to emerge into more flowered and rewarded use of our selves in ways denied to them;—and by our achievement bearing witness to what was (and still is) being lost, silenced. (*Silences*, ix)

The recognition of omission, the need to articulate life comprehensions: these then are the recurrent life dynamics of a writer whose body of work is small but whose power is indisputable. These, too, are the dynamics that led Olsen to write the five short stories for which she is best known—"I Stand Here Ironing," "Hey Sailor, What Ship?" "O Yes," and "Tell Me a Riddle" (all published in *Tell Me a Riddle*, 1961/62), and "Requa I" (1970).[8]

"Circumstancing" the Writer

I wanted to understand more fully what made these powerful stories possible, despite Olsen's difficult circumstances, despite the negative historical context, which was especially hostile to her and her politics during the 1950s when Olsen wrote the four collected in *Tell Me a Riddle*. I wanted to understand something more of the way in which her context and her texts were related to each other. Knowing the hazards of simply reading texts as personal statements of a biographical subject—a hazard identified as an "intentional fallacy" by New Critics and made still more hazardous by poststructuralist denials of authorial "presence"—I was nonetheless convinced that Olsen herself could provide insights into how her texts were situated historically and lead me toward the kind of awareness necessary for a meaningful literary critical response. This is a commitment I share with many other feminist critics, identified by Cheryl Walker as a claim on relationship between women: "Though I may not wish to treat texts as the private property of their authors, I am unwilling to lose the vital links between women that only a practice which preserves authors in some form can provide."[9] Beyond that, I share a commitment to those same "vital links" between readers and writers—across possible divisions of gender and race and class—in pursuit of shared insights into history and language and culture and politics.

I therefore undertook a series of interviews with Olsen—distilled in part 2 of this book—asking with regard to each story: What were the circumstances of its writing and what effect did those circumstances have on its form? How did personal and historical context seem to shape the particular text in question? I knew I was not asking for simple "context," but I did not yet comprehend just how complex this relationship between text and context is. "Circumstances"—a crucial word for Olsen—became the centerpiece of the resulting interviews; indeed, in the first series of conversations she scarcely ever left this question. In her comments, everything in her prior life, everything in her experience of the world around her, everything in her understanding of history and human commitments—*everything* was a part of the circumstances of her writing.

When she talked, then, of circumstances, she never approached the simple glossing of dates and events as context; she talked, instead, of the past and the present, the personal and the historical, in wide, wandering, unpunctuated phrases that arced and rarely concluded. She talked of context as text, of text as context. She talked, for example, about her father's secret departure from czarist Russia under threat of imprisonment following the 1905 revolution. She talked of her own attendance at the Calvary Baptist Church in Omaha, Nebraska, where she fell in love with gospel music as a child. She talked of hearing the voices of immigrants, the distinctive uses of language, in socialist meetings when she was very young. She talked of her own struggles with motherhood—single motherhood, framed by impoverished struggle for survival during the infancy of her first daughter—and then shared parenthood, shaped by community participation and activist involvements in subsequent years. She talked of the bombing of Hiroshima and the personal pain of first seeing that newspaper headline. She talked of specific friends, of her children, of comrades in the Young Communist League, of PTA involvements, of specific terrors during the McCarthy years, and even of memories of political repression during the Palmer raid period—the Red Scare of 1919, when the U.S. attorney general, A. Mitchell Palmer, coordinated a campaign against American Leftists.

All of these—and many more memories and events and observations—were woven together with references to items from the previous day's San Francisco *Chronicle* and that week's *Nation*, to current events in a grandchild's schooling or a daughter's work life, to recent reading, to friends and neighbors in St. Francis Square, the cooperative apartment complex where she has lived for decades—and with references to characters and phrases from the stories that prompted our conversation. The past commingled with the present, the personal with the historical, the textual with the contextual; the common threads were woven into our conversation—the living presence of this person and the concrete texts of *Tell Me a Riddle* and "Requa I" that lay on the table between us—a continuous web of words spun in response to the questions of circumstances and form, history and story, context and text. Occasionally, she claimed a direct connection, as, for example, when she identified the "crack" in the form of "Tell Me a Riddle" and traced it to the intervention of four crucial deaths in her life. But she often merely pursued her own associative response to the question of circumstances, leaving to me the connections and interconnections that are part of her life history, part of the context for her stories' evident concern with racism or perceptions of children or knowledge of immigrant experiences.

In these conversations, Olsen drew many times upon the circumstance of socialist and feminist commitments, as she had in her earlier urgings to write the "life comprehensions" of people whose lives had not been written into literature. Although she never espoused the formulaic assumptions of what is usually called "socialist realism," her commitments are, in some sense, suggestive of a "proletarian realism" that prevailed when she began her writing career in the 1930s with the early sections of *Yonnondio*: "that fiction should show the sufferings and struggles and essential dignity of working-class people under capitalism and allow readers to see the details of their lives and work" (Rosenfelt, 388). By the time that she wrote the short fiction for which she is best known, this context was no longer available: "the concern for working-class life and for understanding the relationship between gender and politics was suppressed in the fifties as anti-communism, suburbanization, and consumerism controlled the environment," and Olsen, like many others, was "subjected to public attack" by the forces of McCarthyism.[10] But the commitment remained: to write of people's lives despite the difficulties of writing of lives that had not yet been conveyed in literary forms. Similarly, Olsen's feminist commitments persisted, especially her commitment to break the silence about female experiences and to provide, as she has said, "some sense of the lives of most women."[11]

The response to Olsen's fiction by an early and emergent feminist criticism in the late 1960s and early 1970s arose from a similar set of commitments: a concern for women's lives, for finding "female experience" in literary expression. Thus, especially during the 1970s, Olsen herself was active in initiating such projects as the Feminist Press's reclamation of the work of "lost" women writers, reissuing it in the hope of restoring to us a fuller understanding of women's lives in previous periods.[12] And Olsen's fiction was itself claimed as a powerful portrayer of lives previously unportrayed.

Language and Experience, Inseparable

The assumption, implicit in much of the early feminist criticism and in definitions of "proletarian realism," is that experience itself is somehow separate from language, there to be either represented or denied representation.[13] Although Olsen seems to embrace this assumption in some of her statements, her fiction and her more extended comments on the circumstances of her writing and on the difficulty of coming to voice suggest a much more complex interaction between language and experience. Throughout her writing life, begun in the 1930s, Olsen retained her powerful commitment to politics, to struggles for social change. But she did so in the knowledge that the language and the context for the writing of her own insights about human experience were not immediately available. I agree with Deborah Rosenfelt that *Yonnondio* came out of Olsen's struggle to write fiction that is political without being polemical and that this same dynamic also shaped Olsen's later fiction (Rosenfelt, 394). More crucially, however, the struggle was a struggle with language and form, a struggle to find a form that would respond to previously unarticulated "life comprehensions." For her, she says, the form always comes out of what she wants to get said; she is not a writer who sits down with it all worked out (see conversation 4). She is not, in other words, a writer who sets out to experiment with form or to write in deliberately new ways. Nor is she a writer who begins with an understanding or a clear plan "prior" to language. Rather she is a writer who begins with those "life comprehensions"; from this struggle arises the distinctive form of her short fiction, a form that is decidedly not polemical, a form that is also not overtly political, but a form that is nonetheless deeply shaped by political convictions.

Recent literary criticism has emphasized the difficulty of writing about the experience of people rarely portrayed in literature. It sees this difficulty as being shaped not just by politics and active directives but also and more complexly by the difficult intersections of language and experience. Feminist criticism, like much literary criticism in general, has grown skeptical of any assumption that experience is prior to language—there to be either represented or denied representation—and it has undertaken an active interrogation of the relationship between language and experience. Poststructuralist critics suggest that

10

experience is always already interpreted, never simply *there* prior to expression in language. Even historians are rethinking the relationships between language and experience, text and context, and asserting, for example, that "the context does not simply exist as a prelinguistic reality that language faithfully describes."[14] In this view any attempt to make women's lives or working-class lives central to narrative form—as Olsen has claimed to do—is at risk of being reassimilated into patriarchal constructions and prevailing definitions of the meaning of those lives, to the forms and linguistic expressions that are already prevalent in society. The experiences of such people—"complex, inchoate and not confirmed by outer reality,"[15] as Olsen says—cannot be simply conveyed in the language or literary forms of the dominant culture.

Virginia Woolf voiced the problem this way: " 'I have the feelings of a woman,' says Bathsheba in *Far from the Madding Crowd*, 'but I have only the language of men.' From that dilemma arise infinite confusions and complications. Energy has been liberated but into what form is it to flow? To try the accepted form, to discard the unfit, to create others which are more fitting, is a task that must be accomplished before there is freedom or achievement."[16] What Woolf calls dilemmas, confusions, and complications constitute, then, the underlying concern of much recent work in feminist literary criticism. In these terms, feminist energy has no previously accepted form; women's lives have no available language. And in these same terms, neither could the lives of most working people find comfortable voice in available forms.

The powers of language and of prior narrative forms are enormous. I agree with Roger Fowler—and numerous other theorists of literature and language—that one effect of language is to draw the individual into "conformity with the established systems of beliefs of the society into which s/he happens to be born" and that "all language . . . constantly drifts towards the affirmation of fixed, and usually prejudicial, categories."[17] Furthermore, this capacity of language for reinforcing conformity does make it risky to pursue "experience" as a basis for literary form, since "the politics of experience is inevitably [or at least may become] a conservative politics for it cannot help but conserve traditional ideological constructs which are not recognized as such but are taken for the 'real.' "[18] To claim to write of the experiences of women and the working class, in this view, is to succumb to prior societal beliefs about what those experiences are.

Narrative forms are similarly implicated in current constructions of reality, particularly through notions of what is "real." Traditional narrative authority, especially, is very much a function of communal standards, the shared assumptions of a culture, a kind of "general consciousness."[19] As Elizabeth Ermath defines it, its basic premise about reality is "not 'it exists, therefore we agree' but the reverse, 'we agree, therefore it exists' " (5); the very capacity to represent experience, to give it substance within a framework of "the real," requires a prior agreement. And the authority of "the real" is the authority of what people already "know" to be the case, the authority of a culture's commonly held assumptions about human experience— about women, about children, about work, about political convictions. This, again in Ermath's terms, is the authority of consensus, capable of making "invisible any view that seriously challenges it" (9).

Such agreement inevitably resides in the ideological framework of the author's and/or the reader's culture, and though a culture's ideology is scarcely univocal—indeed, it is more properly referred to in the plural as ideologies—its fundamental premises have a kind of cognitive priority; we can hardly help hearing the voices of prevailing ideas about communism or about feminism or about family even in language and narrative forms written in resistance to them. Both writers and readers, in other words, interpret their reality through the pattern of available cultural assumptions. Thus ideology, presenting itself "as 'life,' " is the basis for the "privileged epistemological standpoint of realism."[20] The traditional narrative voice of realist fiction—fiction that claims to represent people's actual lives—must apparently be grounded in the predominant values of that fiction's culture.

This, then, is the problem that haunts Olsen's fiction, that haunts critical response to her fiction: how to voice alternative perspectives in the language and literary forms of the prevailing culture, how to convey previously unvoiced "life comprehensions" when the context is unreceptive.

Olsen's comment to me in conversation about feminist criticism indicates that the problem persists and even that it must be addressed more insistently in the face of poststructuralist theories about language and reality: "It's important not to follow this recent deflection of focus—in feminist criticism—away from the actual, the real, the situation of most women."[21] I agree. But the questions remain. Can women interpret their own experience, or is experience itself always already interpreted? Is narrative form bound into the status quo by its conventions of language and form or even by its very textuality? Or can it, through a reshaping of the language of a male-dominated culture, participate in a commitment to understanding women's lives, a feminist commitment to a reshaping of the dominant culture?[22]

More immediately for my purposes here the question becomes: can Olsen's fiction provide us with an understanding of the lives—both male and female, adult and child—that has not prevailed in most literary forms? Or rather: how is it that her fiction has succeeded in conveying such understanding, despite the limitations of language and form? For readers repeatedly attest to the kind of personal connection with which I began my discussion. We *do* find in these fictional pieces new understandings of human lives, especially of the lives of women and working-class people—men, women, and children.

Perhaps, however, these questions are misleading in their implication that we must choose to see one or the other—experience or language, life or narrative, context or text—as somehow prior. Language does have a conservative force—as, for example, in our inclination to "see" things as we have heard them described—and narrative form often participates in this conservatism.[23] But language and narrative form are both also multiple. Cultures, too, are not singular but multiple, and can even be seen as "fora in which many voices are raised and dissensus rather than consensus prevails."[24] And fiction can be written beyond the apparently singular authority of one narrative voice. This is the quality of fiction that Mikhail Bakhtin associates with the modern novel when he calls it "polyphonic," a form in which "a *plurality of independent and unmerged voices and consciousnesses, a genuine polyphony of fully valid voices . . . with equal rights and each with its own world*, combine but are not merged in the unity of event."[25] He sees in the modern novel "the expression of a Galilean perception of language, one that denies the absolutism of a single and unitary language."[26] He also claims that language "is never unitary" (288) and instead serves as "a working hypothesis for comprehending and expressing reality" (61).

In my mind it is this quality of complex narrative forms that enables fiction such as Olsen's to include "confusions" and "contradictions"— to go beyond the apparently singular claim on given cultural "truths" of experience. Although language is often intertwined with what Fowler calls "prejudicial categories" (34), it is never bound by those categories, frozen into cultural assumptions about such crucial categories as gender, race, and class. Instead, as Fowler also says, both literature and criticism have important "roles in combating this tendency" (34). Similarly, Susan Stanford Friedman has made an appeal for "the nineties to be different" in its feminist criticism as we seek new forms

13

of political engagement in a post-poststructuralist environment (465). Significantly prior to poststructuralist inquiries into language and form, Olsen's distinctive narrative form emerged from this same set of tensions, insights, and commitments and from her own urgent desire to articulate the "life comprehensions" of "silenced" people.

Even her own weaving of words in the conversations I had with her, the web of personal history and linguistic self-presentation and awareness traced in language as we conversed—and the rich and dense verbal constructions that are the five published stories—suggest this intertwined understanding: a crucial resistance to separating experience and language, to seeing them as polar categories. In Olsen's own speaking and writing, neither experience nor language seems to have priority; neither can be seen as separate from the other. What emerges instead is a recognition that we might understand a good deal about both—about social forces *and* linguistic patterns—if we examine how they come together and why they are inseparable.

Closely centered in people's lives, Olsen's pieces, then, can never be seen as raw "transcriptions of life," even by those who think such transcriptions might be possible. Her fiction is not only "realistic" but also innovative in form, not only embedded in history but also textured by the sounds and structures and metaphorical possibilities of language. It is shaped by what she calls "the absorbing real need and love for working with words" (*Silences*, 29) in interaction with a commitment to finding words for that which has been previously silenced, a commitment to giving form to that for which previous forms are falsely constraining. And it is shaped by her finding in the complex and inchoate lives of women and working-class people the prompting toward a narrative form that disrupts culturally dominant assumptions while conveying experiential understanding. Olsen, I believe, shares Bakhtin's consciousness of the rich multiplicity of language itself and thus of narrative forms. She shares as well Woolf's insight, in the passage quoted above, that formal innovation is necessary: "To try the accepted form, to discard the unfit, to create others which are more fitting, is a task that must be accomplished before there is freedom or achievement."

From "Life Comprehensions" to "Fitting Forms"

Olsen has suggested that the extraordinary compression of her short fiction—noted by nearly every critic who writes about her work—has a strong experiential basis: "first because I have such an overload over the years of too much material" and second because of "problems with my time . . . taking it up and putting it down again."[27] This, of course, indicates a basis in her own immediate circumstances for writing: the multiple demands of her life as a worker, a mother, a member of a community, a participant in social change. But these same circumstances suggest an additional understanding of the experiential basis of form: "Written from, rather than just about working women's lives, the unique, wrenching angle of vision, the wonderful concentration of the writing which can catch in a phrase a whole lifetime's lost possibility, has been lived and worked for."[28] The actual life she has lived not only silenced her through its material circumstances—as she has attested in *Silences*—but also led her to create forms "more fitting" for developing insights about that life.

What, then, are these "more fitting" forms? In brief, these are the qualities that make Olsen's fiction more novelistic than most short stories and that simultaneously make them "pieces" in the other sense of the word: pieces of a larger understanding that requires an awareness of the historical world (conversation 2). These are the qualities that give Olsen's work the "polyphonic" quality that Bakhtin associates with the modern novel.[29] These are the qualities that differentiate her short fiction even from other innovative modern or contemporary short fiction, that make her stories instrumental in the development of contemporary short fiction. More than 30 years after the publication of *Tell Me a Riddle* in 1962, these stories are still being singled out for "advancing the art of short story writing." In a 1994 Dungannon Foundation announcement identifying her as recipient of the Rea Award, a major prize for short fiction, the selection committee—Charles Baxter, Susan Cheever, and Mary Gordon—attributed to her work "the lyric intensity of an Emily Dickinson poem and the scope of a Balzac novel,"[30] qualities that mark the power of these stories with each new reading.

Like much modern and postmodern short fiction, Olsen's form *is* "lyrical"—given to images and associative patterns—and her plots elliptical, able to include the range of Balzac even in their brevity. But the urgency of "getting said" what she wants to say, the urgency of expressing new insights into human experience and forceful convictions about human capabilities and cultural change, give distinctive power to her language and form. For she has found a way to resist entrapment in the limiting language of description and proclamation even as she retains experiential understandings and political convictions at the core of her writing. As Constance Coiner puts it: "Olsen's sociopolitical vision has enabled her to write what cannot be written" (281). And she does so through the complex intersections of language, form, and history.

A first feature of Olsen's form, then, is its resistance to plot: the compression of her pieces is such that whole life histories—Balzacian in scope—are sometimes evoked through scattered phrases, interjected references. Lives are not presented as either fragmented pieces or rounded wholes but rather as interconnected human experiences not susceptible to "plotting." Eva's life in "Tell Me a Riddle" is particularly exemplary, for the reader must wait until nearly the end of the novella to comprehend her village childhood and her early political activism. Furthermore, her life can only be "comprehended" in intersection with other lives, especially David's and Jeannie's, and hence must be rendered through those intersections. A similar effort of reader construction is essential for any of the pieces. Because the stories' concerns are not with plot but rather with the complex intersections that shape lives in powerfully interactive ways, they cannot be plotted. To plot such lives would be to oversimplify the workings of cause and effect and to put these lives at risk of seeming to fit into the dominant paradigms, stereotypes shaped by gender and class.

Similarly, the experiential grounding of each piece suggests the impossibility of "character analysis," of focusing on a single protagonist. Rather each character suggests a human history and a human depth that do not allow the usual separation of material reality and individual psychology. For these characters, experience is not a given, prior to language, or an enactment of personal identity; it is conveyed, as Teresa de Lauretis says, as "a *process* by which, for all social beings, subjectivity is constructed." Olsen's characters are, as de Lauretis suggests all of us are, shaped by social and historical realities, and their subjectivities exist as intersections of "material, economic, and interpersonal" forces.[31] In no way does Olsen's rendering of this insight make her characters any less "individual." It only ensures that we must confront the complex of conditions that contribute to the subjectivity of such characters as the mother-narrator in "I Stand Here Ironing" or Whitey in "Hey Sailor, What Ship?" or Stevie in "Requa I."

Finally, the narrative voice in these stories is not a single voice, suggestive of a single truth or definitive judgment—even in "I Stand Here Ironing," the one instance of first-person narrative. Rather the voice suggests human interaction, even community, and is always attentive to the qualities of spoken language, particularly to the interaction of sound and meaning in the workings of human community. It is multiple, multivocal, comprising often the voices of several members of a family or a range of cultural perceptions. The family dialogue in the middle of "O Yes" and the exchanges about racism between friends, black and white, voiced and unvoiced, exemplify the ways in which Olsen developed a polyphonic narrative voice to say what could not otherwise be said.

These three broad qualities of form, which I explore much more concretely in the remainder of part 1, all require an unusually active participation by the reader.[32] In stories like "O Yes" and "Requa I," we cannot be lulled along by our assumptions about plot and character or even reality; we cannot simply await the expected denouement or thematic resolution. Instead we must be constantly engaged in *constructing* a version of human experience in interaction with the words on the page, reaching our own insights into the concerns that center each piece. In Olsen's fiction—as in Woolf's—we can find those alter native forms by which to validate "our different sense of reality, to help raise [our] own truths, voice, against the prevalent" (*Silences*, 264) and thus to identify how we ourselves participate in our culture and might wish further to participate in changing that culture.

A thoughtful reading of Olsen's stories requires us to join her in realizing that language and experience are integrally related, that literature and history, text and context, exist in interaction. My own pursuit in the remainder of part 1 is to develop this understanding, an understanding to be found on "the boundaries between text and context." My purpose is not simply to restore context as part of my inquiry but rather to *probe* actively those boundaries.[33] Refraining from positing a fixed hierarchy of cause and effect, I seek the knowledge of how social forces and linguistic patterns interact, in Olsen's stories, in readers' responses. The textual analysis I undertake doesn't merely illuminate historical circumstance; nor does it exactly reveal "the behavioral codes, logics and motive forces of a whole society."[34] Instead, it negotiates those circumstances, those behavioral codes and the available linguistic codes, identifying the intersections between the particular and the general, the public and the private, the social and the linguistic, the text and its contexts.[35]

Olsen's stories, then, do derive from "life comprehensions"—ways of seeing human experience—even if we can never claim that they "comprehend" such lives fully. Especially centered in the comprehensions of family life and political activism, they are also written in language and form derived from those comprehensions—they enact the inseparability of language and experience. Readers, in turn, must take on this interactive understanding. The crucial response is not that the stories are *about* people but rather that they facilitate how we as readers think about people: about ourselves, our society, and the people around us. Our own reading of the stories will then help us, as active participants, to develop new understandings of work and community, of motherhood and childhood, of family life and public events, of gender and race and class. These will not be understandings delivered to us by an authoritative narrator or a decisive conclusion, but they will be understandings nonetheless, understandings derived in partnership with Tillie Olsen, the writer, and with narrative form itself.

"I Stand Here Ironing"

"I stand here ironing, and what you asked me moves tormented back and forth with the iron." The beginning of Tillie Olsen's "I Stand Here Ironing," as she says in *Silences*, is "no accident" (19). The context for her remark clarifies what she means by "no accident": her life circumstances required her, often, to do her thinking and her writing at the same time that she performed ordinary household tasks. But the beginning is also "no accident" in another sense: it is carefully crafted, responsive to the "life comprehensions" that inform it and evocative of the distilled narrative form that follows from it.

The craft of the narrative form is so effective that at first impression the narrative seems nearly artless, almost as if readers are simply being given a literal transcription of a mother's private thoughts, without mediation, as she reconstructs her daughter's past in an attempt to explain present behavior. Under the pretense of silent dialogue with a teacher or school counselor, the mother's first-person narrative moves chronologically through a personal past that is gauged and anchored by occasional intrusions of the present: "I put the iron down" (4); "Ronnie is calling. He is wet and I change him" (9); "She is coming. She runs up the stairs two at a time with her light graceful steps, and I know she is happy tonight. Whatever it was that occasioned your call did not happen today" (11). The present references keep us attuned to the immediacy of the mother's experiences; she is engaging in her private thoughts while simultaneously carrying on with household tasks and family interactions.

Her memories, too, at first suggest a lack of mediation, a reconstruction of lived experiences in chronological order not for the sake of dramatic story line but for the sake of her own probing of personal histories. Through these memories we gain what again seems like direct access to the experiences that weight her self-definition as Emily's mother: her difficulties as a young mother alone with her daughter and barely surviving during the early years of the Depression; her painful months of enforced separation from her daughter; her gradual and partial relaxation in response to a new husband and a new family as more children follow; her increasingly complex anxieties about her first child; and finally her sense of family equilibrium, which surrounds, but does not quite encompass, the early memories of herself and Emily in the grips of poverty. Similarly, we gain an apparently direct access to the experiences she sees as weighted in Emily's development: the stressful growth of the daughter from infancy through a troubled and lonely childhood, an alienating relationship to schools and friends, an unsettled adolescence—and finally development into the present nineteen-year-old, who "needs help," as the inquirer insists, but who has also found a strong inner resource in her gift for mime and in her sense of self.

In this initial reading, the form seems very simple: a mother, standing at the ironing board, performing a routine task, responds mentally to a difficult question put to her by a relative stranger. She silently rehearses a past that is "tormented" by difficult circumstances, as she proceeds with ordinary daily life.

A perception that the story is "autobiographical" reinforces the temptation to see it as an artless portrayal of "life." Like the narrator-mother in the story, Olsen did much of her thinking as she stood at an ironing board. Furthermore, her own immediate circumstances at the time of writing "I Stand Here Ironing" seem to have an almost direct correlation to the circumstances in the narrative. She was, for example, the mother of an older teenaged daughter as well as several younger children, the youngest of whom was born many years after the oldest. She had first become a mother at age 19, struggled singly to sustain herself and her daughter, experienced poverty and separation, come into a fuller family life with a new partner and additional children, and always struggled to balance the conflicting needs of a working mother. Her oldest daughter, Karla, "had not come up easy," as Olsen says she wished to explain to Karla's teacher; more crucially, however, she knew that Karla was a "viable" human being with her own life to live—a talented dancer, gifted in movement, a person capable of making her own way (personal communication, summer 1988).

Such parallels lay powerful claim on readers' imaginations, as does Olsen's assertion that this is the most autobiographical of her stories.[36] Indeed, many readers slip into the tempting equation of Olsen with the story's narrator. But the equation is false and distracting, for the literal parallels are inexact and decidedly not the real issue. Their interest resides, instead, in the recognition that the emotional power of the story derives from "life comprehensions." As Olsen wrote soon after completing it, "The emotional tone of the story came as the story became my own, not in the incidents in which the story was clothed, but in those emotions of a parent whose tasks are finished with a particular child."[37]

The compelling "reality" of the story, then, derives from its complex positioning at the intersection between "life" and "art," at the juncture between the urgencies of life understandings and circumstances and the complications of rendering those understandings into language. As it examines this intersection, my own analysis here becomes an inquiry into how this text emerges from its particular context and how its narrative form is necessarily both derived from and illuminating of that context.

Life Circumstances

In our conversations, Olsen suggested the conditions of her own motherhood experiences as the most crucial circumstances of this story's writing. She insisted on the primary importance of material conditions: "the writing time available to me; what is happening in my work and family life, and in the larger environment, in society" (conversation 1). And she suggested what insights emerge from motherhood as well as how difficult it is to find the circumstances in which one can articulate these insights. Most immediately for this story, she cited a slight easing of her family responsibilities: she had found a more comfortable child-care arrangement that gave her "comparative peace," and her eldest daughter was essentially grown while the youngest had entered first grade. She repeatedly situated her work on the story within her own particular circumstances as a mother: "written and rewritten and rewritten on the ironing board late at night. . . . The very timbre, rhythm of the piece, the back and forth movement as the iron itself moves" (conversation 1).

Olsen also suggested as a first specific prompting for the story a feature of the context that is not apparent to many readers: "the realization after Hiroshima that I had in some way to try to write again and to write on the side of life against death. . . . the dearness and transitory nature of life." In telling of her memory, she contrasted the feeling of her small daughter in her arms—"that wonderful feeling of the warm body surrendered against you"—and the horror of the newspaper headlines: "I . . . knew that death had entered the world in a way never had it been before" (conversation 1). That contrast between nurturing care and incomprehensible destruction, then, is a central part of the emotional context for the story: not only the mother's resistance to Emily's comment, "in a couple of years . . . we'll all be atom-dead" (11), but also the story's overall commitment to resisting the negative circumstances of the social environment in which Emily must make her way. In short, she claims as a crucial prompting for the story the understandings that evolve from living as a caring parent in the midst of societal circumstances that constantly threaten harm; and she makes such understandings integral to the entire narrative: a resistance, as a mother, to "the institutions and the people who have determining power" (conversation 1).

As a second specific prompting for the story, Olsen cited a different and more obviously personal situation: one night she stayed up nearly all night talking with a friend whose son, Freddy, had been picked up by the police and who needed to appear in juvenile court the next day to "explain" the circumstances of Freddy's life.[38] From this experience Olsen became acutely aware of the difficulties of trying to communicate one's life circumstances to authorities who lack the context for understanding: "the difference between the way you're judged from the outside and the true reality. I wanted to write those realities in a way to *inform* the kind of people who had the power to take away one's child" (conversation 1). As she proceeded with writing the story, she came closer to integrating details from her own experience, "borrow[ing] externals from our daughter who was that age" ("Writing," 135). But the story itself was not her own or her daughter's except in the "life comprehensions" that were deep among its roots.

The narrator-mother's torment, then, has the weight of lived experience, and her narrative has clear connections to the lives of many women as well as to Olsen's own life. But however frequently they may occur, these experiences have rarely been part of literature: the dailiness of many women's lives, the anguish of parental responsibility in an unsupportive society. One of the shocks in an initial encounter with "I Stand Here Ironing" is the actual rendering of a mother's voice. This is a voice both familiar and strange, both immediate and alien. As readers, we might or might not pause to ponder this contradiction, but we almost certainly experience some version of it. For all of us have heard not only a mother's voice but many mothers' voices; we cannot move through daily encounters in public and private places without hearing choruses of such voices: nurturing, cajoling, berating, admonishing, instructing, explaining. Yet we have almost never *read* a mother's voice, sustained for the length of a story, telling her own experiences, giving her own perspective on the world around her.[39] The narrative voice in "I Stand Here Ironing" communicates directly with us, as a voice we might encounter in one of those public or private places in which we spend our days. Simultaneously, it communicates deeply with us as a voice we have rarely heard in literature and hear now with the power of a voice released from silence.

The unliterariness of the experience is brought home within the story itself when Emily says to her mother: "Aren't you ever going to finish the ironing, Mother? Whistler painted his mother in a rocker. I'd have to paint mine standing over an ironing board" (11). Her light-hearted irony reminds us: sons may paint their mothers, especially in repose, but we do not think of women's daily tasks as literary subject matter and even less do we think of mothers as narrators of literary forms. Mothers, in short, are more likely to be images than to be active narrative agents. To portray these unfamiliar literary experiences, the narrative must therefore do much more than simply "record" what happens or might have happened. It must instead develop its own form, its own context, and its own voice by which to make the experience both compelling and "real."

What enables this voice to speak here? What circumstances prompted this narrative form to emerge as early as 1953–54 when we still feel the shock of its newness four decades later?

"And all that time I was ironing too," Olsen remarked in speaking of her late-night conversation with Freddy's mother (conversation 1). Slightly earlier in our conversation, she referred to "I Stand Here Ironing" as "I Stand Here Writing," a slip of the tongue, as I note there, that neither of us noticed at the time but one that suggests the powerful mental links between ironing and writing: the deep processing of life experiences that she associates with both.[40] This slip, then, becomes a suggestion for how the story moves beyond simple life parallels, either Olsen's or her friend's, and toward its own distinctive narrative form. For the real issue here is not the question of how to narrate literal life events—how to tell Karla's story or Freddy's—but rather how to understand, how to communicate inchoate life comprehensions, how to shape human circumstances into narrative forms that evoke the complexity of people's lives and elude the available cultural constructions of those lives. Who *is* Emily? How did she come to be who she is and how might she be helped toward future growth? How *are* we to understand "all that compounds a human being" (12)? The question itself is "tormented" and cannot be answered by any simple linear construction of life events.

Constructing a Maternal Narrative

Because the question cannot be answered simply, we are again brought to the realization that the narrative form cannot be simple. Rather it is shaped to the requirements of the human understanding that is always at stake in creating a life history, as it is always at stake in parenthood itself. But more than that, the story reveals the ways in which narrative construction might benefit from the insights of parental understanding.[41] It uses the unfamiliar narrative voice of the mother to convey "unliterary" comprehensions of women's and children's lives, and it does so with the narrative self-consciousness that is itself integral to the life comprehensions it conveys. The voice of the thoughtful mother-narrator is thus both an unusual literary subject matter and a powerful narrative innovation.

The process by which Olsen arrived at this voice and this form illuminates the complex interaction between experience and story. Shortly after writing "I Stand Here Ironing," she published a brief description of the process that lay behind its writing. In this essay, she describes the movement away from the initial prompting of the anticipated interview with the probation officer and her shift to "a school setting": "Give it a school setting, drop the trouble with the authorities, focus on the growing human being, make it a mother-counselor interview and use flashbacks" ("Writing," 134). She then went on to tell of her dissatisfaction with this resolution, not because of a dislike for the change of setting and content but because of a difficulty with the narrative voice: "That counselor kept getting in the way of the story with the necessity of creating him and his school background properly, and with the questions he asked. Just as a help to me in the whittling down of the counselor, I thought of writing down what the parent would have to say and think—in the first person. Immediately it felt right. I saw it was the mother, the one who cared so intensely, who must tell it" ("Writing," 134–35).

Olsen's description of the process emphasizes two key points about her narrative choices. First, she came to the realization that the mother herself is the most appropriate narrative voice, the one who "cared so intensely" and the one most in touch with "the growing human being." Second, she transformed the audience from a potentially hostile probation officer to an increasingly sympathetic school counselor, whom she defined as the projected audience in parentheses: "(Here I thought of an actual person, my daughter's English professor, the kind of person who would summon out of the mother the best kind of 'sifting' she could do. Important not in the reading but the writing of the story that it be said to some one who could care and understand.)" ("Writing," 135; see also conversation 1). Only with a projected audience responsive to the mother's narrative complexities and life comprehensions could Olsen effectively write the story of the growing human being. In other words, the explaining cannot be accomplished unless the anticipated audience is sufficiently prepared to "hear."

Olsen claims that this projected audience is important only to the writer, not to the reader (see also conversation 1). In one sense, this seems accurate: the reader needs only to sense a sympathetic ear, not to know whose ear it is. But in another sense, the projected audience *is* important, precisely because the reader needs to be part of that sympathetic context; like the listener that Olsen imagined, we too must be "sensitive listeners" (Faulkner, 119). Civil authorities—teachers and counselors and officers of the court—are rarely familiar with the pertinent "realities." Nor are they usually prepared to hear a fully contextualized explanation. Readers, too, often lack the previous experience of pertinent realities that might make an explanation comprehensible—that is, they have rarely read about the kinds of human experiences at stake in this narrative: about routine tasks such as ironing or about a mother's need to interpret her daughter's difficult growth. But unlike most civil authorities, readers may want to "hear" a fully contextualized explanation, particularly if they realize that their own lives do not quite match the comprehensions they most frequently encounter in literary form. Like Olsen, they are likely to have experienced "the difference between the way people were in books and the way they were as I saw them" (personal communication, summer 1988)—a difference not unlike the difference between people's lives and the expectations held by authorities. For either audience, the narrator—the person who explains—must simultaneously convey realities and reshape the expectations of the audience.

In this context, the act of constructing narrative—"I Stand Here *Writing*"—supersedes the act of ironing for Olsen, who is simultaneously the friend and the mother, the writer and the perceiver. As such she enacts the cognitive processes by which human beings come to terms with their lives: "And all that time I was ironing too"—working out with a friend, as she later worked out in fictional form, a response to the "tormented" question of how to comprehend the development of a young person within a given set of social and economic circumstances.

The mother is, of course, a privileged narrator of her daughter's life experiences; she is, after all, the only person to have been present throughout her daughter's 19 years. But even she is inevitably separate from her daughter, from the life that has been lived "outside," "beyond" her ken. The mother's insistence on this separateness removes any sense of omniscient authority from her understandings and from her narrative voice, but it creates an alternative source of authority: the teller who gathers the facts and empathetically constructs a narrative coherence that is revealing though always hypothetical. Searching for causal connections, she says, for example, "I think I said once: 'Why don't you do something like this in the school amateur show?' " (10) and follows with the telling of Emily's first successful performance. Each construction, then, is hypothetical; each is subject to the fallibility of memory, the incompleteness of information, and the uncertainty of causation.

Consider again the opening of the story, this time not as simple transcription but instead as response to both a parental and a narrative problem. The initial sentence immediately invokes a dual time frame, both past and present, and a necessarily double consciousness. It begins with present action—"I stand here"—and projects the dialogue that prompts the narrative construction—"what you asked me." Following from that, the subsequent paragraphs confirm the dialogical structure: not only do we have the presentation of the background question— presumably posed via a telephone call from teacher or counselor—and thus the projected dialogue with the external voice but also the sense of the mother's internal dialogue. Her first responses are addressed to the "you": "You think because I am her mother I have a key, or that in some way you could use me as a key? She has lived for nineteen years. There is all that life that has happened outside me, beyond me." She follows with the increasingly internal dialogue with herself, between past and present, between self and self: "And when is there time to remember, to sift, to weigh, to estimate, to total? I will start and there will be an interruption and I will have to gather it all together again" (1). In this way, the story asserts from the outset that narrative construction of past experience is necessarily tentative and arbitrarily shaped by present circumstance.

The opening page thus immerses us in a self-conscious narrative process that persists throughout the story—an immersion that takes place not through any metafictional devices but through the mother's own experiences. The interaction between daily tasks and mental constructions of events necessitates this self-consciousness; this same interaction facilitates the comprehensions of human development.

Interruptions are an obvious manifestation of how this interaction works. The initial statement—"I will start and there will be an interruption"—conveys an experience common to anyone who has been responsible for children. What parent is unfamiliar with the ever-present possibility of interruption? As Olsen says in *Silences*: "More than in any other human relationship, overwhelmingly more, motherhood means being instantly interruptible, responsive, responsible. Children need one *now* (and remember, in our society, the family must often try to be the center for love and health the outside world is not). . . . It is distraction, not meditation, that becomes habitual; interruption, not continuity; spasmodic, not constant toil" (18–19).

But that same awareness defines the narrative context required for understanding how children grow: the interruptions remind us continually that new experiences follow old ones, that children grow and develop and intrude on daily life with their own perceptions as well as their own needs. Ronnie, with his cry, his need for a dry diaper, for example, first intrudes his insistent presence into his mother's thought processes, interrupting her narrative thread. This leads her to a general observation about her own changing circumstances: "That time of motherhood is almost behind me when the ear is not one's own but must always be racked and listening for the child cry, the child call." The observation is a painful one, as it reminds us of how the mother is denied the opportunity for pleasurable solitude, for "meditation" and "continuity." But it also speaks to the recognition that circumstances do change. Furthermore, the interruption itself has positive effects, creating for her an island of comfort as she comforts him—"I hold him, looking out over the city spread in charcoal with its soft aisles of light"—and finally suggesting an insight that not only gives comfort back to her but also redirects her narrative in important ways: "'Shoogily,' he breathes and curls closer. . . . *Shoogily*. A funny word, a family word, inherited from Emily, invented by her to say: *comfort*" (9).

From this interruption, the mother returns to her narrative with new insight and a shift of emphasis, thus highlighting the intersections between maternal experience and narrative form. Immediately prior to Ronnie's call, she had been pondering the self-consciousness of adolescence, "the unsureness . . . the constant caring—what are they thinking of me?" (9). Returning to her thoughts once Ronnie has fallen asleep, she does not lose that concern, but she redirects the narrative line: "In this and other ways [Emily] leaves her seal, I say aloud. And startle at my saying it. What do I mean? What did I start to gather together, to try and make coherent?" (10). What Ronnie's interruption has reminded her of is Emily's presence in the world, Emily's strong sense of self, her capacity to "leave her seal." Emily is not, in this context, merely an unsure adolescent, constantly judged from the outside; rather she is an integral person, able to help shape the world around her. After the mother's self-questioning, she returns to the narrative thread of "the terrible, growing years" and insists that Emily suffered for lack of her mother's time—that she "set her seal" because she "had to." Nonetheless, the interruption and the mother's interrogation of her own meaning have broken that narrative thread and suggested an alternative rendering of the same information. The interruptible narrative voice yields an awareness not likely in a concentrated and consistent perspective.

Emily's arrival home—the intrusion of her physical presence into the narrative that is being constructed around her—represents most insistently the value of interruption for narrative construction. When she comes in, her mother has been thinking about the neglect of her talent: "the gift has as often eddied inside, clogged and clotted, as been used and growing" (11). But the actual interaction with Emily produces a different tone: "She is so lovely. Why did you want me to come in at all? Why were you concerned? She will find her way" (11). Again, this is not a final judgment and is not alone a sufficient rendering of Emily's "story." But it is an important refusal of the "clogged and clotted," of the notion that Emily is permanently scarred by a life of neglect or denial. And it juxtaposes two possible understandings of Emily's present self, of her beauty and her talent, in such a way that neither has the authority of absolute truth. The "mother's own voice" merges the awareness of experience and form in a complex rendering of a child's life.

Throughout the story, each interruption operates similarly to create a shift of emphasis or an alternative interpretation, reminding us that the narrative is only an interpretation of events, never a total rendering of them. In this way the story never becomes "fixed." Each new gathering together reminds us that coherence itself depends on how one interprets initial experiences, that wholeness is not the most crucial narrative value.

Similarly, the repeated use of questions and the denial that there is any single "key," even within the mother, derives from the mother's perspective and reinforces the notion that the narrative is a hypothesis, one possible answer, not an actual transcribing of life events. The first series of questions seem to foreclose possibility, being posed more as answers to the telephone inquiry than as actual questions: "what good would it do?" or "when is there time . . .?" (1). But subsequent questions follow from the mother's first real question to herself: "Why do I put that first? I do not even know if it matters, or if it explains anything" (2). The issues of selection, order, and meaning are the defining issues of narrative form: which facts "belong" in the story, which facts lead to other facts, which ones are significant to the understanding one is trying to achieve? By raising such questions explicitly, the mother makes us aware of the tentativeness of her own construction. By raising them in the context of probing her own memory, seeking poignantly to understand her own daughter's development, she draws directly on the understandings implicit in parental experience and reminds us that these narrative processes are central to human living.

When we turn our attention to the use of questions in the narrative, we can see that the use of chronology as an ordering device is merely incidental: the primary ordering of the narrative follows from the mother's self-questioning instead of from any sense that one event leads inevitably to the next. Questions such as "Where does it come from, that comedy?" (4) or "without money or knowing how, what does one do?" (11) have no easy answers, perhaps no answers at all. But they open the narrative to interactive response, to speculation based on the insights drawn from memory. These questions are not completely unlike Emily's own question—"Why, Mommy?"—asked to try to understand why the boy she liked "still liked Jennifer better'n me" (7–8). That is, they are questions that have no obvious answers, and they are questions whose possible answers are often painful. But the questions that drive the narrative *are* unlike Emily's own question—which the mother understands is the "kind of question for which there is no answer" (8)—precisely because the narrative itself pursues possible responses to them, responses that weave their way between the difficulties of circumstances and the capacities of human growth.

The interruptions and the questions, then, become primary prompt-ers for the nonlinear structure of the narrative, a structure that probes beyond "what seems obvious on the surface" toward "what is not obvious" (8–9) by using parental experience itself as basis for a more effective narrative form. In her comments on the crafting of the story, Olsen emphasizes the importance of narrative selection and of deep knowledge of her characters: "It was a very long story. It filled a paper bag with what was cut afterward, . . . I learned in cutting the dangers (and strengths) of borrowing too directly from life unless there is exact knowledge of what one is trying to say. I used as a guide for selection what would best show 'all I did or did not do, what should have been and what cannot be helped' and 'all that life that has happened outside me, beyond me' " ("Writing," 135). The two thematic concerns—the mother's anguish about societal harms and the daughter's increasingly independent existence—emerge as far more crucial guides for narrative selection than any concern with plot or narrative chronology.

The initial summary of past events that I provided thus falsifies the story's actual structure, its concern with connections over time, by blurring these thematic emphases and by neglecting to address the central attention the story gives to process and to interactive response. Let one passage serve to exemplify the basis of these narrative choices:

> But never a direct protest, never rebellion. I think of our others in their three-, four-year-oldness—the explosions, the tempers, the denunciations, the demands—and I feel suddenly ill. I put the iron down. What in me demanded that goodness in her? And what was the cost, the cost to her of such goodness?
>
> The old man living in the back once said in his gentle way: "You should smile at Emily more when you look at her." What *was* in my face when I looked at her? I loved her. There were all the acts of love. (4)

Instead of a progression, what this passage suggests is a web of interrela-tionships: comparisons between Emily and the other children, the interjection of the mother's present response into the narrative of the past, the searching for possible causes and interpretations. The memory of the old man's comment has no specific time frame but is instead a part of the mother's recurrent self-questioning: "What in me demanded that goodness in her?" and "What *was* in my face when I looked at her?" And her answer is a pervasive context, not a narrative event: "I loved her. There were all the acts of love." Considered in light of a parental selection process, the remembered incident takes its place within a deep understanding of a child's development through interaction with her circumstances rather than being a simple incident within an overall chronology or clearly traceable causal pattern.

The mother's questions and responses, her present circumstances and her memories, are then part of an overall claim to her own agency as narrator and as parent: her capacity to select, to describe, and to interpret based on a much richer and more empathetic knowledge than would be available to any other narrator. As a mother, she responds to immediate circumstances and interruptions; she pursues alternative understandings; she investigates possible networks of causality in the past. Resisting both the impositions of traditional coherence and the simple renderings of a monological voice, the narrative becomes an internal dialogue capable of rendering vividly the interactions between human hopes and possibilities and the constraints set by circumstances.

On the one side of this interaction, the narrative takes as its underlying grid the immutable force of circumstances. It recognizes the power of material conditions: war, poverty, nuclear threat, economic depression, inadequate child care, insufficient time; these are the circumstances that "could not be helped." It recognizes the power of institutional authority in the lives of ordinary working people: the "they" of the medical establishment that tells a mother how often to feed her baby, the "they" of the clinic that dictates a mother's separation from her child, the "they" of the convalescent home that denies children even the possession of their own small personal "things," the "they" of an unresponsive social order, including those teachers who haven't time or insight and the counselor who inquires without really understanding. These, too, are beyond the reach of the mother's efforts.

But the narrative does not yield control to those circumstances. From its dialogical form emerges the other side of this interaction, the capacity to act in response to the immutable, to develop despite circumstances that impede development. For Emily, "what should have been" is not attainable, but the process of the mother's telling reveals some sense of what might yet be. For this, the dialogical structure is particularly fruitful, for it enables the mother to look back at the controlling power of what could not be helped, and yet to discover what can still be changed. Hence each of the key moments at which the present voice and circumstance of the mother break through the narrative coherence of the past becomes an opening for alternative understanding, for identifying capacities to change. This is the central significance of such insights as "she leaves her seal" and "She is so lovely": Emily is not bound by the negations she has experienced.

Because the mother's narrative voice *is* dialogical and is shaped to the distinctive qualities of her own circumstances, she is able to convey Emily's experiences beyond the fixity of expected narrative form, beyond the "unity" or "identity" of traditional understandings of character. Instead, we come to see Emily in context and to recognize her multiple ways of being. When the mother recalls the first performance she herself was able to attend, the recollection is centered in this multiplicity: "I only recognized her that first moment when thin, shy, she almost drowned herself into the curtains. Then: Was this Emily? The control, the command, the convulsing and deadly clowning, the spell . . ." (11). *Is* this Emily? Or rather *who is* Emily: the introvert or the performer, the school child who is "not glib or quick" (8) or the teenager "with her light graceful step" (11), the "beautiful baby" who "blew shining bubbles of sound" and "loved motion, loved light, loved color and music and textures" (2) or the two-year old "walking quick and nervous like her father, looking like her father, thin, and dressed in a shoddy red that yellowed her skin and glared at the pock marks" (3)? Is she the child with a face "closed and sombre" or the performer with "fluid" face (4)? All, of course, are Emily, but no one of these images can alone represent the whole Emily. Hence the significance of her gift for pantomime: she is visibly and perpetually transforming herself before our very eyes; she is both all of these selves and none of them.[42]

Metaphor and Metonymy

The insights of the narrative voice, derived especially from the insights of the narrator's experiences as a mother, are underlined and reinforced by the story's embedded metaphorical insights.[43] Because the language of the story is so immediate and seems so experiential, readers often tend to think of its primary metaphor as the directly claimed one of the iron as the force of circumstances: "Only help her to know—help make it so there is cause for her to know—that she is more than this dress on the ironing board, helpless before the iron" (12). This metaphor, of course, lays direct claim to the experiential context of ironing, as it does to the thematic concern with the power of circumstances and the power of people to resist and to change.

But embedded in the story are other metaphorical insights, such as the intersections between pantomime and transforming selfhood, suggested above, or the pervasive concern with nourishment and food pointed out by several critics,[44] or the concern with growth and blossoming, present in the final paragraph as well as throughout: "Let her be. So all that is in her will not bloom—but in how many does it? There is still enough left to live by" (12). What is particularly intriguing is the story's capacity to intertwine its metonymic qualities with its metaphoric depths: its powerful surface of "realism" is never disturbed by its complex claims on metaphorical insights. Thomas McLaughlin asserts the traditional distinction between metonymy and metaphor: "Metonymy places us in the historical world of events and situations, whereas metaphor asserts connections on the basis of a deep logic that underlies any use of words."[45] But in Olsen's fiction—especially as evident in this story—it seems to me that the distinction is a false one: here the historical world itself yields and intertwines with a "deep logic." Furthermore, this intertwining of the metonymic and the metaphoric is yet another way of drawing on the insights of parental experience to shape the narrative's capacity to say what cannot easily be said in a particular cultural environment.

To exemplify this process, I want to explore briefly the ways in which a repeated concern with "eyes" draws together the story's metonymic concerns—its textures of realism and its connections with our own possible experiential realities—and the story's metaphorical concerns with the determining power of circumstances and the human capacities to grow and change and resist. In doing so, the concern with "eyes" also further emphasizes the intersections between the distinctive experiences of motherhood and the distinctive capacities of this narrative voice.

The mother, in fact, is authorized as narrator in large measure because she has been the primary observing presence in Emily's life. Her eyes have always been the most watchful, the most attentive to the transformations in Emily that are the ostensible concern of the story's progression. Her first recollection, taking us back to Emily's infancy, derives from her parental role as observer: "She was a beautiful baby. The first and only one of our five that was beautiful at birth. You do not guess how new and uneasy her tenancy in her now-loveliness. You did not know her all those years she was thought homely, or see her poring over her baby pictures, making me tell her over and over how beautiful she had been—and would be, I would tell her—and was now, to the seeing eye. But the seeing eyes were few or nonexistent. Including mine" (2). As the initial paragraph in Emily's narrative history, this recollection confers the narrator's status on the mother—the primary observer of her daughter's experiences—and simultaneously acknowledges her insufficiency in that role. She is the primary "seeing eye" even as she realizes that she could not always be that seeing eye. She is also the primary explainer, not only to the inquiring "you," who is invoked twice in this short paragraph, but also to Emily herself, telling what was, what is, and what would yet be. Through the mother's observation, we have access to the protean sense of self that is necessary to Emily's performances; through the mother's observation, we recognize that a protean self is inherent in every human being's growth from infancy to adulthood. This too is an insight grounded in parental experience, learned through participation in a child's developing life.

Even as they help to define the mother's narrative presence, her "eyes" are a part of a metaphorical pattern that shapes the narrative itself according to constantly shifting process rather than fixed definition. The eyes observe multiplicity and can never *see* everything that might be pertinent to a full rendering of Emily's "story." The eyes also express emotion, but never unambiguously. Again: "What *was* in my face when I looked at her?" (4). They acknowledge that appearance is both unstable and an incomplete expression of selfhood but also that what we see is one of our primary means of interpreting other human beings.

The eyes are thus a part of the story's other metaphorical patterns that invoke change, process, flexibility, and resistance to fixity: growth, nourishment, and interaction rather than rigidity, hunger, and separation. The food at the convalescent home—"runny eggs" and "mush with lumps" (7)—is part of the same pattern of cultural denial as the "invisible wall 'Not To Be Contaminated by Parental Germs or Physical Affection' " (6): neither nourishes or sustains growth even as both pretend to be part of an atmosphere of convalescence. Similarly, the breast feeding according to the decree of the clock denies the full nourishment that might be possible because it is part of the "rigidity" of what the authorities dictate in the books (2). Emily's pantomime expresses the same resistance to rigidity as does the mother's narrative:

she has no single "key" to Emily's character; what she has is an understanding of human development through possibility despite the blighted context of the larger culture: "So all that is in her will not bloom—but in how many does it? There is still enough left to live by. Only help her to know—help make it so there is cause for her to know—that she is more than this dress on the ironing board, helpless before the iron" (12).

This final claim, as both metaphor and metonymy—both symbolic expression and lived experience—becomes the distilled claim of parental insight: threatened always by a culture that denies and that will not allow full blossoming—"She is a child of her age, of depression, of war, of fear" (12)—a child nonetheless will grow and change, if helped to know her own capacities to act for herself in resistance to helplessness. The story's final claim also becomes the distilled claim of narrative insight. Constructed in multiplicity through a complex recognition of how external forces shape but do not fully determine selfhood, Emily's "character" is not bound into a simple linear development; the mother's narrative web enables us to see that Emily need not be "helpless before the iron."

This process of both describing and reshaping, then, is the narrative process of "I Stand Here Ironing," an interactive process that conveys to us experiences that are unusual in literary form even as it opens those experiences to alternative interpretations. For the requirements of this dual-narrative construction are strikingly similar to the requirements of nurturant parental understanding. In neither case can the interpreter afford to deny the power of material and public constraints, but in both cases the process requires active construction of events in the effort to enable change.

"I Stand Here Ironing" was written in 1953–54, a time of powerful cultural emphasis on nuclear family life, a time of denial of movements for social change—issues about which I will have much more to say in my analyses of the other three stories in *Tell Me a Riddle*. But even in this first and "simplest" narrative, the form must negotiate the cultural silencings of the period, must find ways to voice insights that could not be easily voiced in that period of entrenched individualism, of McCarthyism, of buoyant nationalism.[46] Olsen cited as the story's "failure" its difficulty in making clear her own social and political insights: "the meaning of that cry, that summons of the last sentence"—the capacity of human beings and human societies to grow and change. And she said that this "failure" derives from the fact that "the context had, has not been developed for that comprehension" (conversation 1). But the story does not, in fact, fail to convey this insight, in part because it is so artful in drawing together its own knowledge of the period and its own narrative insights. Instead it conveys to us what Olsen calls maternal "anguish"—not maternal "guilt"—as part of a larger human understanding of the need for social change, for general societal awareness that takes into account the requirements of growing children and caring adults. It does so with special power because it draws on the comprehensions of motherhood and interweaves them with the capacities of a distinctive narrative voice. It does so because it is crafted so precisely to the "life comprehensions" it seeks to convey.

"Hey Sailor, What Ship?"

Speaking of the phrase that provides both title and refrain for "Hey Sailor, What Ship?" Tillie Olsen has suggested its power as music, as poetry, and still more as meaning: "a way of phrasing to myself that question about the place, the direction, of human lives I was encountering" (conversation 2). The question has both beauty and power, particularly as it is embedded in a distinctive rendering of human lives. But it also expresses acute pain: what direction *were* human lives taking in that historical moment in the 1950s? how might we—writer and readers together, whatever our historical context—see the need for place and direction in our lives and renew our valuing of the lives around us?

At Stanford University on a creative writing fellowship in 1955–56, Olsen awed her classmates with the power of this story when the instructor, Dick Scowcroft, read it aloud in the first class session. Its power must have stood out not only as the expression of a writer more experienced than most of the others present but also as the expression of a life lived passionately amidst the efforts of ordinary human beings to create change. Here was a story that embraced its experiential background, claimed its connection to human lives as the pressure that impelled the writing: "I was already so full of what had to be said that wasn't being said—that peculiar pressure." And behind that pressure lay the recognition that the records of human experience have been significantly distorted by the dominant value systems of the culture: "who writes and who doesn't, who gets the right to leave the evidence or to feel their experiences are the important ones."[47] The lives of people like Whitey and Helen and Lennie, like Jeannie and Carol and Allie, are part of that pressure, experiences that have not been given voice, people who have not been granted the right to leave their own evidence in the chronicle of human history.

Chronicling the 1950s

Olsen wrote "Hey Sailor, What Ship?" between 1953 and 1955, in a cultural environment that actively rejected many of her political values and denounced her political activities. Repression and suspicion prevailed and worked to isolate people like Olsen—who had lifelong commitments to social change and socialist politics—from one another and from much of their past. The pervasive and terrorizing effect of Redbaiting existed both before and after Sen. Joseph McCarthy came to public visibility, but so-called McCarthyism did have a particular presence in the 1950s. It took many different forms: the repeated claims (repeatedly disproved) that Communists were present throughout public life, the sustained inquiries by the House Un-American Activities Committee, the imposition of loyalty oaths, the reporting of friends and neighbors as suspected Communists, the extended trials of Communists and "fellow travelers," the terrorizing of large numbers of people whose political views were somehow "suspect." As Olsen says of this period, "hundreds and thousands of people lost their livelihoods, their standing in society, and were at terrible risk of imprisonment" (conversation 3). Charlie Chaplin's characterization of the United States in 1953 is apt: "America is so terribly grim in spite of all that material prosperity. They no longer know how to weep. Compassion and the old neighborliness have gone, people stand by and do nothing when friends and neighbors are attacked, libeled and ruined."[48]

Olsen herself felt the full weight of these terrors of the period. She was followed from job to job by investigating FBI agents (see Pearlman and Werlock, 27). Her husband, Jack, was "McCarthied" out of his warehouse union. She and her family prepared for the possibility of being sent to a detention camp made ready to confine Leftists. Adrienne Rich writes of the latter threat in very concrete family terms: "A daughter of Tillie Olsen recalls going with her mother in the 1950s to the Salvation Army to buy heavy winter clothes because the family had reason to believe that Leftists in the San Francisco Bay Area would be rounded up and taken to detention camps farther north."[49] For Olsen, this terror extended beyond family concerns to community concerns; she cites, for example, her anxiety about implicating other people simply by asking them for recommendations to submit with her application to Stanford: "As I myself was in FBI files, anyone I asked might be implicated—'guilt by association'—might too, if the worst happened, end up in a concentration camp" (conversation 3).

Another central feature of the context for Olsen's writing this piece was a prevailing emphasis on the nuclear family and the sex roles the culture assumed were necessary to its success. In *The Fifties: The Way We Really Were*, Miller and Nowak begin their chapter on family by offering up the broad cultural claim, "Everybody got married in the fifties, or at least it was a supreme sign of personal health and well-being to be engaged in the social act of marriage and family-raising" (147). And indeed that *is* how it seemed: a powerful emphasis—as we can see in "Hey Sailor, What Ship?"—on individual families closed into their individual homes. Young people were urged to marry and have children; the media paid pervasive attention to sex roles, to the conventions of heterosexuality, and to conventional distinctions between males and females; families exuded a sometimes smug togetherness in apparent retreat from a complex and often horrific outside world. Many of us who lived through those years experience the persistent emphasis on nuclear family life as an ongoing legacy from the 1950s. I remember, for example, assumptions about the appropriate division of tasks between husbands and wives, a celebration of domesticity, and endless debates about whether or not a man should "let" his wife work. In the dominant ideology—though not necessarily in people's actual lives—both men and women were judged by their apparent adherence to sex roles; families were a carefully constructed unit.[50]

Outside the barricaded family were the larger threats of world strife and nuclear destruction: the Korean War (which ended in 1953), the Cold War, the accumulation of nuclear weapons. Patriotic fervor was often invoked as a kind of talisman against threats from other parts of the world, including, of course, the possible spread of communism. Claims to international concerns—other than anticommunism—were suspect, as were claims to concern for class differences. Those in political and economic power expended much effort in undermining the strengths unions had developed in the 1930s and 1940s. The retreat inward—into homes and private lives—that was enacted through families was underlined in the affirmations of individualism as the primary cultural norm: a movement away from larger community concerns, away from international awareness, away from political struggles.

"Hey Sailor, What Ship?" is not directly "about" any of the historical phenomena I have just described—risking oversimplification in order to do so. But like "I Stand Here Ironing," this piece too is situated at critical intersections with the context within which it was written and first published: the lives it traces are distorted and threatened by McCarthyism, embedded in the cultural constructions of individualism, resistant to the prevailing gender norms. The story never risks polemics even as it conveys its own complex commitments to union consciousness, to political consciousness, and to an international consciousness, each of which had little support in the surrounding culture. It is formed through its necessary resistance to its context even as it must also draw upon the language and understandings of that same context.

The bleakness of that context pervades the language and imagery of the story. A sense of sorrow and loss prevails from the opening portrayal of Whitey's disorientation and search for what is missing: his money, his friend, the previous owner of the bar. And throughout, the sense of personal loss is augmented by its connection to broader losses. Allie comes to Whitey for comfort from a dream in which "I was losted" (20); Whitey himself experiences children as "lost country to him and unattainable" (20) and then recalls other children throughout the world: "(The begging children and the lost, the thieving children and the children who were sold)" (21). The battles that unions have fought are lost in a different sense, though no less poignantly: "These kids, these cherry pickers, they don't realize how we got what we got. Beginnin' to lose it too" (35). The current struggle is at best a weary one in a hostile context, wanting resources, either personal or cultural. Small wonder that the repeated phrase at the story's end is weighted with such sorrow: *"And the memories to forget, the dreams to be stifled, the hopeless hopes to be murdered"* (37; see also 34).

Other images reinforce the brokenness, the lack of place and direction. Whitey's "sickness crouches underneath, waiting to spring" (16); his body is scarred and battered; he must somehow approach the house by climbing "innumerable" stairs (16); the house itself, by the end of the story, joins "the myriad others that stare at him so blindly" (38). The world in which Whitey roams and seeks is a world that cannot see him, a world that seems to provide no place for him, a world that denies his previous efforts and contributions and precludes his active participation at present. The sense of weary effort and of self-enclosed blindness converge in a particularly pointed image in the middle of the story: "the fire leaps up, kindles Len's shadow so that it seems a dozen bent men cradle a child up endless stairs, while the rain traces on the windows, beseechingly, ceaselessly, like seeking fingers of the blind" (23).[51] The image is a beautiful rendering not only of Whitey's own weary effort but also of the weariness of many, seeking blindly, caring for children, groping for ways to carry on in the absence of a context and in the face of enormous denial.

But through this weary effort there persists a strand of resistance, a refusal to succumb. The effort itself may lack a supportive context, but it has not been fully suppressed. Olsen's prompting question—what place and direction were possible for people at that time?—yields no simple answer. Instead the story probes the intersections of individual lives with this hostile context of denial, thereby enacting its own resistance to that same context.

Whitey: Intersections of Public and Private

At the center of these intersections is Whitey, whose life has been shaped by both a distinctive personal history and the demands of his cultural context. Because he must in significant measure be characterized through the language and assumptions of the prevailing culture, he may first appear to us as a fairly stereotypical drunken sailor, his speech somewhat slurred, his thoughts elliptical, his environment tawdry. He addresses people who have departed without his realizing it, and he is repeatedly confused about where his money has gone, what has been the sequence of events, what time it is. In their familiarity, these cultural signals of drunkenness risk seeming stereotypical even as they are the necessary linguistic indicators of what is in fact a highly differentiated subjective experience, since no two drunks really experience the world in the same way. Some readers, in fact, succumb to the stereotype, claiming, for example, that Whitey is "the least compelling of all of Olsen's protagonists" (Orr, 86) or that his character is an unsuccessful rendering of subjective awareness in the "stage-drunk accents of a Eugene O'Neill character."[52]

These responses suggest the complexity of the problem that Olsen must have had to confront in writing the story: how to convey an apparently broken life in the terms available within the culture—"stage-drunk" and without hope—while simultaneously claiming the value of that life in resistance to the cultural valuation. As she has said, that period of the mid-1950s offered "little in the outer soil" by which to recognize and honor Whitey (conversation 2). To write of him and of her own "life comprehensions" through him, Olsen needed, on the one hand, to portray drunkenness, lost dreams, broken meanings, and disconnected friendships; but she also needed, on the other hand, to reveal a complex humanity in resistance to many of the available external judgments, a person whose inner dignity remains and whose life has been shaped by ideals the story honors.

Olsen makes a pointed claim on what Whitey has lost in describing a photo of him as a young man: "Under the joyful sun, proud sea, proud ship as background, the proud young man, glistening hair and eyes, joyful body, face open to life, unlined" (31). "M. Norbert Jacklebaum never saw the guy," Whitey asserts in response, simultaneously invoking his own false name and his own lost connection with the young man in the picture. He then ponders the changes: *"Tracing the scars, the pits and lines, the battered nose; seeking to find"* (31). "Seeking to find"—Whitey's pursuit is ours as well. Behind and within the drunken broken man, we too seek the "proud young man" still integral to the character we encounter.

But the story does not pursue this understanding by giving us character descriptions or linear plot; it does not even give us evident flashbacks and explanations. Because Whitey is not the product of a linear history, not the inevitable result of a series of linked events—an interpretation of his development that would imply that he is now at a dead end—such narrative strategies would be insufficient to the task. Because he is, instead, a complex expression of multiple experiences, all of which are part of him, none of which fully "explain" him, the story must actively enlist us in the pursuit, our "seeking to find." It requires us to ferret out the knowledge that is integral to Whitey's development as the complex human being that he is.

Well before reaching the photographic image, we need to have begun the effort of active construction, gathering from embedded references and allusions to past experience the information that we must assemble if we are to understand who Whitey really is. Even in the story's opening, of course, Whitey is no mere stereotype, no simple unhistoried presence. We not only have an eerie sense of his distinctive physical reality as we see his "face flaring in the smoky mirror. The veined gnawing" (13), but we are also given significant particulars of his history in the inventory of his pockets: his status as a working sailor who has been recently paid, his extensive travels, including Manila and Managua, his union involvements, his likely frequenting of prostitutes. We have encountered as well the repeated reference to "Lennie and Helen and the kids" (13, 15) and the refrain that will acquire increasing significance as the story proceeds: *"Hey Sailor, what ship?"* (13, 16). His near-despair at the end of part 1 already has emotional resonance— premised on the yearning for place and direction—before the story goes on to probe this complexity through interaction with his old friends: "He only sits while the sickness crouches underneath, waiting to spring, and it muddles in his head, *going to see Lennie and Helen and the kids, no presents for 'em, an' don't even feel good"* (16).

Though part 1 may seem like a preliminary character sketch, then, it has, in fact, gone much beyond simple external description. It is instructive that Olsen moved even more strongly in this direction in the one major revision made between the story's first appearance and its publication in the *Tell Me a Riddle* collection: in the earlier version we first see Whitey from the outside, stumbling along a traffic-ridden city street and then spotted by Lennie in a passing car, whereas in the version we now read, we struggle with his consciousness and his embedded history from the very opening scene.[53] Here we are provided with key pieces of Whitey's history and presence from which we must begin to piece together the complexity of his character.

The remainder of the story develops this complexity and emotional resonance still further as we continue in our reader commitment to seek the "real" Whitey, to understand him beyond the threatening stereotype of the drunken sailor. We learn of his personal history with this family through the children's memories of emotional intimacy, stories told, games played. We learn, too, that he has been an important contributing member of this household, not just an occasional visitor: the material evidence of the toys repaired, the paint job that has survived many years (25), and his history of *"much help given, much support"* (37). Lennie thinks of him as someone who had a "tough mind" (37) with whom to ponder and interpret a mutual social world, and Helen recalls his capacity for sensitive listening and empathetic help: *"the ear to hear, the hand that understands"* (37).

Whitey's public presence, his existence in the world beyond the household where we come to know him, further deepens our knowledge of his character. His status as "ship's delegate" (22, 30) emphasizes his commitment to union activities and the respect he has achieved among coworkers. His efforts on behalf of one, a "kid, overtime comin' to him" (35), emphasize that his commitment is actually to workers' needs, not to the bureaucratic process that was relatively new to union structure in the 1950s. He is someone who at least used to have "drag" (18), and the willingness, though not always the ability, to help out someone else through his own influence. Furthermore, his travels have taught him much about the world. He has seen the "begging children and the lost, the thieving children and the children who were sold" (21) and has, in his response to them, intertwined his knowledge of Lennie and Helen's children: Allie on his lap, "this helpless warmth against him, this feel of a child—lost country to him and unattainable" (20), becomes a reminder to him and to us of the begging and starving children throughout the world. He has stories from many different places, especially from East Asia, and he knows about political struggles around the world through the lives of people encountered at work.

Exceeding any particular description or simple labeling process, Whitey becomes a distinctive individual. Two examples of his emergent complexity suggest how the stereotypes built into our language, as in "drunken sailor," are disrupted in Whitey: his reopening of notions of "masculinity" and his enacting of a much broader and more empowered definition of sailor. Whitey is *not* in any simple way defined by his gender since he is simultaneously and without contradiction tough, active, and "masculine" as well as empathetic, domestic, and nurturing. In conversation, Olsen has pointed out that the "Whiteys" who were part of her own life were "the only men I knew then who were truly helpful and thoughtful when it came to housework, or looking after the children for a while—with utmost respect for and delight in children" (conversation 2). Similarly, he is not the rootless, carefree wanderer we often associate with the sailor; he is integral to this family's life and is also their source of connection to a larger international world, with which he is deeply concerned: he brings stories and information about distant places such as Korea and the Philippines. Olsen affirms this role as well: "the seamen and the refugees . . . brought a wider world; they brought the news; they also brought me literature. . . . I learned about the real situation in the Philippines and about José Rizal, heard El Ultimo Adiós, from Filipino seamen. From seamen I learned the truth about what was happening in Central America, Chile, the Banana Republics, so much of the world" (conversation 2).

The "real" Whitey—the one we come to know through attentive reading of the story—gradually takes on a powerful and complex presence. He is actualized for readers who have known sailors like him, as is evident in the phone calls Olsen has received from people who ask her urgently, "Where's Whitey?"[54] and in the letters citing experiences with "such men" who were, especially for children, "the gift-givers, the adventurers, the wider world" (conversation 2). Furthermore, he is actualized for readers who have *not* known sailors like him. All of the features of Whitey's public life suggest a quality we might label "idealism," but they do so in a way that embodies rather than labels his commitments to resisting and changing the political and work structures of the world around him. He is not presented as a political activist or an idealist; rather his piecemeal history is resonant with the effects of those commitments. From a careful and active reading, we may well generate our own labels for Whitey; some of the qualities I have come to attribute to him are activism, idealism, empathy for others, and unquenchable dignity. But this understanding of him has emerged from my active engagement with his story, not from any easy labeling process.

A second effect of our active construction is that we begin to tease out—through seeing the connections between Whitey and this family—the intersections between private realities and public events. Lennie and Helen and their children are themselves at risk for seeming to be a stereotypical nuclear family, comfortably making their way as an isolated emotional unit. But through their history with Whitey, the story shows as well the ways in which this ostensibly "private" reality is deeply connected with a public reality, a world of political events and international concerns. Both Whitey and the family with whom his history is woven together are situated at this intersection of public and private, are themselves markers for the fact that the private is not and cannot be isolated from the world of public events any more than the public can be seen as distinct and separate from the private. These lives are rendered within and against the context of a McCarthyism that denies claims on "brotherhood," the context of union breaking, of hostility to internationalism, of pressures to lead a self-enclosed family life, of imposed norms for gender. Private lives take shape amidst the forces of this public context. Olsen has said, "So many human beings in my life . . . were experienced by me not only in their personal life, but also in their work, neighborhood, activity setting— and of essential importance, as public events profoundly affected their personal beings" (conversation 2). So too with the characters in this story: they live in the intersections of public and private.

The suggestions of political, union, and international consciousness further weave across the boundaries of public and private as they weave Whitey's history into the history he shares with Helen and Lennie. We learn, for example, that Whitey is credited with having saved Lennie's life in the general strike of 1934, in which some workers did lose their lives to police violence. Though the reference is made only in passing, invoked snidely by Jeannie—"Now you're going to tell me the one about how he saved Daddy's life in the strike of 1934" (34)— it is a crucial marker for what the reader must construct of the shared political past that has helped to shape the friendship, a past of union activism and commitment to social change.

Most readers are probably unaware that Whitey still pays a price for his political activism, since that information is only tangentially evident in references to his being shipbound off the coast of the Korean port of Pusan or to his pleasure in finally being able to sail again, "after Pedro" (21). As Olsen explains it, "Most of the seamen who were not permitted to sail because of the McCarthy years were drydocked in San Pedro, as were the seamen who were given temporary and limited clearance and had long waits for ships" (conversation 2).

But the context for noting such buried references *is* there: not only the direct claim to the strike of 1934 but also the repeated references to lost dreams and *"The death of the brotherhood. Once, once an injury to one is an injury to all. Once, once they had to live for each other"* (35). His meaning to Lennie, too, invokes this political past: *"To Lennie he remained a tie to adventure and a world in which men had not eaten each other"* (36). The slogan, central to union history—"an injury to one is an injury to all"—and the memory of vital participation in a movement toward "brotherhood" are crucial reminders of the interconnectedness of these characters' lives.

Whitey's emotional rendering of the poem "Crown 'n Deep," or The Valedictory, is particularly powerful because it is situated at these intersections: the public and the private, the community and the individual, this family and Whitey. As the words express José Rizal's personal strength and sorrow as he faced his death by firing squad in 1896, Whitey's recitation expresses his own investment in movements against imperialism and against tyranny. It also expresses his long and intertwined history with Lennie and Helen and the children, the many levels, both political and personal, of that history. The "garden of Eden" of which the poem speaks is not only to be lost to Rizal in death but has also been "forfeited" by all Filipinos to the impositions of imperialism, with consequences in the Philippines of 1953 and beyond.[55] The "vision" Rizal claims as the guiding force throughout his life is the vision of a people's self-determination, a vision that he sees as yet possible through continued struggle: "That the vision may rise to fulfillment" (32). Both the garden and the vision are under seige in Whitey's own time, in Whitey's own country. Both also represent social and political convictions that Whitey has shared with Helen and Lennie more actively in the past than is possible in the present.

In Whitey's recitation, the lyrics both mourn the loss and honor the struggle: Rizal, in his martyrdom as in Whitey's imagination, is emblematic of the conviction and urgency behind the ongoing struggle for self-determination in the Philippines and, more broadly, of the conviction and urgency behind the shared struggle for social change. Whitey's recitation is both painful and incomplete; it is also "special" as it honors not only Rizal and the Filipino struggle but also Li'l Joe, from whom he learned the poem and who "Never got back home" (32), who never himself returned to the "forfeited garden of Eden" (32). Whitey's inability to complete the poem is, of course, a part of his current physical decline and is again potentially explicable by simple drunkenness, as he stands there "swaying," in need of Lennie's help. But, more than that, it situates Whitey at the node of the story's many intersections: human connections to people like Li'l Joe and Helen and Lennie and their children, work experiences that are integral to social consciousness, political convictions in a context that actively silences them, publicly voiced idealism on the verge of destruction in the midst of these private tensions. As the recitation pulls all of these intersections together, it draws on the awareness we have previously developed and prepares us for the eventual conclusion in a similar configuration of loss and vision. Like that ending, it immerses us in our own struggle with these intersections and these entangled understandings.

Narrative Voice, Family Dynamics

The story's evident avoidance of the narrative conventions of both plot and separable protagonist, then, is not so much a strategic choice as it is a response to the pressures of its own context, even as the characters' lives are visibly shaped by the pressures of that same context. Olsen had no choice but to write in the times, even as she was fully committed to writing *against* the times, in resistance to the constraints of culture, of language, of politics. Her further strategy for writing both in and against the times was to use a complex and subjective narrative voice that draws on multiple points of view. She has suggested that this was not a deliberate choice—"I was certainly not trying for a more experimental form or multiple points of view" (conversation 2)—but has also affirmed that her choice of voice was closely tied to "what I was trying to say" (conversation 2).

Of particular interest, then, is that her choice of narrative perspective—multiple and personal—is closely aligned to the dynamics of the family within which the story takes place. Most immediate is the realization that family life itself is implicitly structured on the presence of multiple points of view. In a traditional patriarchal family structure, the pretense is one of unity, the claim to a singular point of view shaped to the authority of the father. But in most real families, the notion of a singular point of view is almost certainly a pretense. And in some families, struggling to redefine notions of authority and to realize the complexities of human experience, family life itself is instead premised on multiple points of view. The latter sort of family is what we encounter in the domestic situation in "Hey Sailor, What Ship?" Lennie has no singular claim on the authoritative view, and there is no pretense that everyone agrees in their perceptions of the circumstances at hand. Instead Lennie and Helen each has a distinctive set of memories connected to Whitey, the children have their own memories, and the five family members have differing judgments as to what is important and how they ought to react to such unusual events as the mixed pain and pleasure of Whitey's visit.

I have already pointed out that we begin the story with Whitey's point of view, away from the household that is integral to the remainder of the narrative. Such an opening initiates a sense of multiplicity and alternative perceptions, as he brings with him into the household a range of experiences and perspectives to which it is unaccustomed: Whitey's visits to prostitutes, his broad travel to other cultures, his witnessing of extreme poverty among children elsewhere, his experience of living with men, separated from women for extended periods of time. All of these experiences surrounded and framed family life in the United States in 1953; all of these experiences existed in contrast to the apparent insularity of that same family life, the safety and certainty of family roles and of protection from external intrusions. For the narrative authority in the story, it is crucial that we take into account an often negated reality outside the family, that we not begin with any sense of certainty that one view will prevail or that the life of any single family will construct a complete and reliable reality.

This same goal is addressed from *within* the household in the remainder of the story, especially through a strategic use of dialogue. Though the primary internal perspective of part 2 remains Whitey's, most of this section consists of unmediated dialogue—without quotation marks—that simply puts forth each person's observations in interaction with the others. This narrative strategy conveys the literal effect of children all talking at once—"surging around him" (16)—each from an individual concern of the moment, at the same time that the adults persist with their own multilevel interactions. Carol, for example, comments that "Mommy oughta quit work" by way of explaining why Helen has responded with tears to Whitey's arrival; "she's tired. All the time" (17). Her older sister, Jeannie, has already responded by assertively marching her mother into the kitchen; her younger sister, Allie, responds primarily to the excitement: "Whirl me round like you always do, Whitey" (17). Although Lennie issues orders—"Cut it, kids, not so many questions, orders Lennie" (17)—his is not the patriarchal command but rather the urging of one voice among many in the midst of turmoil; the verbal surging of the children persists and any notion of simple and singular paternal authority is oddly undercut further when Carol repeats the directive: "Not so many questions" (17). Lennie's concern is with the emotions of the situation—including Whitey's visible illness and Helen's sorrow—not with the authority of his own voice. This is a family of active and multiple voices rather than a singular perspective.

This narrative strategy opens onto one of the central insights of the story and, indeed, of the entire collection: "Children of different ages perceive differently" (conversation 2). From the moment of his arrival, the children respond differently to Whitey; more crucially, the differences in their responses can be situated in terms of the children's relationship to the culture around them. Allie, in first grade, responds with the sensory and intuitive pleasure of a young child; she persists in wanting games and songs and touch and cab rides and is unselfconscious in her mimicry of Whitey's language;[56] she notices the new scar on Whitey's cheek and is anxious about the pain it implies (22). She is the least integrated into the larger cultural perceptions. Carol, age 10—"too big to bounce any more" (27)—who is especially attentive to her parents' and her older sister's responses to Whitey's arrival, nonetheless still wants presents and wants even more to hear stories and to renew her memory of the past through hearing "Crown 'n Deep": "I try to remember it and I never can, Carol says, softly" (32). She hovers between the unstudied responses of a young child and the attentiveness to the judgments of those immediately around her more typical of adults. Jeannie, the oldest, on the verge of graduating from junior high school, is most judgmental: she disdains Whitey's language, cannot excuse his drunkenness, and sees him through the eyes of her friends—and hence through the external judgments of the culture. She, too, recalls the past but rejects the story of her love for Whitey when she was four years old (30); she momentarily renews her potent memories when she "kneels down beside Whitey, and using his long ago greeting asks softly, Hey Sailor, what ship?," and then "without warning, with a touch so light, so faint, it seems to breathe against his cheek, she traces a scar" (22). But her primary response returns and prevails throughout the story: a judgment on Whitey's unacceptability in her cultural context.

Olsen's acuity in seeing these children and their differences is striking. But even more intriguing is how valuable this knowledge is to the narrative form. The sense of multiple perspectives that is first enacted through dialogue is reinforced through this perception about children: each sees the world from a distinct vantage point; adolescent children are particularly susceptible to the powers of peer pressure and cultural judgment; each of us, from childhood on, alters our perspective and shifts the basis of our judgments. Through this experiential understanding of children—Olsen attributes it directly to parenting experiences (conversation 2)—she embeds in the story the deeper knowledge of empathy and judgment. Jeannie remains primarily rigid and judgmental; we last see her "silent and shrunken into her coat" on the final page of the story (38). But we also see within her the Jeannie that has been, the child who was devoted to Whitey, as Allie still is. And we see the Jeannie "that may yet be," evident particularly, as Olsen says, in the moment when "she traces the scar on Whitey's face and the tenderness and regard and understanding with which she speaks to him" (conversation 2). From these portrayals, reinforced by the Jeannie that we come to know in "O Yes" and "Tell Me a Riddle," we are placed fully within the story's narrative knowledge: people always see from within their own circumstances, and, even more important, "people can and do change" (conversation 2).

This important thematic knowledge, linked to Whitey and Helen and Lennie as well as to the children, is inseparable from the story's narrative construction. The multiple perspectives within the narrative not only suggest the necessity of seeing Whitey and indeed all people from multiple perspectives, including their own, but also point to the necessity of not closing any one person into a single point in time: again, "people can and do change."

The brief part 3, narrated solely from Whitey's perspective when he wakens to the empty house, renews our focus on his understanding of his circumstances. By this time the house itself is full of multiple voices and memories, including the unsigned note that Helen has left, but Whitey's outsider's perspective must be a part of what we take with us into the final part 4. He "reads" the house, noting signs of current economic fragility and of partial neglect of household matters in the face of insufficient time. We experience him standing alone in the empty house, noting his own contributions from the past, reliving his "old vision" (24) of being able to say "the house is clean, and there's steak for dinner" (25). By the time this short section ends with the same phrase that has ended each previous section— *"Hey Sailor, what ship?"* (25)—we have experienced with him his own simultaneous presence in and exclusion from the current domestic arrangements; the question about his own direction, his own ship, intensifies the contradiction.

That contradiction emerges completely and painfully in the most fully multiple narrative perspective of part 4. Here we have not only the intensive use of dialogue, as in part 2, and the focus of issues through "Crown 'n Deep," as I have already discussed. We have as well a heightened sense of Whitey's alienation, drawing upon and deepening his experience in part 3, and a fully developed sense of multiple points of view through the inclusion of both Helen's and Lennie's thought processes.

Whitey's alienation, the painful edge of his exclusion, is rendered most immediately through two parenthetical expressions of his thought, both of which suggest that he is feeling something quite different from what his words—as well as others' words—convey: "(Oh feeling good, come back, come back)" (30) and "(Not what he means to say at all. Remember the love I gave you, the worship offered, the toys I mended and made, the questions answered, the care for you, the pride in you.)" (30). The latter in particular suggests poignantly the near impossibility of translating emotions into material objects even as it reminds us of the emotions Whitey has invested in such objects. Although his internal perspective here remains partial and fragmented, it is essential to the overall narrative perspective.

Essential also is the dialogue between Jeannie and Helen that then distills the sense of overall dialogue throughout the story between the voices of judgment in the culture and the voices of empathy in resistance to the culture. Here Jeannie voices the cultural perspective— judging Whitey's language, his drunkenness, his carelessness with money—speaking these judgments in the language of adolescent resistance to a parent. Here Helen voices the empathetic perspective— speaking of Whitey's integral participation in their family life, of their shared history, of his knowledge, of his place in the world of sailors whose language *is* distinctive. In isolation, this dialogue seems to see judgment and empathy as mutually exclusive, to set Jeannie and Helen in decisive opposition to each other. But within the story as a whole, it portrays both perspectives as components of complex understanding; it honors Helen's empathy without discrediting Jeannie's perceptions. Resonant with parental concern and personal friendship, the dialogue concludes with a simple phrase, ambiguously offered as either thought or spoken words but decisive in honoring empathy: "To understand" (34). Predicated on Helen's previous assertion—"Jeannie, I care you should understand. . . . You've got to understand" (34)—the phrase leads directly into the crucial italicized portions of this final section and establishes the necessity of empathy in resisting negative cultural judgments.[57]

Understand. The italicized portions of the text, interspersed among ongoing fragments of speech from all five characters, delve deeply into the necessary roots of empathy in Whitey's history and in human caring. They are in no clear and unambiguous voice, though they decidedly follow from Helen's argument with Jeannie and therefore from her consciousness even as they also draw directly on Whitey's consciousness and merge into a broader and more inclusive perspective premised on the entire preceding story. The first segment cites a *"beginning"* in *"youth and . . . that curious inability to take a whore unless he were high with drink"* (34) and moves directly into the much more powerful prompting: *"And later there were memories to forget, dreams to be stifled, hopes to be murdered"* (34). What is left out, like what Whitey cannot voice but can only think and feel, is the entire intervening history, the complex web of conviction and knowledge and activism and shared experience. The second of these italicized segments begins *"Understand. The death of the brotherhood. Once, once an injury to one is an injury to all"* (35) and moves through the experience of sharing resources, of mutual work, to the current *"dwindling"* presence of the union, the threat of a destroyed brotherhood, not just in the union but in any kind of community.

The remaining italicized segments, then, draw on the entire story's dialogical quality, its complex intertwining of many perspectives. These sections voice Whitey's 23 years of painful memories, such as the exclusions by virtue of class (*"only so far shall you go and no further, uptown forbidden, not your language, not your people, not your country"* [36]). But they also voice both Lennie's and Helen's memories and valuing of Whitey: their shared youth, their adventures and conversations, their intertwining lives. The last of these sections concludes by reiterating the self that Whitey now feels nearly trapped within: *"Now the decaying body, the body that was betraying him. And the memories to forget, the dreams to be stifled, the hopeless hopes to be murdered"* (37). The loss, of course, is far more significant than the destruction brought about by alcohol; the addition of the one adjective—*"hopeless"*—in the second instance of the phrase *"hopes to be murdered"* underscores the enormity of the loss, as does its framing by reference to Whitey's decaying body and the implicit recollection of the "proud young man" in the earlier photograph. What we experience here is the enormity of the personal and historical affronts to the integrity of that young man in the photo, the enormity of the multiple losses we have seen twisted into the lives that the story conveys.

But the story does not end with *"hopeless hopes to be murdered"* (38). It does not end with a claim to personal tragedy. Instead it ends with a judgment on the culture that has isolated and nearly destroyed Whitey and finally a renewal of the plaintive question that speaks both to that culture and to the life history that has been explored. As Whitey walks away from the house, he experiences directly the painful shift in cultural context, from a world of shared activism to a world of blind individualism:

> He passes no one in the streets. They are inside, each in his slab of house, watching the flickering light of television. The sullen fog is on his face, but by the time he has walked to the third hill, it has lifted so he can see the city below him, wave after wave, and there at the crest, the tiny house he has left, its eyes unshaded. After a while they blur with the myriad others that stare at him so blindly.
> Then he goes down.
>
> *Hey Sailor, what ship?*
> *Hey Marinero, what ship?*(38)

While sobering in its social vision, the passage does not close upon a Whitey in despair. His yearning for a private place "where he can yell or sing or pound and Deeck will look on without reproach or pity or anguish" (38) and his resistance to the eyes that stare blindly at him, failing to see his wholeness, his humanity, are both strong affirmations of what he has known and lived. And our own active participation in having constructed his history and his humanity—seeking, with him, to find that previous self—further affirms the integrity of his life and being.

Part 1

Finally, the sailors' greeting with which the story ends affirms most pointedly the necessity of pursuing both place and direction, of finding within this blindered culture a claim on genuine connections and shared values. Its reiteration—and the shift in its final formulation to include the mellifluous Spanish version *"Marinero"*—connects Whitey back into the community in which he still works and connects him as well to the idealism that reenters the story through its concluding dedication:

> *For Jack Eggan*   *1915–1938*
> *Seaman. Volunteer, Abraham Lincoln*
>   *Brigade*
> *Killed in the Loyalist retreat*
>   *across the Ebro, Spain.* (38)

Volunteer in the Spanish Civil War—a war emblematic to many of a fight against fascism—Jack Eggan, Olsen's friend and partner in political struggle, a seaman like Whitey and many other friends, here invokes the active participation in efforts to transform the world. The ending, like the interwoven voices of the story itself, thus articulates not only the enormous sense of loss—shared historical struggle, human lives, political idealism all lost to the forces of political repression and cultural blindness—but also the persistent awareness of human needs and human resistance.

"O Yes"

These stories are of the 50s, I have said of both "I Stand Here Ironing" and "Hey Sailor, What Ship?" When we turn to "O Yes" (written in 1956), we may be more skeptical of such a claim, for historical references here are even more oblique than in the first two pieces. But like them, this piece is profoundly shaped by the issues and experiences of the period; and like them, it too is enriched—not limited—by its historical specificity, as it generates understanding of the social dimensions of our "individual" lives. In "O Yes" this understanding emerges from—shapes and is shaped by—its experiential context: the social forces at work to separate people and the urgency and possibility of human resistance to those forces. Olsen's own claim is revealing here: "I realized—understood in the writing of this—another important factor, for these stories are so much, so deeply out of the fifties: the human hunger for community . . ." (conversation 3). What, then, were the forces at work to deny human community at the time the story was written? What were the sources for resistance, the ways in which human beings nonetheless laid claim to this powerful human hunger for community? And how does the story both reveal this hunger and generate new understandings of its roots and possibilities?

Hunger for Community: Text in Context

To pursue these questions, I want to begin by drawing together some of the particulars of the story with some of the particulars of the historical moment at which it was written. In doing so, I will be frequently at risk of oversimplification, but I want to take that risk in order to provide some specific contextual information and a broad sketch of issues of the period. As with "Hey Sailor, What Ship?" I wish not so much to make detailed correlations as to identify crucial patterns for how individual perceptions are embedded in a social context, how language choices are necessarily shaped by prevailing cultural values and concerns, and how broad issues of historical context have been integral to Olsen's realization of "the human hunger for community." I do not,

55

of course, mean that Olsen's writing is based on any uncritical acceptance of prevailing values but that her writing necessarily speaks to and against her cultural context. All five of the issues I will discuss are related to one another and to the concern for human community; in my characterization of them, I draw primarily on Olsen's comments in interviews and on my childhood memories of the 1950s, supplemented by general historical sources such as those cited in my discussion of "Hey Sailor, What Ship?"

First, the issue that most readers identify as central to the story: race and racism. This concern is scarcely specific to the 1950s—witness the ongoing power of racism in the 1990s—but it was a central reality with specific historical forms in the 1950s. In the years prior to and during which Olsen wrote "O Yes" there took place, for example, the Supreme Court decision in *Brown v. Board of Education of Topeka*, rejecting the "separate but equal" doctrine in public education (May 1954); the racial murder of Emmett Till, a 14-year-old black boy who had allegedly "whistled at a white woman" (August–September 1955); the initiating of the Montgomery, Alabama, bus boycott, when Rosa Parks was arrested for refusing to yield her bus seat to a white man (December 1955); and the emergence of Martin Luther King, Jr., as a powerful leader in the civil rights movement.

Olsen herself has a strong history of resistance to racism: "The struggle against racism, the evidences of the workings of it, have been a part of my life from the beginning, growing up in the neighborhood in which I did, and with my Socialist parent background" (conversation 3). She tells of growing up in a racially integrated neighborhood and sometimes attending a black church in the neighborhood; of her father's participation in a caravan to rebuild the black community after "terrible, terrible race riots in Tulsa" (conversation 3); of her two oldest children's "natural relationships with Black children because part of their lives had to do with neighborhood, union and movement friendships and activities, and we lived in San Francisco's Fillmore and Mission mixed working class districts" (conversation 3); of her immersion, through her political involvement in the Communist party, in "that whole ideology of 'Black and white, unite and fight' which we used to not only proclaim but try to live—the whole focus on the situation of Black people in this country and the side-by-side association one was fortunate to have with others of every human hue" (conversation 3). She tells, too, of a specific impetus for this story: "In San Francisco, in the late forties, early fifties, I would sometimes go on Sundays to church with a friend, one of the few Black women in our neighborhood. I took it for granted that going to the same schools, being neighbors, her children and my children would also be friends, as she and I were. Part of what also fed 'O Yes' was seeing what happened to those kids when they reached junior high. Separation again" (conversation 3).

As Olsen says, Parry in "O Yes" is "pre-Civil Rights time," though the story was written in such a way that readers might "envision her in the later Civil Rights time" (conversation 3). It was written from the deeply felt knowledge of Olsen's personal history and a strong consciousness of racism: the racism that Parry experiences at school when her teacher questions her relationship with Carol—"Does your mother work for Carol's mother?" (57)—and implies that she will behave irresponsibly in retrieving Carol's books; the racism that helps to break up the friendship between Carol and Parry; the racism that gives emotional force to *"the religion of all oppressed peoples"* (60); the racism that is intertwined in Alva's entire personal history. The story was likewise written with a strong consciousness of the emergent civil rights movement of the period: the strengths inherent in Alva; the empathetic understanding in Helen's thoughts at the story's end; the recognized need for resistance to all the social forces at work to deny Parry the opportunities that are available to Carol.

A second issue of central concern in the 1950s, though again not exclusive to them, was education and the sorting process enacted through the schools, where children were often tracked according to social categories such as race and class. At the time "O Yes" was written, the United States had not yet experienced the educational crisis often attributed to *Sputnik I*: the anxiety about Russian superiority in science education resulting from the Soviets' successful launch in October 1957 of the first human-made satellite. But the anxiety about education in the internationally competitive world of the Cold War was powerful throughout the 1950s (as indeed it remains in a different version in the economically competitive 1990s). Circling around and framing this anxiety was the attempt to associate communism with earlier educational reforms. Claims were made that the philosophy of progressive education and the teachers who embraced it—that is, those who attempted to break down previous barriers to individual student development—were subject to insidious infiltration by "foreign" political systems (see Miller and Novak, 248–68). (This leads us to a third issue, McCarthyism, which I will take up shortly.) There was a consequent "sorting" that took place in public schools in the 1950s—a new emphasis on college preparatory and advanced placement courses for certain students—that led to "competitiveness, judging, tracking" (conversation 3). There was a recurrent turn to traditional forms of academic programs, even in the midst of ongoing democratic reforms in education, as evident in the educational possibilities opened up by the explosion of community colleges and the passage of the GI Bill. Integral to this sorting and tracking were the powerful forces of conformity at work in the youth culture of the mid-1950s. Often reinforced by the threat of being or seeming to be a "juvenile delinquent," this thrust toward conformity was then (as now) especially potent in the years of early adolescence and took its shape from often unacknowledged class divisions.

In "O Yes," issues of economic class are closely tied to the role of public education in an overall societal sorting process. This is the process, of course, that is central to the separation of Parry and Carol—linked in their instance with particular racial expressions of class separation. The awareness is first made specific by Carol's older sister, Jeannie, recalling her own loss of a best friend during the crucial junior-high years: "It's like Ginger and me. Remember Ginger, my best friend in Horace Mann. But you hardly noticed when it happened to us, did you . . . because she was white? Yes, Ginger, who's got two kids now, who quit school year before last. Parry's never going to finish either. What's she got to do with Carrie any more? They're going different places. Different places, different crowds. And they're sorting. . . ." (53–54; Olsen's ellipses).

When Helen, Jeannie and Carol's mother, insists that Parry's capacities are equal to Carol's, Jeannie continues, making her own experiential attributions to the forces that work on sorting children, particularly in the years of early adolescence: "They're in junior high, Mother. Don't you know about junior high? And it's all where you're going. Yes and Parry's colored and Carrie's white. And you have to watch everything, what you wear and how you wear it and who you eat lunch with and how much homework you do and how you act to the teacher and what you laugh at. . . . And run with your crowd" (54; Olsen's ellipsis). The pressure to conform rises along class lines: clothing and behavior patterns and homework choices and the need for *your own* crowd all converge in the name of avoiding a "bad reputation for your school" (54).

Helen's own thoughts and recollections underscore Jeannie's point. She remembers Carol telling her about the Welcome Assembly, in which they were told "How to Dress and How Not to Dress," a description surrounded now in memory by "a mute cry of violated dignity" (54)—what Olsen elsewhere calls the "reaction against shame" and the "shaping character of class" (conversation 3). Helen recalls as well the help she has been able to give with homework and the knowledge that there are other children who receive no such help. Like Olsen, she feels the wrenching pain of unequal opportunity. In Olsen's words: "I have never gotten over having to live through knowing wonderful kids, as bright as my kids or brighter—or some of them not as bright but needing special help—and seeing what happened with most of them because they were denied enabling circumstances" (conversation 3). The sorting, Helen too realizes, is done along both race and class divisions.

The subsequent summary of the events that develop between Carol and Parry emphasizes the economic context for much of this sorting:

> And after school? Carol is off to club or skating or library or someone's house, and Parry can stay for kickball only on the rare afternoons when she does not have to hurry home where Lucy, Bubbie, and the cousins wait to be cared for, now Alva works the four to twelve-thirty shift.
>
> No more the bending together over the homework. All semester the teachers have been different, and rarely Parry brings her books home, for where is there space or time and what is the sense? (56–57)

Again the observations are embedded in the story, the particulars of the development of these two young girls, the separations that distort their friendship. But the knowledge of the social context that enacts the sorting is an essential dimension of the narrative richness.

A third issue of historical import, McCarthyism, is one I have already cited as vital to the context for "Hey Sailor, What Ship?" Olsen claims its background presence in "O Yes" as well: "So the McCarthy period is also part of the personal background, although not specifically in 'O Yes,' . . ." (conversation 3). Olsen dedicated the piece to Margaret Heaton, with whom Olsen had discussed the "torment and soul-searching" surrounding the state-imposed demand that Margaret sign the loyalty oath—swearing never to have belonged to a subversive organization—in order to continue teaching: "Many human beings in the fifties felt terribly alone, particularly caring, conscientious people like Margaret, for all the fact that they had friends and people who loved them.

They saw how quickly people were being isolated, excommunicated, condemned; and that does something to the human fabric, to trust. . . . It does not enter into 'O Yes,' but separation in *this* terrible sense was certainly a characteristic of that time" (conversation 3).

Though not directly evident in "O Yes," that political terror, that isolation, that terrible aloneness *are* visible as the background against which the story comes into focus. In the story's concluding section, this terrible anguish is surely what frames Helen's painful inability to voice possible explanations of the experiences of racism and of Carol's emotional turmoil. The affirmed need for community, with which I began this discussion of "O Yes," also emerges from the pain of broken human connections, such as those in "Hey Sailor, What Ship?" Of these concerns, I will have more to say later in the discussion of narrative voice; for now I want to return to my interview with Olsen to bring in another strand of the story's historical context: "the McCarthy period . . . had partly to do with my deciding to write of two youngsters who were Black and white instead of two white youngsters. I greeted the fifties' Civil Rights movement, then in its first stages, with great hope and joy. Here was the first real break against the fear and the prevalent feeling that one must not involve oneself in activity against the powers-that-be" (conversation 3). That is, the emergent civil rights movement—as powerful evidence of *resistance* to the political terrorism of the period—was itself a prompting for the story's concern with racial issues. In the struggle to change a racist society, Olsen saw the possibilities for human community and evidence of the human capacity to move beyond the isolation imposed by FBI files and political trials and mistrust of friends and neighbors.

A fourth issue of historical context is religion. Religion seemed to be everywhere during this period: religious movies—such as *The Robe*, *The Ten Commandments*, and *A Man Called Peter*—were a strong presence in popular culture; the newly published revised standard version of the Bible repeatedly headed the best-seller list; radio and television evangelists enjoyed widespread popularity; Congress legislated the addition of "under God" to the Pledge of Allegiance in 1954 and adopted "In God We Trust" as the national motto in 1956. All of these evidences of a pervasive religious presence suggest a national unity and a commercialization of religion. In this version of popular culture, an almost monolithic Judeo-Christian tradition prevailed, and an intertwining of patriotism, religion, and capitalism characterized the 1950s for many people.

As she wrote this story, religion was a more complex part of the context for Olsen. She could not have helped being aware of the prevailing national concern with religion, but she was not likely to have participated in its popular manifestations. Her Jewish heritage was more cultural than religious and was inextricably linked with a political and secular concern to transform human institutions: "I was the daughter of atheists who understood and who tried to understand but were inalterably opposed to the opium and the divisive kinds of religion" (conversation 3). She was deeply aware of the harms that have been done in the name of religion.

At the same time, Olsen was equally aware of the strengths available through religion, especially in African-American communities:

> not only the hunger of people for a place where they feel they belong and are treated with dignity but the special character of Black churches and the other churches that *are* people's solace, source of community, source of strength and keep alive the human spirit of resistance, of deeply felt song, of joy. What was the basic institution that made the Civil Rights movement, the human rights movement possible? Where was its major fortress? The churches, the Black churches. . . . [T]he religion that I was writing of was the religion that was people's solace, and again source of strength, of human resistance. (conversation 3)

She was also personally attuned to the music of black churches and to the powerful expressions of language she had observed in her long personal association with them, begun in her childhood attendance at the Calvary Baptist Church, where she fell in love with the music and then began to sing herself.

This complexity of response is pervasive in the story itself: the carefully observed opening of the story in the concrete realities of the church; the story's building in religious and emotional intensity toward the moment when Carol "is drowned under the sluice of the slow singing and the sway" (48); its embedding of Alva's memory-vision, including her acknowledgment, *never really believing, as still I don't believe all, scorning, for what have it done to help* (51), as well as her powerful religious experience; and its ending with Helen's thoughts and feelings about religion, half-formulated in response to Carol's need and Helen's emerging recognition of her own need. All of these experiences and particulars are integral to the narrative; all emerge from, are "wrenched out of" (conversation 3), the complexity of the cultural context from within which Olsen wrote.

Finally, a fifth issue of central concern to the 1950s and of consequence to "O Yes" is an emphasis on the nuclear family and the sex-based roles assumed necessary to its success, again a concern cited as part of the context for "Hey Sailor, What Ship?" The negative effects of the turn inward and of gender constraints are also pertinent in this story. Here we see as well the added concern with how these shape adolescent experience. I remember, for example, the highly gendered conventions of the dress codes (not unlike those articulated at the Welcome Assembly in "O Yes") and the constant reminders of what a girl should do and not do when she was with a boy.

The emphasis on the nuclear family, however, also had its affirmative expressions, prompted in part by the end of World War II and what Olsen calls "a hunger for domesticity" (personal communication, summer 1988). Like religion, the family is in many ways a traditional source of human community, a place of comfort and companionship, especially when the "larger" world seems fraught with divisiveness and hostility: racism, class divisions, political repressions. Family life, then, can genuinely be a context for understanding and solace and strength—as the church often has been for oppressed peoples—in spite of the distortions of its cultural reinforcements. Olsen speaks of her own yearning for time with her children, for the kind of intimate engagement in human lives that she too associates with family. Her comments about her husband and her daughters—though relatively infrequent and often protective of their privacy—reflect a deep commitment to the bonds that she herself lived within, even in the midst of the turmoil of so many other crucial commitments; and in the 1950s, in particular, she experienced the external silencing and repression as so powerful that the embrace of friends and family was especially sustaining.

The story suggests this emphasis on family in its narrative events. The initial visit to the church—part 1 of the story—is arranged for the daughters by the "mommas" (50) and is in many ways shaped by a whole series of interactions between each mother and her children. Part 2 of the story is, then, framed and introduced by the attempt to understand and interpret Carol's resulting crisis through the lens of family understanding: the discussion among Carol's parents and older sister—Helen, Len, and Jeannie. And the story's conclusion takes on the rhythms and emotions of the mother-daughter embrace: "Rocking and strangling the cries . . . Clinging and beseeching" and eventually

"Caressing, quieting . . . Sheltering her daughter close, mourning the illusion of the embrace" (60–62). The embrace *is* an illusion in the sense that it cannot convey complete understanding, cannot in itself heal the grief and pain in Carol's experience, or in Helen's; but it is *not* an illusion in the sense that Helen and Carol struggle together, in silence and partial communication, through touch and shared sorrow, toward the cry that echoes in Helen's thoughts at the story's end: *"caring asks doing"* (61). This is decidedly a story formed to the concerns of family life.

Olsen's comments about the importance of motherhood in "O Yes" suggest the complexity of these concerns: "You really only know a society, what kind of a society it is, who it benefits, who it harms, how the harm happens, when you have to do with life from the beginning and live how it is shaped and misshaped, when you learn what power you have and don't have, how much more power the outside world has" (conversation 3). That is, insights into public negations derive explicitly from intimate involvement with children: the harms of the public, social environment are visibly and painfully enacted through children's lives and are integral to the "private" lives of family relationships. The conflicts people experience within their families and friendships, then, are not merely private but are inscribed in cultural patterns through forces that are both subtle and potent. As Olsen goes on to say, "It's hard to hold onto motherhood truths and understandings against the outside realities that determine so much about what is going to happen with your children" (conversation 3).

Understanding through Writing

How, then, does one not only hold onto alternative understandings but even find ways to articulate them in resistance to the prevailing culture? Keeping in mind the overview of historical context, I want to return to a statement by Olsen cited at the beginning of this discussion: "I realized—understood in the writing of this—another important factor, for these stories are so much, so deeply out of the fifties: the human hunger for community" (conversation 3). This is a statement not only about thematic content and historical context but also about how writing and understanding are inseparable. That the writing itself *yielded* the understanding, instead of being derived from it, is a crucial reminder of how experience and language interact, each shaping the other, neither with a clear and unchanging priority. And more: this observation speaks for the social dimension of language as our access to perception itself, even to "experience" itself. The "human hunger for community" is simultaneously an experience that prompted the story and an experience that emerges from the story; it is simultaneously prior and subsequent to the writing. It is of the historical context and points the way toward resistance to that context.

This knowledge of the complexities and contradictions, of the inextricable intertwining of public and historical context with personal and private lives, is thus crucial to "O Yes" itself, as well as to the analysis of it that I am proposing. For the remainder of this section, I want to examine how this knowledge shapes the narrative form itself, how the form is both of the times and against the times, and how the language and narrative voice of the story are themselves responses to the urgency of the human knowledge from which the story arises and to which it aspires.

Consider, first, the central "event" of the story: Carol's near-faint. On the face of it, the event is a young girl's simple response to an unfamiliar experience; she is overcome by the intensity of the religious experience to which she comes unprepared by previous experience: "the thrashing, writhing body" and "the torn, tearing cry" (48) of her classmate are the climax of the emotions that have swirled around Carol since her arrival. Though she now tries to close out this experience by closing her eyes, she "still can see . . . and hear" (48), just as throughout the service she had been torn between immersion and resistance.

Examining the context for Olsen's decision to make this event central to the narrative may help to enrich our response to it, for Olsen has woven into this one incident a whole fabric of concerns. Most immediately, she identifies a specific experiential prompting for the event: Margaret Heaton's attending with Olsen the black church of Olsen's friend, Katherine. The experience was unfamiliar to Margaret: "She had never been to the kind of Baptist church most Black people attended. She had never heard that music. She had never heard the sermons. She had never been exposed to all that intensity. Well, she fainted. Some of it, of course, was physical reaction—the sheer battering of those great waves of sound. But the largest part was the exposure to the intensity, the beauty of expression, the extremity of emotion" (conversation 3). Olsen goes on to describe further roots of this event: "There is another semi-autobiographical root and that is the experience of my third daughter, Kathie, who, as in the story, had gone from grade school with her friend to a junior high, where the friendship became so changed. She came with us also to church. But she didn't faint, although she too was frightened, deeply affected by what took place. It was Margaret who fainted" (conversation 3).

As Olsen says later on in the interview, "I didn't write about Margaret or Katherine and her family or my own Kathie except in the way that you take from here and you take from there and you don't tell everyone's truth or a single individual's truth—but it is a compound" (conversation 3). The decision to weave these truths together—to merge in particular the experience of fainting in response to unfamiliar intensity and the separation of two junior-high-school age friends—suggests a necessary distillation of insight, a bringing together of the powerful forces of change that shape any adolescent's life (sexual development, for example, and physical growth and attentiveness to peer judgments) with the powerful forces of religious experience and of cultural contrasts, as well as with the social pressures of racism and class "sorting." Recall, as well, that Margaret Heaton was in Olsen's mind emblematic of the isolation people felt during the McCarthy years, the breaches in the fabric of human trust and the need to address the hunger for community.

Thus the general issues I have identified as crucial to the period merge with the particularities of individual experiences to shape a narrative event that is far more powerful than simple event but is at the same time thoroughly embedded in the "realities" of human experience at the time. The near-faint that initiates Carol's baptism expresses simultaneously the desire to participate and the desire to resist participation, the immersion in this particular experience and the withdrawal from it, and it also foreshadows the anguish that shapes the conclusion: *"caring asks doing. It is a long baptism into the seas of humankind, my daughter. Better immersion than to live untouched. . . . Yet how will you sustain?"* (61). In drawing together this "compound" of human experience, both individual and historical, the story probes the complexity of precisely those forces that thwart the potential for human community and those that foster it.

The human knowledge that shapes this narrative event is grounded in the recognition that the problem is not merely a narrative problem, that human lives are themselves "a compound": "rise or not, Parry forever is part of Carol, as is Alva. And they have lived what inequality of circumstance is about. Consciously or not, they know: I might have been she; she might have been I" (conversation 3). Because it is framed by an unresponsive public context, Carol's baptism cannot be simple

65

baptism into human community. It must be both immersion and resistance. It must be identification with her classmate: "She acts so awful outside but I remember how she was in church and whenever I see her now I have to wonder. And hear . . . like I'm her, Mother, like I'm her" (61). It must also be a distancing from the experience. It must be new knowledge of the forces that prevent human community and the human bonds that nonetheless weave lives together. Like Carol's, Helen's need is unmet: "While in her, her own need leapt and plunged for the place of strength that was not—where one could scream or sorrow while all knew and accepted, and gloved and loving hands waited to support and understand" (62). Like Carol, Helen can only continue the anguished struggle both to care and to do, despite the denials implicit in racism, class separations, and loss of the fabric of trust among human beings.

That key "event" of the story, then, opens onto its entire structure. Carol's baptism begins when she arrives at the black church, where she and her mother are the only white people present, and continues beyond the story's end. Although the actual shift in consciousness seems to occur in midstory, it moves outward in multiple directions from the baptismal immersion when Carol is "drowned": "So high up and forgotten the waves and the world, so stirless the deep cool green and the wrecks of what had been" (48). Patterns of loss and separation and community are integral to patterns of water imagery, as they are to patterns of religious imagery, of music, of children's games.[58]

The suggestiveness of the water imagery, as it links shifts in consciousness with Christian baptism, and with baptism into a complex human community that involves both responsibility ("doing") and nurturance ("caring"), is one response to the need to speak both in the language of the culture and in resistance to that culture, to voice unarticulated life comprehensions even when a supportive context is absent. A second response is the narrative structure that opens out from an apparently simple event—the baptism—into a whole network of interconnections rather than pursuing what might be the culturally expected sequence of beginning-middle-end. A third response—and one that I want to explore at some length—is the claim to a narrative voice capable of making the social connections that language makes possible without necessarily accepting the social assumptions of the cultural context. Like the voice Olsen develops throughout her fiction, the voice here rejects cultural authority; like the voice in "Hey Sailor, What Ship?" the voice in "O Yes" resists the prevailing values of the 1950s, partly by drawing on the insights derived from family life and pervasively by affirming multiplicity.[59]

Though readers for whom the situation is unfamiliar sometimes feel a little lost at the beginning of the story, the voice there, at least, seems to be the voice of traditional narrative authority, describing the scene and the context with an explicit certainty about the setting and an implicit certainty about the emotional dynamics within that setting: "They are the only white people there, sitting in the dimness of the Negro church that had once been a corner store, and all through the bubbling, swelling, seething of before the services, twelve-year-old Carol clenches tight her mother's hand, the other resting lightly on her friend, Parialee Phillips, for whose baptism she has come" (39). The passage includes two slightly jarring notes, one cultural and the other stylistic. First, for the culture of the 1950s, particularly for a white readership, there is the probably unexpected racial designation of Carol and her mother as white, when there is no racial designation for Parialee, whom we must assume to be black. Olsen thus makes race an issue for whites whereas it is usually understood as an issue only for people of color. Second there is the unusual stylistic choice to use gerunds more as adjectives than nouns, suggesting an intensity that is not yet defined "bubbling, swelling, seething"—and initiating the pervasive link between water and human community. But beyond these slight disruptions, the narrative authority seems intact, congruent with a version of reality familiar to a general culture: reality resides in the external and shared context of place and event.

Through the remainder of part 1, the narrative perspective becomes increasingly focalized in the consciousness of Carol. The implicit authority of the opening statement gives way to Carol's fragmented state of mind as we witness the difficulty she has assimilating both her emotional and physical surroundings: she wants to be part of this religious experience but is terrified by its emotional power and its unfamiliarity. By the time she faints from emotional distress, we have moved from the omniscient voice of the narrator at the story's opening to the confines of Carol's consciousness. The narrative, however, has not yet broken the boundaries of its implicit assumptions; it has merely focused on one possible frame of reference within the omniscient sensibility. Part 2 then moves to a second frame of reference within this sensibility as it shifts to emphasize Helen's consciousness when the story relocates in their family home and assesses the dissolution of the friendship between Carol and Parialee. The narrative voice, in other words, explores the perspectives of two primary characters and places those perspectives in an overall frame of narrative description. Although some of the techniques for conveying consciousness draw on the insights and innovations of modernist narrative—particularly the compression of Virginia Woolf's explorations of consciousness—the overall narrative strategy appears reasonably conventional, with authority apparently vested in an external "reality" and hence in communal assumptions about that reality.

But in order to summarize, I have already distorted the patterns of the narrative voice; indeed, I have omitted some crucial contributors to the way in which the narrative is simultaneously able to speak and to disrupt. I want now to go back and address the disruptions. The first and most dramatic disruption occurs very early when, at the end of part 1, Alva's voice suddenly erupts. Hers is a perspective that has been hitherto suppressed. Mother of Parialee, a member of the black community, Alva has no clear place in the "general consciousness"[60] that seems to define the story as a whole: white onlookers, sympathetic but participant in the dominant culture rather than in the black religious experience they are witnessing. We make the shift to Alva without preparation, without any attempt to reconcile it with the dominant perspective; at the end of part 1, we are simply given an extended italicized paragraph providing her very different response to the situation that causes Carol to faint. For Alva, the situation prompts first a series of explanations, offered to Carol, and then the "dream vision," which Olsen says she has heard versions of several times over the years (conversation 3): beginning with the memory of religious skepticism, the italicized dream vision moves into a still more powerful memory of religious experience in a time of intense need, when she was pregnant, young, alone. Her thoughts place us directly within the dialectic of religious faith in the black community and especially among black women—*"what have it done to help"* in tension with *"Free, free, I am so glad"* (51–52)—the simultaneous and irreducible need for a solace beyond the harsh material world coupled with the irrepressible recognition that the harshness persists. More crucially, those thoughts serve as an insistent reminder of a perspective unavailable to Carol and unassimilable by the dominant perspective.

A second dimension of the narrative voice is more diffuse but shares in the capacity to disrupt: the ways in which the story draws on spoken language, particularly within the black community. As Olsen has indicated, Alva's "dream vision" is itself a part of her drawing on oral traditions—"long, long rhyming poems would be recited from memory or 'prose' recitations like this one of Alva's" (conversation 3); other ways include her extensive quoting from the sermon and the congregation's response, her attention in the dialogue to the kind of "jivetalk" (53) that is prevalent in Parialee's conversation—"the new way she likes to talk now" (40)—and her weaving of song into the narrative reality of the story. The sermon becomes, for Carol, a "voice of drowsiness and dream to which Carol does not need to listen" (42) and is woven into her emotional sense of comfort and memory of warmth and shared experience with Parry. The choir's singing and the congregational responses, similarly, weave in and out of the narrative voice as Carol dreams and remembers the past and takes in the immediacy of the service at present. All of these dimensions of oral expression emphasize the way in which the narrative voice is *of* the context, integral to it, rather than merely describing it, and thus begin to suggest that the voice itself is more complex than either omniscient description or limited expression of a single consciousness.

It is, in fact, the *voices*—the plurality around her—that shape the emotional intensity for Carol. As she begins to "go under," to relinquish controlled consciousness, these voices take on an increasingly powerful presence: "Behind Carol, a trembling wavering scream. Then the thrashing. Up above, the singing. . . . Powerful throbbing voices. Calling and answering to each other" (46). The call-and-response form integral to such services—and indeed to prevalent notions of communication in many black communities—is thus made explicit in the narrative voice and points to some of the reasons that the service is so threatening to Carol: something is being asked of her; to be genuinely present, she herself needs to participate actively. But her own understandings of language and community and religious experience have not prepared her for this intensity or this expectation of involvement. To her, it looks like weakness, like a relinquishing: "Alva Phillips, strong Alva, rocking too and chanting, *O Yes*. No, do not look" (47). Thus when she sees her own classmate—with whom she later confesses to identify despite her distance from her by virtue of class distinctions and behavioral codes—succumbing to this power of communal feeling, she herself succumbs to her own "drowning," at present the most available escape for her. The voices in which she has been immersed and the call-and-response form of the service, with its reiterated refrain—"*Yes. Yes. . . . O Yes*" (45, for example)—suggest a much more complex rendering of narrative voice in communal interaction than the simple claim on observation that at first seems to be its definition.[62]

When we turn again to part 2, we see there a similar complexity, merged with its context and suggesting a multiplicity of perspectives in interaction: dialogue, as a third way in which the narrative voice both conveys and disrupts notions of reality. Indeed, the immediate response to Carol's fainting in part 1 is conveyed through this quality of dialogue, where we can see the conflicting perspectives and concerns of Parry, Carol, Helen, and Alva in unreconciled interaction: Parry wanting to restore simple order and comfort, Carol wanting primarily to go home, Helen wanting to attend to Carol's physical and emotional distress, and Alva wanting above all to explain, even when Carol does not want to listen (50–51). Each of these voices asserts a perspective that the narrative credits, even as no single perspective has priority.

Part 2 reinforces the sense of multiplicity: the family, in its own polyphony, even provides an explicit model for the narrative voice. This section opens with a family conversation, including disparate perspectives, not a univocal claim to any one interpretation of the story's central "event," Carol's baptismal faint. Len's concern seems primarily to moderate the tensions and to ease Helen's anxiety: "She seems good as new. Now *you* forget it, Helen" (52), or "Don't you think kids like Carol and Parry can show it doesn't *have* to be that way" (54), and then "Too much to talk about for one session. . . . Here, come to the window and watch the Carol and Parry you're both all worked up about" (56). And the scene out the window seems to legitimize his view: "Leaping, bounding, hallooing, tugging the kites of spring. In the old synchronized understanding, Carol and Parry kick, catch, kick, catch" (56). But at the same time, Helen's view is in reiterated tension with Len's: her response, in tears, introduces the conversation; her thought processes predominate in the crucial middle of the conversation (54–55)—shaped by her "foreboding of comprehension" (54); and the final idyllic description is already shadowed by the narrative voice interjection in parentheses: "(the last time)" (56). And in interaction with these two perspectives—the one reasoned and optimistic, the other emotional and apprehensive—we have, as well, the perspective of Jeannie, who speaks, as neither parent can, from her own recent experience with the "sorting process" she so soberly and painfully describes. The conflict she attributes to Carol—having to

"Be a brain—but not a square. Rise on up, college prep, but don't get separated" (55)—is her own conflict: the pain of both resisting and succumbing to social pressures at school, the opposing pull of the values of home and those of peers, the warring values within herself.

This sense of conflict is the underpinning of the narrative voice: perceptions of the social environment that are all accurate but not susceptible to reconciliation. Hence the peculiar appropriateness of the call-and-response background for part 1 and the centrality of dialogue for initial interpretation. Each allows for the inclusion of multiple voices without requiring that the perceived reality be congruent. A further dimension of this capacity derives from the narrative inclusion of what *doesn't* get spoken as well as what does. Alva's "dream vision" in part 1 is a central part of this pattern and significantly intervenes between the two dialogues, reminding us of perspectives that are unassimilable even to the process of dialogue, perspectives even less susceptible to articulation within the shared discourse. The narrative voice further acknowledges such unspoken understandings through Jeannie, Parry, and finally Helen herself. Although the family dialogue first seems to be framed around Helen's emotional needs and is centered on her thoughts, it also includes two crucial unspoken observations from Jeannie: "You don't realize a lot of things, Mother, Jeannie said, but not aloud" (52); "Enough to pull that kid apart two ways even more, Jeannie said, but still not aloud" (53). Jeannie's unvoiced thoughts thus make their own contribution to the conflicting insights that surround our interpretive response and shape the narrative voice.

Similarly, in part 2, which is centered in the white family home, Parry's presence and voice are given a disruptive and partially silent presence in an indented section that resists the closure of the sentence that precedes it: "the sorting goes on and seemingly it is over" (57). Parry's section is presented without quotation marks, but it appears primarily in her words and is shaped to her realities, conveyed in the rhythms of her speech, including the parenthetical singing: "*whole lotta shakin goin on*" (57). Parry's suppressed voice, like her mother's, then actively disrupts any threat of "general consciousness." Although the forces of racism try to exclude her, she is not a silenced victim; she affirms her presence and agency in her rhythmic and insistent motion and in the ironic stance she takes toward the material objects in Carol's room: Rembrandt, book jackets, fishkite mobile (58–59). Her presence—physical and powerful—also emphasizes the silencing in the

Part 1

section that is further indented within the indentation, the painful context for some of what separates Parry from Carol: *"But did not tell"* . . . (57)—did not tell of the insults, the condescension, the racism. Her silence and her presence thus take their place in a pattern of silences, things not said but included as disruptive understandings within the narrative perspective.

In this context, Helen's final pattern of thought at the story's end takes on additional significance, for she too joins the pattern of silent insights, not susceptible to joining the "general consciousness" of shared realities but nonetheless essential to the story's narrative perspective. The repeated phrase—"thought of saying. And discarded" (60)—emphasizes the insufficiency of explanation, the pain and necessity of Carol's own emergent consciousness of racism and her own involvement in the culture of racism. Helen's "And said nothing" (61)—repeated for emphasis—is not, then, her own failure of communication but an acknowledgment that Carol (like her mother) is placed in an untenable position by the culture in which she lives and that she (again like her mother) must find her own way to "sustain" in the face of this knowledge.

The narrative voice is thus developed to express an overall resistance to dominant discourse, an overall resistance to "general consciousness," and an overall resistance to reconciling perspectives that cannot be reconciled. In a traditional third-person narrative, Helen—as both Carol's mother and Alva's friend—might be used to mediate the preceding contradictions. But instead the narrative voice here merely posits her contribution as yet another interpretive response, full of its own contradictions and *not* part of the same "general consciousness" that observes the powerful emotional dynamic in the black church and withdraws when it cannot assimilate that experience—as Carol did in fainting, as the story seems to in its shift to the white family home in part 2. What part 2 adds, instead, is the painful rendering of a perspective defined by its sympathetic understanding of the needs of oppressed cultures and its conflicting sympathetic understanding of the need of a white adolescent girl to be able to live in the world she finds around her. Through Helen's perspective, part 2 thus rests partially on the recognition that neither Carol nor Helen can be full participants in the black community and that the dominant culture impedes their individual attempts to redress the patterns of racism. Helen's concluding thoughts convey the maternal version of the conflict:

72

Thinking: *caring asks doing. It is a long baptism into the seas of humankind, my daughter. Better immersion than to live untouched. . . . Yet how will you sustain?*

Why is it like it is?

Sheltering her daughter close, mourning the illusion of the embrace.

And why do I have to care?

While in her, her own need leapt and plunged for the place of strength that was not—where one could scream or sorrow while all knew and accepted, and gloved and loving hands waited to support and understand. (61–62; Olsen's ellipsis)

Helen's own urgent commitment to cultural change remains in conflict with her protectiveness toward her daughter as she anticipates the difficulty of such change. And more: her own loneliness for community, for shared commitment and for nurturance must go unaddressed so long as her social environment remains unreceptive.

The story then never reconciles these disparate points of view: Carol and Parialee do not fully restore the friendship damaged by a racist culture; Helen and Alva do not develop a communal strategy for resisting the pernicious effects of racism. But through its shifting narrative perspective, the story does disrupt the complacency of a "general consciousness" grounded in racism, as it dispels the notion of interpretive omniscience. Instead of offering the "truth" about the situation at hand, it simply rests silently on the disparate viewpoints of an adolescent white girl, an adolescent black girl, a middle-aged black woman, and a middle-aged white woman, and it makes explicit the necessary contradictions not only among these multiple viewpoints but also within each of them.

In refusing to dissolve or even mute the differences among these women—just as it refrains from reconciling the conflicting needs within each of them—the story makes manifest the impossibility of resolution within their present cultural context. In concluding with the silent embrace of mother and daughter, however, it enacts what narrative assertion cannot: the community of perception that must ground both mother's and daughter's participation in cultural change. The story has no resolution except in yearning; it has no agreed upon version of reality. But in juxtaposing the differences and oppositions in these versions of reality, it suggests the crevices in the "general consciousness" defined by racism and sexism and initiates a hope for a community of people, struggling through the negations of culture, to come to some understanding of their lives—both different and similar. It is this struggling amidst disparate perspectives that grounds the story's narrative voice, that gives it the authority of mutual interpretive effort without imposing a forced consensus.

"Tell Me a Riddle"

Asked about the title of the novella that concludes her first book-length publication, Tillie Olsen renewed the sense of riddle. She first quoted a Randall Jarrell poem, "What's the Riddle . . ."[63] about riddles and aging and uncertainty, calling it "a wonderful way to answer questions about the title." Her first response thus affirmed that life yields no answers, as the poem returns to its own enigmatic refrain—"I don't know." But she added a second response, referring to the title of the song that provides the novella's epigraph: " 'Tell Me a Riddle' was not the best title. I wish ever more I had called it 'These Things Shall Be' but it does also have to do with the riddles of life we grope for the answers to, or whether the answer we come to *is* the right answer" (conversation 4). She thus upheld both the title and the epigraph and renewed the riddle as a paradoxical tension between the assertive certainty of what *shall be* and the groping uncertainty with which we must make our lives.

I have been pursuing riddles throughout my analysis here: how to speak of "life comprehensions" without succumbing to prevailing cultural assumptions, how to write, as Olsen says, "when the context isn't there." The riddle reasserts itself here, returning on itself in the manner of many riddles: the answer reopens the question, as does each new piece in the *Tell Me a Riddle* collection.

In the novella, her "life comprehensions" are centered in what she saw as a "generation of believers," an older generation who had participated in efforts to attain the ideals described in "These Things Shall Be," that "song of their youth of belief" (110). Olsen's response, her way of writing this piece of fiction, takes into account a context that discounts such revolutionary belief, even as she voices her own recurring belief in human capacity and in the possibilities for social change. The riddle, then, is: how to write of the tragic losses and denials suffered by that older generation, to acknowledge their pain and sacrifice and even their uncertainty, and simultaneously to affirm the centrality of their belief in the possibilities of a better world.

Olsen's cultural context at the time of this writing was itself framed by the tension between belief and a cynical denial of belief: "so much of what was happening in the late forties and the fifties was again a test of belief versus cynicism" (conversation 4). She sees these as contending spirits of the period: on the one hand, cynicism, expressed through the Cold War, McCarthyism, the threat of nuclear destruction, and the bigotries and hostilities of the period; and on the other hand, belief, expressed through commitments to human rights, resistance to war, and the idealism evident, for example, in "the 1948 Universal Declaration of Human Rights, . . . subscribed to by every country then in existence, and also in the later UNESCO Declaration of the Rights of the Child" (conversation 4). She speaks, as well, of ongoing convictions, still present in the 1950s, that "war must not be any more, that human life was sacred, that this was the central task and that human beings of whatever color, nationality, or sex—all comprising one human race—had certain universal needs and rights" (conversation 4). She sees cynicism as the more prevalent of the two forces at that time, taking shape as an active resistance to "[a]ny activity of human beings with other human beings to make changes, to do something about wrongs," and she felt the ascendancy of "this teaching of despair" (conversation 4).

Behind Olsen is the older generation to whom she dedicates the novella: her own parents, participants in the 1905 revolution in Russia—her mother as a Tolstoyan, her father as a member of the Jewish Workers Alliance (the Bund); a friend, Seevya, whose wit was like that of David in the novella, who took the leap from ghetto life into a world of literature, music, history; and another friend, Genya, who was as a young woman "a famous orator and national leader of the Bund" and whose manner of dying was the manner of Eva's dying.[64] These members of an older generation suggested to Olsen a human commitment that cried out to be preserved.

Genya Gorelick's life history has a particularly powerful resonance for Olsen, deriving in part from a long friendship with her and with her son Al Richmond as well as from her personal and political history. As conveyed in Richmond's personal narrative, *A Long View from the Left* (1973), Genya's experiences are interwoven with that immigrant and revolutionary context that was such an important prompting for "Tell Me a Riddle." In his first chapter, "Childhood and Revolutions," Richmond recalls his mother, citing her participation in the Russian revolution of 1905, followed by confinement in "Czarist prisons, serving six years in these after 1905, aging and maturing in them, discovering here the world knowledge and the range of human culture that were denied her in the *shtetl*."[65] He also asserts that "[i]n the Czarist prisons, where she received her education, her tutors were the cultured daughters of the aristocracy and middle classes, among them the purest of Russian souls in their time. In their culture was the strong strain of Christian mysticism and symbolism that runs through Russian literature" (20). He speaks, too, of her involvement in "the Jewish Workers Alliance, commonly known as the Bund" (6), "her gifts as a public orator" (8), and goes on to trace his own birth in London in 1914, their eventual return to Russia to participate in the 1917 revolution, their subsequent imprisonment by occupying German troops, and then their immigration to the U.S. in 1922. Clearly, Genya had lived many of the pieces of history woven into Eva's past.

So, too, but differently, had Olsen's own mother. Specifically, of her mother's dying "in the winter of 1955," Olsen has more recently written: "my mother so much of whose life had been a nightmare, that common everyday nightmare of hardship, limitation, longing; of baffling struggle to raise six children in a world hostile to human unfolding—my mother, dying of cancer, had beautiful dream-visions—in color." Olsen describes her mother's childhood: "As a girl in long ago Czarist Russia, she had sternly broken with all observances of organized religion, associating it with pogroms and wars; 'mind forg'd manacles'; a repressive state. We did not observe religious holidays in her house."[66] She goes on to trace her mother's final—and beautiful—dream of three wise men who metamorphose into many women. Olsen's interpretive conclusion is equally beautiful, as it honors her mother's "inexhaustible legacy": "Inherent in it, this heritage of summoning resources to make—out of song, food, warmth, expressions of human love—courage, hope, resistance, belief; this vision of universality, before the lessening harms, divisions of the world are visited upon it" ("Dream," 263–64). It is not hard to see in these poignant claims to memory and heritage the vividness of Eva's life and convictions.

Genya, Seevya, Olsen's mother and father: each in a different way contributed to that rich sense of human reality that prompted the writing of "Tell Me a Riddle." All of them together provide the novella's deep roots in human history.

Socialist Convictions, Cynical Context

As her decision to write in "O Yes" of girls of different skin color was a way to honor the efforts of the civil rights movement and to affirm human efforts for social change, so here her decision to write of a revolutionary generation was a way to honor belief over cynicism. During the 1950s, the prevailing view of the culture was to see those revolutionary efforts through cynical lenses. Khrushchev's speech at a 1956 Communist party conference had focused attention on the horrors of Stalinism, and a large number of U.S. members had left the Communist party. Many socialist convictions were viewed with hostility in the surrounding context of anticommunism. The real issue for Olsen, however, was not party membership but deep friendships and powerful socialist convictions. Despite the hostile context, she still saw in socialist values the seeds of cultural change. Her effort in the novella, then, was framed by this tension: to acknowledge the losses and disillusionments that her parents' generation had lived through—that she herself felt—and yet to affirm their convictions, and her own.

Olsen's initial plan had not been to focus on politics at all but rather to write of "what drives older people apart after being together for many, many years" and "what keeps people together" (conversation 4)—a plan that is evident in the novella's opening on the scene of a marital quarrel. This plan, however, was disrupted by the deaths of people close to Olsen, people like her mother and Genya, who had made the transition from ghetto to revolutionary conviction to immigrant life in a new country and who had lived lives that embodied a resistance to cynicism. Her personal love and respect for the people of "that generation" and "the need, the urgency, to write of them" (conversation 4) are evident when she speaks of them; so too is the painfulness of their deaths.

Although the novella encompasses these deep comprehensions, its characters are not in any literal sense modeled on Olsen's friends and family. Rather they develop from the understandings Olsen acquired in the course of living attentively among those believers; hers is a powerful claim on their legacy. She says of her mother: "she is not Eva; but o she is profoundly present on every page of 'Tell Me a Riddle' " (conversation 4). Eva is not Olsen's mother, nor is she simply Genya or Seevya. She is instead—as Olsen has said of other of her characters—a "compound," written from that knowledge of her mother's life, of Genya's manner of dying and her revolutionary history as activist and orator, of Seevya's sense of humor and shortness of stature, of all those others whose lives are integral to her own understanding of history and political change and human circumstances.

Central to these understandings are Olsen's own beliefs, her own personal and political history. Her childhood in a socialist household, her relationships with many people who were part of movements for social change, her involvement in the Young Communist League and then the Communist party—these were all a part of her personal context for valuing the beliefs woven through "Tell Me a Riddle." Like many Americans of her generation,[67] she had joined the Communist party partly because of a conviction that change for human growth was both necessary and possible. Having drifted in and out of the party a number of times and then finally leaving it in the mid-1950s, she was no longer a party member by the time of writing "Tell Me a Riddle," but she never lost her convictions or regretted her involvement in movements for social change.

Speaking of a book that traced the disillusionment of former Communists, she has said, "I could never have been eligible for inclusion in *The God That Failed* . . . because for me it never was a God and it never failed. I was an atheist's daughter from the beginning."[68] She thus affirms both her capacity to refrain from deifying a party or a particular movement and her ongoing convictions. She also links her own convictions directly with those of the previous generation, particularly Jewish immigrants: "I believe that the heritage of those socialist communist Jews, that heritage that is less than a hundred years old, is in a way our most living heritage. . . . That is part of what I feel is *my* Yiddishkeit, my Jewish heritage, that need to change the world and eradicate those breeding grounds for hatreds and ignorances."[69]

This is the heritage she honors in the novella, especially through the "compound" life of Eva, who resists those old hatreds and ignorances with the vehemence of a life lived among them and the convictions borne of a socialist, communist Jewish history. When she objects to the hospital's labels—"At once go and make them change. Tell them to write: Race, human; Religion, none" (80)—she voices the values of that heritage and her own drive to eradicate hatred and ignorance. Her claim on heritage is decidedly not religious but passionately political, resisting falsely constraining categories of race and gender as it resists the horror enacted in the name of religion and ethnicity: "Religion that stifled and said: in Paradise, woman, you will be the

footstool of your husband, and in life—poor chosen Jew—ground under, despised, trembling in cellars. And cremated. And cremated" (81).
Eva sees the absolute urgency of leaving behind that terrible past:
"Heritage. How have we come from our savage past, how no longer
to be savages—this to teach. To smash all ghettos that divide us—not
to go back, not to go back—this to teach. Learned books in the house,
will humankind live or die, and she gives to her boys—superstition"
(81).

But the horrors are not only of the past: those ghettos still exist, still
divide. And the heritage of resistance must be brought into the present.
The memory of the recent Holocaust in Nazi Germany, the recent
atomic bombing of Hiroshima and Nagasaki, and the threat of nuclear
holocaust—the possibility of the total destruction of humankind—
these were all powerful cultural realities. Eva acknowledges them in
the phrase "will humankind live or die," and she reiterates the knowledge again in her later, halting phrases:

> *Even in reality (swallow) life's lack of it*
> *Slaveships   deathtrains   clubs   eeenough*
> *The bell   summon what enables*
> *78,000 in one minute* (whisper of a scream) *78,000*
> *human beings   we'll destroy ourselves?* (108–9)

The destruction of Hiroshima, the recurrent divisions among human
beings, the destructive capacities of human endeavor: Eva, like that
generation of believers for whom she speaks, knows that these horrors
and injustices must be resisted; she knows the necessity of leaving
that savage past, this savage present—"this to teach."

The most concrete evidence of these convictions and connections
can be found in the centrality that the novella gives to the song that
provides its epigraph, "These Things Shall Be." The song is one that
Olsen learned in childhood and has retained as a powerful expression
of conviction: "it expresses the essence of the aspirations, the hopes,
the beliefs in the future. It is an old Socialist hymn that comes out of
an old religious hymn and I learned it as a child from the Socialist
Sunday School hymn book; in our time it has been adopted as a United
Nations hymn and is sung by school children in some countries on
Universal Human Rights Day" (conversation 4). In her dying days,
Eva sings this song, as David recalls her youthful voice—"a girl's voice

of eloquence that spoke their holiest dreams" (110)—and struggles
with his current cynicism:

> *These things shall be, a loftier race*
> *than e'er the world hath known shall rise*
> *with flame of freedom in their souls*
> *and light of knowledge in their eyes*
>
> *They shall be gentle, brave and strong*
> *to spill no drop of blood, but dare all . . .*
> *on earth and fire and sea and air*
>
> *And every life* (long strangling cough) *shall be a*
> *song.* (110–11)[70]

The song, then, is a powerful connection to Olsen's context as it is
also a connection between past and present for Eva and eventually for
David, too. Most crucially, in the concluding section of the novella, it
becomes a part of the necessary and difficult communication between
David and Eva as he comes finally to his own memory of belief, his
own sense of conviction: *"that joyous certainty, that sense of mattering, of
moving and being moved, of being one and indivisible with the great of the
past, with all that freed, ennobled"* (113).

On the more immediate, physical level, Olsen was at that time
feeling a different threat of loss and disillusionment: the difficulty of
sustaining her commitment to writing in the midst of the other compelling necessities of her life. This deeply felt knowledge lies behind the
connections she makes to other writers in *Silences*, as it lies behind her
acknowledgment, in her 1962 talk published as the first essay in *Silences*,
of harms done to her work. But it is also a powerful shaping knowledge
integral to the writing of "Tell Me a Riddle." Having had to return
to employed work, as well as to family responsibilities, after the respite
of her time at Stanford University, she was forced to put aside the
portion of the novella she had written and to struggle to claim those
brief interrupted periods in which she could only take it up and put it
aside, never sustain the immersion that facilitates creative efforts. As
she indicates, this was also the period in which she was "sometimes
hospitalized—the harm had entered my body" (conversation 4; cf.
Silences, 224). Her response to these losses and harms was to shorten
the piece and to try "to embed all I could in the piece as it turned out
to be" (conversation 4).

"Life comprehensions"—a phrase that embraces so much—are surely a part of the forces that shape the novella, that give it its distinctive compression of form—as they do in all of Olsen's published work. These same life comprehensions suggest a powerful connection between her own losses and denials and the losses and denials in Eva's life. From this knowledge emerges the thematic concern for lost possibilities and denied capacities, not only for Eva but for all of the characters and even for their sense of humanity. Eva's response to the community sing is not grief for herself alone but for pervasive denials: "*Humankind one has to believe* So strong for what? To rot not grow?" And then: "Singing.   Unused the life in them. . . . Everywhere unused the life   And who has meaning?   Century after century   still all in us not to grow?" (99). Her earlier bitter response to David—"Enough unused I have to get used to already" (64)—takes on new resonance not only as her answer to his "Used to can get unused!" (64) but more crucially as her answer to all the unused life in people everywhere: we should not have to get used to so much wasted life. So too with Lennie's grief—"not alone for her who was dying, but for that in her which never lived"—and more—"for that which in him might never come to live" (107)—for that in all human beings which is denied full blossoming.

This was the riddle she faced as writer, the riddle we continue to face as readers. Again, the culture of the 1950s—and in different ways, so too the culture of the 1990s—had a powerful resistance to many of these insights, many of these human comprehensions. The prevailing anticommunist feeling made it difficult to communicate the power of these beliefs, the socialist conviction that human beings must work together in social movements to implement necessary changes. Similarly, readers in the 1990s, especially those lacking in general historical awareness, often have difficulty conceiving of the struggles that took place in Russia leading up to the revolution; instead they often think only of Stalinist Russia as the link to such references as "exile in Siberia" and "resistance to oppression."[71] In either instance, American readers—grounded in the prevailing belief that *individual* effort is what matters and that socialism leads to social control and eventually to such collapses as have taken place in Eastern Europe—often have difficulty discerning the values that are central to the novella or recognizing a socialist value system that is not defined by the abuses that have been enacted in the name of socialism. And yet the novella conveys very powerfully: "this to teach"—to smash the ghettos of human divisions, to affirm the capacities of human lives.

Feminist Insights without Context

As with her socialist convictions, Olsen held lifelong commitments to sexual equality, despite the fact that her cultural context often seemed blind to such possibilities. Here, too, Olsen felt with the "generation of believers" a continuity of insight and conviction. For this generation, "human included women" (conversation 4) and human capacities were to be nourished and developed. By contrast, the culture of the 1950s made marked divisions between men and women and implicitly adopted the equation that to be fully human required that one also be male. The novella itself is embedded in many of those divisions: the expectations of the culture have shaped the lives of David and Eva, as they have the lives of most men and women of the time. To portray those lives, Olsen necessarily describes and acknowledges those sexual divisions in the novella. At the same time, she negotiates that negating context, resisting the culturally imposed losses by tracing and recovering the resistances of "that generation," including its resistance to sexual divisions.

Consider, first, how Olsen conveys an understanding of sex roles, the divisions between men and women. As I suggested in my discussion of "O Yes," culturally defined sex roles were central to assumptions underlying marriage in the 1950s (as in earlier periods, as, still, in our own, despite some significant changes). We see the harms done to Eva in the name of these divisions: the "young wife," faced with an unacceptable choice between her passion for reading and her sexual passion—the reading time too rare, the sexuality too likely framed by the desires of her young husband, who coaxes her away when *he* returns from a meeting "stimulated and ardent" (67); the assumptions of motherhood—*her* parental responsibilities—and the losses that followed from the total commitment of that love that rose "like a torrent [and] drowned and immolated all else" (83); her required domestic role of "housewife," scraping through poverty while caring for seven children, "old humiliations and terrors," managing the insufficient resources, begging credit, salvaging "the old to see what could yet be remade" and begging soup bones as if for the dog (67). Sexual partner, mother, household manager—these are the roles assigned to her as a woman;

these are the roles constructed to meet the needs of this version of marriage.

David, too, feels the pressures of his masculine role. Faced with the knowledge of her illness, he must think: *"The money, where will come the money?"* and reiterate, *"The money, where will I wring the money?"* (78). Although anyone, male or female, might feel such an anxiety, for him—as for many men—the current responsibility is a replaying of a lifetime of this role: "Poverty all his life, and there was little breath left for running. He could not, could not turn away from this desire: to have the troubling of responsibility, the fretting with money, over and done with; to be free, to be *care*free where success was not measured by accumulation, and there was use for the vitality still in him" (64). His wish to enter the Haven is closely tied to his fatigue with his masculine role: "But as *he* had no peace, juggling and rejuggling the money to figure: how will I pay for this now?; prying out the storm windows (there they take care of this); jolting in the streetcar on errands (there I would not have to ride to take care of this or that); . . . he gave *her* no peace" (66).

But the issue is not merely a question of harms done and strife between them; it is also a knowledge of internal conflict and lives lived. Both Eva and David have felt joy, as well as suffered loss, through the roles assigned to them. Each has lived and developed within the intimacy of intertwined lives: "old harmonies and dependencies deep in their bodies; she curled to him or he coiled to her, each warmed, warming, turning as the other turned, the nights a long embrace" (75). Each has felt, too, the energy of the pleasures of their respective roles—beyond or in addition to the harms imposed by those roles. Hence his wish to go to the Haven, where he can be the public and social person he has grown into in his masculine role; hence her pleasure in the extension of her caring roles as she prepares for family guests: "With a kindling of energy for her beloved visitors, she arrayed the house, cooked and baked" (75).

Eva's inability to touch or hold her newest grandchild suggests the complexity of both the pleasures and the losses associated with her sex role. For her response is full of the intertwined richness and harms of motherhood as she experienced it:

> It was not that she had not loved her babies, her children. The love—the passion of tending—had risen with the need like a torrent; and like a torrent drowned and immolated all else. But when the

need was done—oh the power that was lost in the painful damming back and drying up of what still surged, but had nowhere to go. Only the thin pulsing left that could not quiet, suffering over lives one felt, but could no longer hold nor help.

On that torrent she had borne them to their own lives, and the riverbed was desert long years now. Not there would she dwell, a memoried wraith. Surely that was not all, surely there was more. Still the springs, the springs were in her seeking. Somewhere an older power that beat for life. Somewhere coherence, transport, meaning. If they would but leave her in the air now stilled of clamor, in the reconciled solitude, to journey on.

And they put a baby in her lap. Immediacy to embrace, and the breath of *that* past: warm flesh like this that had claims and nuzzled away all else and with lovely mouths devoured; hot-living like an animal—intensely and now; the turning maze; the long drunkenness; the drowning into needing and being needed. Severely she looked back—and the shudder seized her again, and the sweat. Not that way. (83–84)

The power of that "torrent" is indisputable: a power beyond individual human needs, a power in conflict with other powers, other needs: "coherence, transport, meaning."[72] One feels its indisputable priority, even as one feels its capacity to drain away the mother's life, to diminish her to a "thin pulsing." It is not so much that the demands of motherhood are harmful as that they are all-consuming, immediate, insistent. She is not disputing her love or the value of her energies spent in caring for her children; she is acknowledging her need for *other* values as well, other powers, earlier commitments that were lost and overshadowed because her experience of motherhood was too consuming. Now she needs that "older power that beat for life"—that resurrection of another self that was "immolated" in her motherhood.

Throughout the novella Olsen conveys the complexity of the ways sex roles work. We are never led to see Eva as having made "wrong" choices; rather, we come to see her as a person interacting with circumstances over which she lacks full control. Like the mother in "I Stand Here Ironing," Eva realizes her motherhood is defined by this power of external circumstances in her children's lives—"lives one felt, but could no longer hold nor help"; similarly, she recognizes in her own life the shaping power of cultural circumstances. Rather than presenting Eva's losses and denials as personal concerns, the novella embeds within it the consciousness that these are cultural circumstances and that they persist even in the present. As Olsen points out, the easy assumption that Nancy, Eva's daughter-in-law, rather than Paul, her son, will arrange for the doctor's appointment, is another reminder of how sex roles are lived and reinforced: "It was Paul who loved his mother, but it was his wife he expected to take her to the doctor, do other such tasks" (conversation 4).

Even more poignantly, these divisions are reenacted in the youngest generation: "Eva of that generation, her consciousness of the little granddaughter, the little grandson, in the process of being 'crucified' into a sex—'Dody hunching over in pretend-cooking' while Richard ('Watch me, Grandma') is 'snaking up the tree, hanging exultant, free.' The cry within Eva—'Climb too, Dody, climb and look'—seeing the little ones already acting out according to old, old circumscribed and in certain periods of human history probably somewhat necessary ways of being and doing" (conversation 4; text excerpts, 86). Thus when Vivi remembers her own childhood, her own experience of the mother that Eva had been (87–89), we recognize the intertwined values and losses in this role, the impossibility of seeing it singly and clearly. Vivi's "spilling memories" (89), the grandchildren's questions—these are vivid and real; so too is Eva's own compelling need to "leave that time" (88), to find in solitude an alternative way to understand herself and her past. Braiding and unbraiding the sashes as she sits alone in the closet, tracing "the pattern on the hoop slips" (89), she seeks to twine together other memories, other understandings, to form some further pattern, woven out of these conflicting understandings.

The reading of Eva as "a frustrated career woman, a woman embittered because she did not have time for herself" (conversation 4), can be constructed from the novella's implicit critique of sex roles, the limitations placed on human capacity. But that is not the Eva Olsen intended to write:

> In dying, her anguish was not for her woman's life, gone into (loved) children and tasks, but about what was central in our time. That "still, century after century," the failure to make the changes that would enable human potentiality to flower, the torment as to whether or not humanity would be able to do away with the nuclear threat of extinction, the other threats of war, injustice, reaction, ghettoization, the barbarities of the past still so present. She "accepted," I say accepted in quotes, what her woman's working-class life had been. Indeed, she saw herself in the context of her own generation, including her own generation of women. (conversation 4)

As readers, then, we must circumstance Eva within her own generation: a generation capable of seeing the difficulties of imposed sex roles, of living beyond them when granted a context for doing so, but also of knowing the values to be claimed from the life that has been lived.

The conflicts surrounding the thematic concern with motherhood are again embedded in particular cultural contexts. I have already spoken of the complexities of Eva's response to memories of her experiences as a mother: these are both central to her, a valued part of her personal history, and harmful to her, a confinement within only one dimension of her human complexity. Olsen herself speaks contradictorily of motherhood in *Silences*, where she calls it both a source of oppression and an experience of "transport" for some women: "an almost taboo area; the last refuge of sexism . . . the least understood, least and last explored, tormentingly complex *core* of women's oppression (and I believe, transport as woman)" (202).

Similarly, she makes this contradictory understanding central to her analysis of the difficulties faced by women writers. On the one hand, she raises legitimate objections to women's centering literary work on the "stereotypic biological woman (breeder, sex-partner) sphere" (*Silences*, 42); on the other hand, she calls for women writers' inclusion in literature of all those specifically female experiences that have been omitted from literature—most notably the experience of motherhood (*Silences*, 42–43). This is a riddle, indeed: for an experience to be simultaneously at the core of oppression and the wellspring for transport of self, to be simultaneously a limitation on a writer and a vital inclusion in literary form. But the riddle is not Olsen's construction; it derives from its patriarchal context: to make motherhood central to any literary form is to risk "essentializing" women within patriarchal language and thought—that is, to define women solely by biological or reproductive traits—but to ignore motherhood is to deny a central fact of many women's lives. Motherhood *is* both: a central and sometimes positive fact in many women's lives; a central and sometimes fatal tool of women's oppression. As Deborah Rosenfelt says, "All of Olsen's work . . . testifies to her concern for women, . . . her sense of the deepest, most intractable contradiction of all: the unparalleled satisfaction and fulfillment combined with the overwhelming all-consuming burden of motherhood" (397).

Because we are ourselves embedded in these cultural contradictions, we often have difficulty escaping either the essentialism (mothers are *only* mothers and women *should* be mothers) or the denials (don't think or write of women as mothers because then we accept the patriarchal judgments that womanhood equals motherhood). From this context, readers have difficulty determining how to think of Eva's motherhood: her inability to hold her newest grandson must either be a judgment on her inadequacies or a judgment on the horrors of motherhood. Her daughter Clara's poignant claim—*"I do not know you, Mother. Mother, I never knew you"* (107)—becomes for some readers a further judgment on her coldness, her inadequacy as a mother.[73] But the response that Olsen offers elsewhere—"Daughter—you knew yourself. Without knowing, you knew me"[74]—becomes an acknowledgment of a more complex motherhood experience rather than a judgment on a particular mother, as does her son Lennie's comment: *"good-bye Mother who taught me to mother myself"* (108). In both of these responses to motherhood we can see that much of the accomplishment of motherhood will go unacknowledged, will exist only in the lives that a parent has helped to bring to adulthood: the daughter and the son both take with them the unacknowledged experiences and knowledge derived from the mother's life. The resulting insight is contradictory but vital: motherhood is simultaneously premised on the denial of the mother's selfhood and on the enactment of that selfhood through connection in human continuity. But the "journey to her self" that Eva pursues *cannot* be premised on motherhood; each human being is entitled to make that journey beyond the limits of culturally imposed roles.

Form as Resistance to Context

Olsen's work as a whole is testimony to her life comprehensions and convictions and to their effect on form and linguistic expression. As she says in summary response to my overarching question about circumstances: "Well, the circumstances of writing very much affected its form" (conversation 4). This integration of personal and historical comprehensions and the recognition that external factors become integral to how writers write, then, become one explanation for the distinctive quality of her work. As Olsen says of the first three pieces in the collection, "They were not what was being written in that period" (conversation 4). They *were*, however, by 1957 published work, and this factor too helped to shape Olsen's interaction with her form and with her expectations of readers. As she continued her work on "Tell Me a Riddle," she had reason to think of readers of published work—readers who would not have immediate knowledge of her or her specific context. She knew that her work was unusual for the 1950s; she knew that her subsequent work needed to bridge the distance between her own life comprehensions and the context of the culture around her, even as she retained the compelling need to write of that which the culture might not yet be ready to comprehend.

My final entrance into the riddles of this novella, then, derives from these insights into cultural contradictions and pursues an understanding of how the novella itself is constructed in resistance to imposed meanings. For it is through its form that it finds ways to speak on many levels, articulating realities that expand our knowledge beyond what our context expects us to understand. In doing so, the novella is able to convey its "life comprehensions," to express immediate "realities" while simultaneously opening out toward alternative realities.

The novella's opening paragraph points toward the complexity of the narrative form that follows. As it conveys crucial specific information, it also introduces a powerful metaphorical pattern and an equally powerful narrative perspective: "For forty-seven years they had been married. How deep back the stubborn, gnarled roots of the quarrel reached, no one could say—but only now, when tending to the needs of others no longer shackled them together, the roots swelled up visible, split the earth between them, and the tearing shook even to the children, long since grown" (63). The metaphors are those of growth and those of bondage, of harms that spread across generations but also of deep and powerful interconnections. The narrative perspective draws on these same metaphors as it claims a basis beyond any single character, probing interconnections that extend in many directions and speaking through the voices and understandings of many characters.

Consider first something that I have noted in all of the stories in the collection: there is no clear protagonist, no single character on whom we are asked to focus our attention. Although most readers see Eva as a central character—and clearly I too have been speaking of her as such—we also see David as central and come to see Jeannie as central in part 4. From the opening paragraph, we see that the story talks only of an unnamed "they"; and when, immediately following that paragraph, we turn to a series of responses from the "children, long since grown," we are further diffusing our focus of attention. When we do, then, attend directly to David's and Eva's responses, we receive his perspective first—and for neither of them are we yet given names.

Many readers first take David to be the protagonist.[75] Having come to expect a single protagonist, they readily accept that it should be the character whose perspective they first enter into at length. They join him in his frustration and judge her for her resistance to both his arguments and his voice. When the story turns away from his perspective—"And now it was he who turned on the television loud so he need not hear" (66)—they feel his justification. But, of course, the story immediately shifts to Eva's perspective: "Old scar tissue ruptured and the wounds festered anew" (67). Her consciousness surrounding their dialogue provides a basis for beginning to see *her* as central. Her solitude newly frames the issues of their conflict: "She would not exchange her solitude for anything. *Never again to be forced to move to the rhythms of others*" (68).

These opening pages, then, suggest the centrality of both characters. Readers very likely choose one or the other as central depending on their own histories in reading and in living. Expectations of a single protagonist may first join expectations that that protagonist will be male—or that that protagonist will be of the same sex as the author. Such expectations will then be joined by understandings derived from having listened to such quarrels among people that we know, from having participated in decisions about where parents or grandparents ought to live, from our own assumptions about how marital differences ought to be resolved or which burden is most in need of easing—the burden of financial responsibility or the burden of nurturing responsibility. But however we negotiate these disputes as we first read the story, we almost certainly come to realize that the intertwined lives of these two characters are the central concern, not the exploration of one set of conflicts for a single protagonist.

This realization may dissipate to some extent in the lengthy part 2, where so much of our attention is focused on Eva—her interactions with her grandchildren, her fragmented memories, her claims on solitude.[76] It may further dissipate in the shorter part 3, in which the perspective emerges from her sensory impressions and the prose mimics her distinctive gasping for breath and in which we build toward her painful realization: "And looking for answer—in the helpless pity and fear for her (for *her*) that distorted his face—she understood the last months, and knew that she was dying" (99). But that realization comes to her through reading *his* face and the realization that emerges from the subsequent part 4 is indeed a shared realization, a knowledge of the anguish and convictions of their shared lives that eventually she is able to reach and to communicate to him.[77]

No single protagonist: indeed, what we are moving toward is the understanding that must emerge through interaction—between characters, between each character and his or her material circumstances, and even between generations. Hence the importance of Jeannie in part 4—"I had always intended to go on with Jeannie, with that family" (conversation 4); Jeannie not only elicits important understanding between David and Eva but is also a central source of support and love for each of them. Furthermore, she brings connections to other people's understandings, as in her gift of the "Rosita" bread, and helps to extend the story well beyond the immediacy of one generation's experiences. By the end, indeed well before we have actually learned their names in the novella's final pages, David and Eva have long since moved beyond an anonymous "they." But they also remain thoroughly entangled in each other's lives, each other's perceptions, each other's emergent knowledge. No longer can we easily return to an initial assumption that either one or the other must be the protagonist; no longer can we easily see the story as the history of the conflicts and perceptions of *any* single character.

The novella's capacity for conveying complex insight and probing interconnections is enriched by a second narrative strategy. Not only does the novella have no single protagonist; it also has no linear plot that builds from conflict to resolution. Although the story does begin with a decided conflict and even has a sense of resolution at the end, the understandings do not evolve from any linear transmission of events as causal sequence. Crucial causal events are, in fact, withheld from us, and only gradually revealed in the progression of characters' thoughts and observations. The effect is to reveal the characters as shaped by their circumstances but also as they interact with those circumstances, both past and present. Neither David nor Eva can be simply contained in a "coherent" character description. We must rather develop a complicated and sometimes contradictory understanding of them by assembling the circumstances that have framed their lives.

A roughly chronological sequence of events in Eva's life and then their shared lives can be constructed from embedded references: a childhood in the impoverished Russian village of Olshana, with "round thatched roofs" (83) and children playing jacks (89); reading lessons from the "noble" Lisa, a Tolstoyan of high birth (103); involvement in and orator of the 1905 revolution—*"hunger; secret meetings; human rights; spies; betrayals; prison; escape"* (95) and "a girl's voice of eloquence that spoke their holiest dreams" (110); the "springtide" love between them (92); a year of solitary exile in prison "when only her eyes could travel, and no voice spoke" (83); immigration on a steerage ship; young married life of poverty and struggle; the responsiblities of a large family—nursing a baby, sewing, washing clothes, singing, laughing, cooking; the death of a son in World War II, in Stuttgart, "where Davy has no grave" (104); books, music, arguments—extending the "stubborn, gnarled roots of the quarrel" (63) and of their shared and disparate lives.

Knowledge of these past circumstances and experiences helps us to go beyond the conflicting roles in which we first encounter them, helps us to understand more fully their points of connection and of conflict; but the chronology can neither "explain" them nor provide a simple causal sequence by which we move toward a resolution. Instead, the very effort of constructing such a chronology and the elliptical way in which events are conveyed to us through characters' own connections in shared memory and private thought suggest to us the complexity of lives that can never be fully known, whose richness and depth intensify the coming together that we witness in the final pages, where we experience "the ever heightening consciousness of the significance, the meaning, of what was happening around her, and remembered from the past—the new experiences also evoking, drawing on what had been" (conversation 4).

The associative structure of the novella, like Eva's probing of memory and braiding together of past and present experiences, thus prompts connections and insights that would be lost in a chronological narrative. It does not deny history; rather, it renews a more complex sense of history that incorporates the webbing of interconnections among which human beings actually live. As Eva hunches in the closet, she recalls deep and overlaid memories: her grandchildren's game of jacks the previous evening and her own long-ago games of jacks in her village, "though there was no ball, no jacks. Six stones, round and flat" (89). The associative pattern then moves through her grandson Richard's school lesson on three kinds of stones toward a series of memories mixed with metaphors in interwoven mental process, including the mythical claims on Sisyphus—"a great rock that crashed back down eternally—eternal labor, freedom, labor"—and on the biblical David, "who with a stone slew . . ." (90). The associative pattern takes Eva back to Lisa in the prison of deep personal memory and forward to the connection to the grandchild who finds her hiding in the closet. The "stone" of memory is layered and fossilized with history, both personal and cultural. Nothing is to be omitted in the process by which Eva braids and unbraids the images and thoughts that construct her subjectivity and that pervade and construct the entire novella.[78]

A third narrative strategy in a sense embraces the first two that I have identified: the novella's complex narrative voice—both multiple and interactive—draws on its dispersed character consciousnesses and its resistance to linear plot. The initial claim on the narrative voice comes with the first use of narrative collage on the opening page of the novella. Instead of telling us the reactions of the grown children to this new strife between their parents, the narrative voice simply lays before us a series of concrete responses, questions and assertions that simultaneously situate the parents and their children:

> Why now, why now? wailed Hannah.
> As if when we grew up weren't enough, said Paul.
> Poor Ma. Poor Dad. It hurts so for both of them, said Vivi. They never had very much; at least in old age they should be happy.
> Knock their heads together, insisted Sammy; tell 'em: you're too old for this kind of thing; no reason not to get along now.
> Lennie wrote to Clara: They've lived over so much together; what could possibly tear them apart? (63–64)

Hannah wails; Paul comments, almost bitterly; Vivi *feels*; Sammy insists; Lennie questions, in written interaction with Clara, who is herself silent. All six living children are situated in reaction to their parents' turmoil. And the questions first posed implicitly by the narrative voice—how far back does the quarrel reach and how far does the damage now extend—are now reframed by the children's needs as well.

The collage technique that from the beginning makes possible this complex and multiple understanding is used differently but repeatedly throughout the story, especially as a way of initiating possible conceptual patterns that help us to understand the characters. Experiences that are not consecutive or linked by narrative connections are simply enumerated as part of a broader pattern that is being explored: conversations associated with David's attempts to draw Eva into social interaction (73); examples of her behavior that stand as exceptions to her more general calm ("Musing; gentleness—*but for the incidents of the rabbi in the hospital, and of the candles of benediction*" [80])—followed by the repeated phrase, "Otherwise—musing; gentleness" (82); incidents of the grandchildren's pulls on her emotions (86–87); and a series of memories gathered from Vivi's invoking of the past in multiple conversations (87–89). All of these passages resist expectations of narrative links and instead bring together disparate incidents as part of broader patterns that form the context for our understanding of these two characters and the strife and interconnections between them. Although the incidents are conceptually framed, however, they are not presented as illustrations of points in an argument; they are instead explorations of pieces of understanding that we may find pertinent to our overall understanding.[79]

A second way in which the narrative voice is multiple and exploratory rather than singular and explanatory is in its use of dialogue. Dialogue is of course a traditional narrative device—and one that makes many narrative forms capable of including multiple perspectives without needing to develop experimental forms. But its use here is distinctive. The opening section is again revealing. Immediately following the collage of the children's voices, we enter not only the literal dialogue between David and Eva but also the larger dialogue between their two divergent perspectives. His perspective comes first, as I discussed above, but even in that we have the use of dialogue between the two of them, each circumstancing his or her own understanding of their distinctive human needs. Because the surrounding narrative seems to come primarily from his perspective, we may, as I suggested, initially credit his views more strongly, but the dialogue itself opens those views to question. Then, when her perspective follows, dialogically resituating us in an alternative understanding, we experience directly the tension that results from these two disputing views.

Olsen has prepared for the concluding section of the novella with all of the intervening uses of dialogue. In the conclusion she draws most directly on the dialogical process of thought itself, here in David's perspective. David's dialogical thinking as Eva lies dying exemplifies the novella's capacity to incorporate increasingly complex and interactive understandings:

> Escaped to the grandchildren whose childhoods were childish, who had never hungered, who lived unravaged by disease in warm houses of many rooms, had all the school for which they cared, could walk on any street, stood a head taller than their grandparents, towered above—beautiful skins, straight backs, clear straightforward eyes. "Yes, you in Olshana," he said to the town of sixty years ago, "they would look nobility to you."

> And was this not the dream then, come true in ways undreamed?
> he asked.
> *And are there no other children in the world?* he answered, as if in her
> harsh voice.
> *And the flame of freedom, the light of knowledge?*
> *And the drop, to spill no drop of blood?* (112)

His internal thought processes not only have integrated her voice but now turn on the very questions that lie between them, the larger questions that frame the narrative as a whole and move both them and it beyond the personal quarrel and into the difficulties of historical change. The thinking David pursues seems to require a dialogical form and to yield the interactive understanding that is necessary to the novella's knowledge of human complexity and its voicing of belief in human capacity.

A third way in which the novella's voice opens onto complexity results from its intertwining of physical and psychological realities. In discussing the narrative voice, Olsen first cites the centrality of physical realities—"I had to keep reminding the reader that she was deaf, almost blind—and that she was *dying*"—and then suggests the interconnection between the physical and the psychological: " 'The great ear pressed inside her . . . the sweat . . . the long shudder seizing' are not only the body response to profoundly emotional happenings,—they are the workings of the cancer, growing" (conversation 4).

The concern with hearing is particularly pertinent as it provides a powerful metaphorical pattern without ever losing its physical basis. She experiences the emotional claims of family as *"a great ear pressed under her heart"* (86), and she experiences the cancer as "the great ear pressed inside" (90). The cancer is thus linked not only to her physical loss of hearing but more crucially to her heightened emotional attentiveness to her own needs: she dare not respond to the "tendrils," the "knocks" that pursue her from others' needs, insisting *"let me in, let me in"* (86). Instead, she must follow the emotional pattern set by her physical experiences: *"Being able at last to live within, and not move to the rhythms of others*, as life had forced her to: denying; removing; isolating; taking the children one by one; then deafening, half-blinding— and at last, presenting her solitude" (68–69). This solitude is hers alone; won at the cost of both physical and psychological losses, it is the foundation for her "reconciled peace" (69).

The ear then images her pain, her inwardness, her solitude, and her intensely focused listening. On her final sickbed, she continues her listening—to music on Jeannie's radio, to her own inwardness when she silences the radio; she has *become* the ear: "She would lie curled on her side, her knees drawn up, intense in listening (Jeannie sketched her so, coiled, convoluted like an ear), then thresh her hand out and abruptly snap the radio mute—still to lie in her attitude of listening, concealing tears" (102). But it is from this listening that she develops as well a voice: "She, who in her life had spoken but seldom and then only when necessary (never having learned the easy, social uses of words), now in dying spoke incessantly" (103). And she voices some of the crucial interconnections of her life, placing Jeannie in a lineage that includes Eva's own mother and grandmother and that identifies her with the noble Lisa (103–4). Her speaking now, in the fragments of delirium and memory, connects her listening and her voice and her dying effort to comprehend: "All that happens, one must try to understand" (104).[80] Her deafness now is not hers alone but the hazard of human loss and denial that we all must face: " 'The music,' she said, 'still it is there and we do not hear; knocks, and our poor human ears too weak. What else, what else we do not hear?' " (105).

In this way, the narrative voice has dissolved the distance between the physical and the psychological, the personal and the larger patterns of history. When Eva reaches across the bed to hold David's hand (105), she initiates the patterns of connection that not only rejoin her to David but also weave into their shared lives the historical significance of persistent belief. She has struggled throughout the novella, throughout her emergent knowledge that she is dying, to retrieve an earlier sense of belief, to plumb her solitude for its resources in meeting her death. Her prior turning away from the pull of motherhood, of grandmotherhood set the stage: "Not there would she dwell, a memoried wraith. Surely that was not all, surely there was more. Still the springs, the springs were in her seeking. Somewhere an older power that beat for life. Somewhere coherence, transport, meaning. If they would but leave her in the air now stilled of clamor, in the reconciled solitude, to journey on" (84). During the subsequent portions of the novella, she *has* journeyed on; she has pursued that "older power that beat for life."

In the novella's final pages, Eva renews her connection to her earlier self, a connection via voice and meaning—"a girl's voice of eloquence that spoke their holiest dreams" (110)—a connection via song—"a song of their youth of belief" (110)—and a connection through both

David and Jeannie to a capacity to resist the harms she has witnessed in her lifetime. In the end David and Jeannie must articulate these connections for us, but they emerge only through Eva's prior immersion in "listening" to her past, to her solitude, to her fragile but persistent belief.

The final pages of the novella are thus in some sense a resolution, but they are not so much a resolution of the initial conflict as they are a resolving of the many narrative strands into historical insight. David's cynicism—echoing the prevailing cultural ideas of personalism and lost belief—dissolves into a claim on the persistence of belief:

> The cards fell from his fingers. Without warning, the bereavement and betrayal he had sheltered—compounded through the years—hidden even from himself—revealed itself,
>> uncoiled,
>> released,
>> *sprung*
>
> and with it the monstrous shapes of what had actually happened in the century. (111)

He struggles in his own solitude, in facing her death and the dying "with her [of] their youth of belief" (112), and he continues his dialogical response:

> And he yearned to package for each of the children, the grandchildren, for everyone, *that joyous certainty, that sense of mattering, of moving and being moved, of being one and indivisible with the great of the past, with all that freed, ennobled.* Package it, stand on corners, in front of stadiums and on crowded beaches, knock on doors, give it as a fabled gift.
>
> "And why not in cereal boxes, in soap packages?" he mocked himself. "Aah. You have taken my sense, cadaver." (113)

His self-mocking response, however, does not return him to a pervasive cynicism; instead, it leaves him open to Eva and to his own need to reconnect with her and with himself, his own belief: "*Still she believed?* 'Eva!' he whispered. 'Still you believed? You lived by it? These Things Shall Be?' " (113–14).

Finally opened to her, he reaches toward necessary reconnection:

And instantly he left the mute old woman poring over the Book of the Martyrs; went past the mother treading at the sewing machine, singing with the children; past the girl in her wrinkled prison dress, hiding her hair with scarred hands, lifting to him her awkward, shamed, imploring eyes of love; and took her in his arms, dear, personal, fleshed, in all the heavy passion he had loved to rouse from her.

"Eva!"

. . . felt that at any moment he would die of what was unendurable. Went to press the buzzer to wake Jeannie, looked down, saw on Jeannie's sketch pad the hospital bed, with *her*; the double bed alongside, with him; the tall pillar feeding into her veins, and their hands, his and hers, clasped, feeding each other. And as if he had been instructed he went to his bed, lay down, holding the sketch (as if it could shield against the monstrous shapes of loss, of betrayal, of death) and with his free hand took hers, back into his. (114–15)

Only in these moments of his return to her does he also return her to herself, calling her, for the only two times in the novella, by her own name. Only in these moments of his return to her does he also return to himself, to a self he too had lost in the years of disconnection and cynicism. Only in these moments of his return to her does he finally realize his need for connection—to her, to his past, to his own sense of belief in change—even as he must now confront as well "the monstrous shapes of loss, of betrayal, of death" (115).

These final pages, though painful, are also healing in their response to the pervasive riddles of the novella. We are not given answers, but we are led to more complex understandings and to responses that resist a simple capitulation to pain and loss. As she comforts David in the final paragraph, Jeannie also comforts the novella's readers and points us beyond the sorrow to her own integrating response: "It is a wedding and they dance, while the flutes so joyous and vibrant tremble in the air. Leave her there, Grandaddy, it is all right. She promised me. Come back, come back and help her poor body to die" (116). The image of the interior experience of her grandmother's dying thus integrates several earlier images: from Eva's childhood village life and the dancing there, from the "springtide love" between Eva and David (92), from the mourning for three-year-old Rosita, whose death is honored with "songs she liked to dance to" (101), from the pervasive role of music throughout the novella.[81]

Jeannie's crucial role here also emphasizes the sense of healing and joy that have been attributed to her in her role as caregiver and in her role as grandchild, heir of those who make change. She had arrived, "the lightness and brightness of her like a healing" (93), and she has now shared the joy she claimed from her grandmother: "Shameful the joy, the pure overwhelming joy from being with her grandmother; the peace, the serenity that breathed" (107). She has provided both the sketch that in some sense "instructed" David in his physical reconnection with Eva and the final return to music and joy. The "scar tissue" that had earlier "ruptured" and "the wounds" that had "festered anew" (67) have, by this ending, responded to Jeannie's healing presence and to the complex intervention of Olsen's narrative response.

The novella's ending is reaffirmed in the concluding dedication:

> *For my mother, my father,*
> *and*
> *Two of that generation*
> *Seevya and Genya*
> *Infinite, dauntless, incorruptible*
>
> *Death deepens the wonder (116)*

The theme of reclamation of lost lives, the healing between David and Eva, the generational continuity embodied in Jeannie, the return to belief that we witness in David through Eva's own reconnection with her youthful idealism—all of these join with the emotional power of the dedication in an integral resistance to despair, despite the harrowing sense of loss in which we have also been immersed as we read through the novella and its approach to imminent death. Themes, phrases, characters, and dedication all acknowledge the tragedy of human waste without succumbing to it; all participate in the complex narrative form in which Olsen has conveyed these lives and their "incorruptible" belief.

The narrative, then, has been structured so as to give form to the riddles of these lives, the complexities of their belief and the difficulties of their resistances to the culture around them. The narrative resists a simple response to the pain and possible despair of facing death as it resists a simple choice between the two primary characters whose lives it portrays. Instead it invites us to be a part of that "common work" of understanding human experiences[82] and to pursue our own living in resistance to simple answers. In reminding us of the riddling of both life and narrative form, it also affirms the power of conviction inherent in the beliefs of "that generation" and in the novella's epigraph: "These Things Shall Be." Speaking beyond the cultural context that frames its meanings and necessitates its riddles, it also affirms its own belief in human capacity for growth and change.

"Requa I"

"Requa I"—Tillie Olsen's fifth and most recently published story—seems at first to depart from the central concerns of the pieces published in *Tell Me a Riddle* a decade earlier. It is set in 1932 rather than in the period of its composition. It traces the experiences of two males—13-year-old Stevie and his uncle, Wes, both white, both working class—rather than giving central attention to women's lives. It immerses itself in the sensory stimuli of the natural world rather than visibly probing societal circumstances. Although it is a "piece" of something larger—as are all the pieces in *Tell Me a Riddle*—in this case, the larger work remains incomplete: "Well, I didn't want it to be published so. I kept saying, this is part of something longer; this is just the first part and everything in it has to do with what is to follow" (conversation 5).

First published as "Requa" in the *Iowa Review* in 1970 and then as "Requa I" in *The Best American Short Stories of 1971*,[83] it has not yet been widely anthologized or published in a book devoted exclusively to Olsen's work; nor has it received the critical attention and widespread reader response that followed *Tell Me a Riddle*. Instead, it remains unknown to many readers of Olsen's earlier work. Nonetheless, "Requa I" renews Olsen's recurrent commitments. It speaks—from a new set of circumstances to a differently situated group of readers—in a language of possibility. It speaks anew: of human harms and human capacities, of the imperatives of social change.

From the beginning, the story is shaped to circumstances, especially to the immediacy of personal anguish. We enter the story through Stevie's distinctive experience of dislocation and loss—most painful in a young person whose own roots in memory are not yet deep resources. The story provides no definition of situation, no clear context; rather, we come to know these experientially, by participating in Stevie's and Wes's dislocation as they travel through a literal fog that reflects their emotional fog of pain and isolation. As in "Tell Me a Riddle," the characters are at first unnamed and are situated more by emotional context than by historical detail. As in "Hey Sailor, What Ship?" the opening seems highly subjective, tied to a disoriented sub-

101

jectivity, and conveyed largely through the sensory experiences and the memories of a particular consciousness.

But Stevie's and Wes's circumstances are not merely obscure or confused. Rather they are distinctive and distinctively rendered: the boy whose mother has just died, riding in a pickup truck with his uncle away from San Francisco and north through California, out of the city and into an unknown geography with winding roads, deer, lumber trucks, great redwood trees. He is displaced from the known, thrown unprepared into the unknown, "without even time to say good-bye to the lamppost that he could hug and swing himself round and round" (237). Even in his own mind, his circumstances are unclear as he struggles with the change from having been his mother's primary caregiver to being alone among strangers and in new places: "Being places he had never been. Waitin   moving   sliding   trying. Staying up to take care of his mother, afraid to lie down even when she was quiet, 'cause he might fall asleep and not hear her if she needed him" (237).

The opening is markedly sensory: readers must experience it first and only later come to understand it. Stevie's fatigue and nausea, his most vivid sensations, are palpable; his grief is omnipresent, submerged, everywhere and nowhere but always experienced in his body. He is mute, exhausted, without purpose or context, uncertain even whether he really *has* left behind his mother and his task of caring for her. The story later puts the situation directly—"this man he hardly knew . . . came and took everything and him and put him in a place he did not know where he was" (243)—but in the beginning we *experience* what we have not yet been told: 13-year-old Stevie's grief for his recently dead mother. The opening sections conclude by distilling the factual context in one brief sentence: "So he came to Requa   March, 1932   13 years old" (239). Even as these opening pages evade interpretive clarity, they nonetheless provide concrete context: both Stevie's personal immediacy and the broad societal circumstances of March, 1932—an implicit invoking of the Depression, the widespread unemployment (then near its peak), the near-end of prohibition, the fractured social fabric.

Olsen's commitment, however, is not only to trace these circumstances—"the soil *out* of which people have to grow and the kind of climate around them; circumstances are the primary key and not the personal quest for identity"—but, as always, to write in resistance, to "help change that which is harmful."[84] It is not that this piece provides a political or social program, any more than do the earlier pieces—and certainly much less visibly so than her novel *Yonnondio*—but rather that it participates in social change through its richly embedded insights into both circumstances and language. As it traces the uneven process of healing that Stevie must undergo following his mother's death, it portrays what such healing must entail and hence what the development of fully human lives must entail; it also portrays societal and economic pressures at work in shaping individual lives. To "help change that which is harmful" is enacted directly through Stevie's personal healing and expressed much more fully through the complex voicing that constitutes the story. Framed by the same human concerns as Olsen's earlier work—the struggles of the working class and the stresses and exhaustions of the working poor, work and the language of work, children's perceptions and needs, the constraints of gender, and the historical difficulties *and* self-affirmations of silenced people— "Requa I" nonetheless becomes a new struggle to articulate the unspoken, a new emergence from silence into language,[85] a new invitation to the reader to help to change circumstances that are harmful to human growth.

The story, then, is both highly specific and deeply rooted in broad human understandings; it is simultaneously about the distinctive pain and healing of this one boy—in the full knowledge of a child's perspective—and also about the conditions of human healing and human growth within particular historical circumstances. When Olsen disclaims an interest in the idea of a "personal quest for identity," she is not disclaiming the distinctiveness of personal human lives, not denying the complex interest we might take in the particularities of a boy like Stevie or a man like Wes. She is rather suggesting that the quest is not for identity and the issues not merely personal; the concern is for meaningful human life in a particular context. Such apparently inconsequential people as Stevie and Wes embrace a wealth of human potential and highlight the need for enabling circumstances.

Why this story at that moment of Olsen's writing life? What does this piece suggest about Olsen's development as a writer? What does its focus on Stevie and Wes suggest about connections between gender and class? How does its attention to nature contribute to its societal understandings? Toward what new insights does it point for our thinking about the relationship between language and experience, text and context?

To address these questions, I want first to situate this piece within Olsen's work life as writer. Second, I want to identify a series of promptings—concerns that Olsen cited in conversation as part of her urge to write "Requa"—and explore the ways in which these concerns are imbedded in the story itself. Finally, I want to discuss the resulting insights into language and form.

Altered Life Circumstances

First, Olsen's own circumstances. "Requa I," begun shortly after she finished the collection *Tell Me a Riddle*, took a decade in the writing, while the still unfinished novella, "Requa," has been in process for another two decades. The length of this struggle is most immediately explained by material circumstances: during these periods she opened her work life onto a number of time-consuming and potentially trans-formative concerns. She took on extensive teaching commitments, in-cluding the development of syllabi that focused on working-class and women writers, writers who had often been excluded from previous course syllabi. She also undertook responsibilities, particularly with the Feminist Press, for facilitating the republication of work by "lost" writers. She moved into literary criticism as well: before publishing "Requa I," she wrote the first of the essays later published in *Silences* (1978), "Silences in Literature," originally an unwritten talk in 1962 and first published in *Harper's Magazine* in 1965; in the period before and after the publication of "Requa I" she also wrote the other sections of *Silences*, repeatedly taking on the question of what enables writers to write and what silences them, especially by force of "circumstances— including class, color, sex; the times, climate into which one is born" (*Silences*, xi). During this same period, especially 1972–73, she rediscov-ered and edited the lost manuscript of her earlier novel *Yonnondio: From the Thirties*, "begun in 1932 in Faribault, Minnesota, when the author was nineteen" (*Yonnondio*, vii). As she reworked it for publica-tion in 1974, "the book ceased to be solely the work of that long ago young writer and, in arduous partnership, became this older one's as well" (*Yonnondio*, viii).

All of these commitments were choices that Olsen made affirming her own urgency to participate in cultural change. But they also became material reasons for the interruptions in her writing of fiction. Although her work life was increasingly focused on literature and language, she was not necessarily enabled in her own writing as she became much more of a public figure, immersed in multiple activities besides the writing itself: public lecturer, teacher, editor. And though her family circumstances certainly changed as her daughters grew older, her powerful commitments to family and the concerns of personal relationships continued.

Still, these involvements, while they took her away from writing, were not simply distractions but intensifications of previous concerns: feminism was now a central and public strand of her work, as it was an increasingly visible presence in the culture at large; reconnecting to the past, both historical and literary, was newly central to her, as is evident in her work on both *Yonnondio* and *Silences*; a retrospective sense of the responsibilities of motherhood gradually supplanted the immediate demands of caring for children; her attention to issues of class was refocused; and an acute investigation of the intersections of language and silence, historical event and personal story wove these concerns together in new and compelling ways. The developments in Olsen's life thus not only delayed but also enriched her work on "Requa."

I will not be able to trace direct causal patterns from these changes in activities to "Requa I" itself—in part because these activities both precede and follow her work on this piece and on the longer "Requa." But I do not wish to do so. What I want to do instead is to situate the story within this fabric of concerns and suggest that it is the *interconnections*, not a simple causal trajectory, that are of interest. For these interconnections converge on my recurrent questions about language and silence, and they speak again to Olsen's commitment to fostering change.

Promptings: A Fabric of Text and Context

Olsen sets the context for the years of work on "Requa" in the epigraphs for the two other works that occupied her during those same years: *Silences*, whose epigraphs about "our silenced people" I quoted in the introduction to this volume, and *Yonnondio*, whose epigraph draws from Walt Whitman's poem "Yonnondio" about the "utterly lost" lives of aborigines. These epigraphs identify her prevailing concerns: the lost, the surviving, the silenced, the voiced—and the urgency to bring to language all that has been "unlimn'd" (see epigraph to *Yonnondio*), all that has not yet been depicted in literature. In our conversations, Olsen suggested a number of such promptings for the writing of "Requa." I want now to pursue my second approach to the circumstances of the story by discussing seven of these promptings and tracing their presence in the language of the story as part of Olsen's commitment to enabling growth.

As first and "immediate impulse" for the story, Olsen cited the response to *place*, the area "on the Smith River, which is the last huge river on the California side of the Oregon border" (conversation 5). She spoke with reverence of the natural beauty of the place and of its power over human response: climbing up past what had been "the old Indian village of Rekwoi (Requa)" until finally reaching "the top with its panoramic view of the forests, the river mouth, and up and down the coast." Later she added, "In a way 'Requa' is my 'Hymn to the Earth' " (conversation 5). The earth, of course, remains, but the threat to its beauty was emerging as a powerful cultural concern at the time she wrote the story and was certainly on her own mind as she experienced "awe" in response.

Olsen's own awe becomes embedded in the significance that nature has in Stevie's healing and in the bridging of emotion that he must undertake as he moves from the city to a natural environment that is almost terrifying because it is so new to him. Nature is at first rather threatening to him. He sees the redwood trees not as beautiful and majestic but as projections of his obsession with death: "The trees *were* red, like blood that oozied out of old meat and nobody washed the plate. Under them waved—ferns? Baddream giant ones to the baby kind they put around flowers for   too sick people" (238). These strange trees can only be assimilated into his thoughts by references to his previous life in the city—and more, by references to the artifacts that surround his memories of his mother's death. His grief cannot yet be voiced and even his knowledge of death is submerged, as indicated by the extra spaces that always precede "too sick people" in these opening pages—suggesting his evasion even as he calls details to mind. But also in these opening pages he is beginning to bridge his city life and his rural life in more positive ways: "Across the creek, just like in the movie show or in a dream, a deer and two baby deers were drinking. When he lifted his head, they lifted theirs. For a long time he and the doe looked into each other's eyes. Then swift, beautiful, they were gone—but her eyes kept looking into his" (238).[86]

Later, when Wes leaves him alone in the woods so he can go to a prostitute—"*Annie Marines*, she sells it" (258)—Stevie again relives the transition from city to country but finds in nature a fuller source of renewal and connection:

Slap. On his face. Another slap. Great drops. *Rain.* . . . Rain, hushing, lapping

City boy, he had only known rain striking hard on unyielding surface, walls, pavement; not this soft murmurous receiving: leaves, trees, earth. In wonder he lay and listened, the fir fragrance sharp through his caked nostrils. . . .

Far down where Wes was, a branch shook silver into the light. Rain. *His mothers quick shiver as the rain traced her cheek. C'mon baby, we've got to run for it.* . . .

Twisting away from the pain: trying to become the cocoa steam, the cup ring marking the table, the wheat wreathed breadbox. *Her shiver.* How the earth received the rain, how keen its needles. Don't ask *me* where your umbrella got put, don't expect *me* to be sponsible, you in your leaky house.

Rain underneath, swelling to a river, floating her helpless away   *Her shiver*

Twisting away from the pain: face contorted, mouth fallen open: fixed to the look on her dying, dead face. (258–59)

The story draws repeatedly on the natural world—river, salmon, sky, sun, rain—and embeds Stevie's sensations within this environment. I quote this passage at length to exemplify how this embeddedness works, how the natural world is shaped to his consciousness—and more: to convey in the words of the text the concreteness of nature's healing powers. The plaiting together of city and natural world, of memory and concrete immediate sensation, of grief and conversation, bring him directly to a necessary acknowledgment of what he has been evading—his mother's death—even as it allows him to treasure his memories of life with her. The "Hymn to the Earth" is not so much a series of beautiful passages of description as it is an embedded honoring of the powers of the earth to heal human suffering. The natural world is integral to saving and renewing the human resources that are numbed in Stevie by his grief and by the harshness of his circumstances.

A second prompting Olsen cited was intertwined with the first—the embedded history of people's lives in the ruined cemetery at Requa that she encountered on a walk up a "little off path": "Climbing up further behind, we saw a lot of bones, a few skulls, also a few upended grave markers just lying there. Already a spell was cast" (conversation 5). She also quoted from her old notebooks, "Larger truths embodied in the real Robert and Alice Spott [two Native Americans, brother and sister] as in the created Stevie. Truth that all of us who live as part of or come from submerged peoples know, capacities expressed in whatever ways they could be, but latent—lost there, untraced" (conversation 5). In this prompting, Stevie's life—and Olsen's too—become intertwined with the lives of other submerged peoples, especially the lives of Native Americans, whose "limning" is barely visible in the broken tombstones and the fight to preserve their cemetery.

In the story, too, the cemetery is nearly destroyed; it becomes the subject of local dispute, with its preservation eventually to become a central concern to Mrs. Edler[87]—friend and boarding house keeper, also called Mrs. Ed. But in this first part of the story it has only an indirect presence as a place that contributes to Stevie's further healing in the final pages. Here again his experiences are "rooting him back into life" (conversation 5) as he learns to acknowledge his grief. The visit to the cemetery is only tangentially connected to the knowledge of the "submerged peoples," through Mrs. Edler's conversation about the Indians' dispute with the sheriff over the rights to their cemetery (265). But their threatened loss—the barely limned lives that these bones represent—is intertwined with the loss and renewal that Stevie himself undergoes throughout the story.

Mrs. Edler and Stevie's excursion to two cemeteries—one Euro-American and one Native American—is undertaken on Decoration Day and thus evokes not only Stevie's dead mother but also his dead father, a member of the American Expeditionary Forces (AEF), killed in World War I ("before he was born . . . AEF" [264]). Furthermore, it draws that grief, those memories, and the renewals of nature into an implicit configuration with the submerged peoples whose cemetery is endangered. The unendangered cemetery of the dominant peoples is more directly restorative for Stevie, as he rests beside a tombstone: "How warm it felt down there in the weeds where nobody could see him and the wind didn't reach. The lamb was sun warm too. He put his arm around its stone neck and rested. Red ants threaded in and out; the smell was sweet like before they set the burn pile; even the crackling flags sounded far away" (264).[88] As Stevie here draws on the healing resources of the preserved cemetery, his renewal suggests the necessity of preserving the other, nearly lost cemetery. Although the fight over the Indian cemetery has a limited presence here—Olsen has said that it takes on a greater significance in subsequent portions of the novella— it is interwoven with Stevie's grief and healing in such a way as to honor the struggles of "submerged peoples" and to highlight the significance of preserving memories of their lives.

A third prompting that Olsen indicated in our conversations was the Depression, not as historical period or economic phenomenon but as "it was lived in and by people" (conversation 5). This sense of people's ordinary lives in daily struggle—not romanticized and not seen in impersonal patterns—is again an experience likely to be unrecorded, lost to history except as embedded in individual memories or in occasional oral histories. In interview, she mentioned in particular the bonus march of 1932, when thousands of World War I veterans marched on Washington, D.C., demanding full bonus payment—an important historical event "lived in and by people" and apparently given greater prominence in subsequent portions of "Requa." But in the first part of the story we experience the Depression through the immediacy of events not often traced in history books: wandering and impoverished people who pass through the gas station, unemployed people who are desperate to make a little cash, people who want to barter anything for a little gasoline, the hungers and yearnings of ordinary people living ordinary lives.

The struggles for food and necessities are an immediate part of people's daily lives, of Stevie's life with Wes, the stress of poverty as lived in ordinary ways. Soon after their arrival, Wes implicitly points toward the Depression as the context for the strange assortment of objects they have brought from Stevie's previous home: "Well who'd I leave them for and I thought they might be worth a dime or two. Listen, you'd be surprised how many's been in tryin to sell Evans their pots and blankets and everywhich things. Even guns and fishin gear, and thats get-by when nobodys workin" (240). When Stevie fails to go fishing with High, another boarder, Wes again responds in terms of economic consequences: "You think the candle fish run is goin to last forever? Maybe you might of brung in a basket or two   Mrs. Ed would've took it into consideration   You cost boy ghostboy   don't you know that?" (244). When Stevie asks Wes to get him a job, Wes responds, "You ARE in a nutworld. Half the grown men in the county's not working, High's down to two days, and this dummy kid talks about a job" (249). When a customer asks for credit, Wes's boss Evans responds, "Pay on the line or no tow. You heard me, no dough, no go. I don't care *how* many kids you got stuck in your jalopy, or how far you had to hitch to get here. Sure we got a used transmission. We got a used everything. But for do-re-mi" (254–55); he rejects a mattress offered in barter for gas and he denies the implicit plea in a customer's response. Someone else comes in to the station, pursuing Wes rather than Evans, asking on the sly for some link chain to make toy trucks: "I might pick up some loose change makin 'em to sell. . . . Evans won't help me out, but you will, won't you Wes. I'm about out of my mind" (255). These are not simple data from another era; rather they are lived connections made across time, even as they are also indicators of a specific historical period: the Depression "lived in and by people."

So too with a fourth prompting: a pervasive concern for class. We are, of course, never told that the story traces working-class lives, or that those lives are at risk for remaining obscure and unrecorded; we are merely given embedded realities in the relationships and experiences within the story, experiences of ordinary struggles to survive, of work for meager pay, of pride in skill and craft. Asked about class, Olsen responds, "it has shaped what I am as well as all I've written." She speaks vividly of Wes's life: "of necessity, of limitation, of hard work and little compensation, little respect." She speaks too of the effects of that hard work on him and on many like him, including Stevie's mother—their "Human tiredness, human exhaustion," regardless of gender. She resists other, sometimes negative, judgments we might be inclined to make of the behavior of men like Wes—"limited, big-oted, and often racist, often in most ways sexist"—and affirms that "we do not have enough of the sense of their lives . . . and how their human need to assert outraged dignity shapes so much of their being" (conversation 5).[89] Most pointedly, she affirms—as does the story it-self—the centrality of Wes's teaching in his caring for Stevie: "he's teaching Stevie skills; he *cares* about equipping him to function in this world" (conversation 5).

These experiential understandings of class pervade the story, not as thematic concerns but as deeply felt human knowledge. We experience that kind of exhaustion directly, through the responses of Wes's body: "The work of the day (of the week, of years) slumped onto Wes. For a minute he let go, slept: snored, great sobbing snores. In a spasm of effort, jerked awake, regarded the shadows, the rumple on the floor by the window" (243). And we further understand physical exhaustion through Stevie's response: "Was that his mother or his uncle sagged there in the weight of weariness, and why were her feet on the floor?" (243). Stevie (con)fuses his uncle and his mother in recognizing similar bodily responses; his nurturing response to Wes relives his nurturing response to his mother:

> How you going to put up your feet and rub on the varicose like you like to, now?
> *(Blue swollen veining) (Are you tired, Ma? Tired to death, love.)* (243)

As Stevie rubs Wes's tired feet, he merges his memories with his current realities; both are grounded in the kind of human exhaustion that Olsen has associated with working-class life. As she has said elsewhere of her own personal experience: "the harm had entered my body" (conversation 4).

The possession of skill and pride in that skill are also integral to Olsen's portrayal of working-class lives. Stevie's rejection of school is necessitated by his grief and his inability, at present, to tolerate the taunts of his peers, but it is also premised on his realization that Wes has much to offer him. When he asks Wes about finding him a job, he calls it "A learn job, Wes. By you." And he reiterates the claim, "You said: I'll help you, Steve. You said it. He don't have to pay me. You hurt me, Wes. A learn job. By you. You promised" (249). Wes himself lays claim to this pride unconsciously as he works: "Singing—unconscious, forceful—to match the motor hum as he machines a new edge, rethreads a pipe" (252). And he claims it consciously in response to Stevie: "Maybe this is better'n school for you Stevie   Keep you outdoors, build you up   I got so much to learn you   All your life you can use it" (253).

Hence a fifth prompting: a need to value and reaffirm and record those skills themselves and the technology that was a part of many of them. "[T]his was a time of fear of and contempt for technology," Olsen says, speaking with reverence for "the human genius for invention, the creation of ever-better tools for various tasks, and of language to describe them" that was "manifest" in the junkyard where she herself, like Wes, had worked. In her respect for the tasks and tools of manual work, she draws especially on the capacities of language to embed history as well as to speak poetry: "[T]he sections of 'Requa' describing these tasks, these tools, have the precision, the rhythm, the sound of true poetry"; and "I live in a period where many kinds of tools . . .—as many kinds of skills—are leaving the world forever—because of new processes. So I was also recording, trying to fix into

111

'art,' that vanishing which had not been recorded into literature" (conversation 5). The choice of a junkyard as Wes's workplace, of course, enabled Olsen to draw on her own knowledge of junkyards, gained from work experience. The junkyard setting also provides a language of work and tools and an integral way to speak of salvaged "junk" as a source of beauty.

These values are vividly rendered in Stevie's and Wes's lives at work. In a passage that distills much of the healing that has been going on subterraneanly in Stevie, Olsen also explicitly honors the tools and tasks of the workplace:

> *But the known is reaching to him, stealthily, secretly, reclaiming.*
>   Sharp wind breath, fresh from the sea. Skies that are all seasons in one day. Fog   rain. *Known weather of his former life.*
>   Disorder twining with order. The discarded, the broken, the torn from the whole: weathereaten   weatherbeaten: mouldering, or waiting for use-need. *Broken existences that yet continue.*
>
> Hasps   switches   screws   plugs   tubings   drills
> Valves   pistons   shears   planes   punchers   sheaves
> Clamps   sprockets   coils   bits   braces   dies
>
>   How many shapes and sizes; how various, how cunning in application. Human mastery, human skill. Hard, defined, enduring, they pass through his hands—link to his city life of manmade marvel. (252)

This is not "found" poetry, but it *is* poetry: the poetry of work and technology as intertwined in the lives of people.[90]

This section of the story thus moves toward its own ending phrases with the deftness of poetry and the distinctive claims on Stevie's healing process:

> Wes: junking a towed-in car, one hundred pieces out of what had been one. Singing—unconscious, forceful—to match the motor hum as he machines a new edge, rethreads a pipe. Capable, fumbling; exasperated, patient; demanding, easy; uncomprehending, quick; harsh, gentle: *concerned with him. The recognizable human bond.*
> *The habitable known, stealthily, secretly, reclaiming.*
> *The dead things, pulling him into attention, consciousness.*
> *The tasks: coaxing him with trustworthiness, pliancy, doing as he bids*
>
>   having to hold up (252)

As we reencounter the final phrase, repeated from the story's opening pages, we realize just how well Stevie *is* "holding up." He is not healed—indeed, the very next section begins with the single word, *"Rifts"* (252)—but by this time we have seen him begin to weave together all of the resources on which he can draw in his grief and recovery, and we have seen the extent to which they are the usually unlimned resources of the lives of working people.

Through the choice of Wes and Stevie as her central characters, Olsen also spoke afresh of an ongoing dimension of her feminism, questioning gender construction, especially for men. Though this process of change, so personal and so incremental, has received some attention in the two decades since the story's publication, at that time it had rarely been depicted in story or even in feminist analysis. When I asked about her explorations of masculinity, her response voiced this sixth prompting and fanned out into a range of ways to inquire: "Exploring. Observing. Including the ways of forming; of resisting; what is already formed; including motherless Stevie, now in an almost stereotypical 'man's world'; including Wes, so little in his life to prepare him for becoming solely responsible for a young human being." Through Stevie's growth, as through the transformation of Wes in his role as caregiver, she expresses a powerful value that helps to drive her writing: "the coming into being of a caring, more fully human male, and the tracing of it in writing is very important to me" (conversation 5).

The men whose lives she is tracing in "Requa" are enmeshed in a value system that hampers the development of that "fully human male." As Richard Sennett and Jonathan Cobb note, this difficulty is one of the ways in which constructions of masculinity are reinforced by an intertwining of gender and class: "Class . . . makes it rational for men to keep their 'soft' feelings to themselves until they are very sure they won't be hurt" (Sennett and Cobb, 218). The boarders at Mrs. Edler's house, for example, impose a harshly gendered value system when they taunt Stevie for his inexperience with "manly" activities: "Would you believe it? He's never been fishin never been huntin never held a gun never been in a boat" (241). Wes, too, responds to Stevie's behavior in terms of gender-based stereotypes, dismissing his grieving as "Bawling now like a girl" (247). He pleads a kind of helplessness of inexperience in trying to guide Stevie through his loss and again resorts to a female stereotype when Stevie refuses to go to school: "Listen, don't pull no girl tantrum" (248).

Worse yet, Wes's own behavior often reflects a worldview that validates male and/or parental violence as a show of authority: he physically beats Stevie—"socking him a good one" (248) and "Really hurting him; pinning him back, banging and banging his head against the wheel, against the seat" (249)—in a vain effort to change Stevie's behavior. This is the "roughness" Olsen speaks of in interview (conversation 5), the behavior expected of men, particularly working-class men like Wes.

But the story puts this kind of behavior in a new context, thereby allowing incremental but essential shifts in our expectations of behavior based on sex. From the opening of the story, Wes's overall caregiving, of course, sets his "roughness" in a loving context. The gentleness Stevie himself expresses in returning caregiving to Wes—caregiving he learned from his mother—also suggests an important redefinition of what is appropriate male or female behavior. [91]

As the story progresses, Wes's character increasingly weaves together qualities that are stereotypically masculine and feminine. When he relinquishes his harshness and responds to "[s]omething in the boy's voice," allowing Stevie to stay out of school, he draws on a new empathy and a new gentleness: "This time Wes's hands on his shoulders are gentle" (249). In the later lessons in target shooting, a necessary part of Stevie's training in masculinity, Wes remains gruff but he again moves away from his old self-definition and toward a new capacity to teach instead of coerce:

> Who barks more, Wes or the gun? If you'd been concetrating if you'd just been concetrating. I want you good as me, Stevie. See? 200 yards right on target everytime.
> The bruise on his shoulder—from when? Wes's beating the day he would not go to school?—purples, spreads. (253)

Wes does not relinquish his masculine self-definition or simply learn a new self-definition. Instead, he gradually and unevenly develops responses that include a traditionally feminine quality: teaching "masculinity," teaching skills, touching harshly, touching gently.

The story further develops this more complex understanding of human qualities—no longer simply masculine or feminine—when it juxtaposes two very different views of Wes's sexual presence. First, it portrays Wes returning from a night of drinking and carousing—"howling"—and then it describes, from Stevie's point of view, Wes's quiescent penis: "His fly was open. How rosy and budlike and quiet it sheathed there" (259). Even his physical "masculinity" is no longer access to sexual purchase and abusive gender privilege; in Stevie's eyes, it has become a gentle claim on the vulnerability of all human flesh and selfhood, budlike, a fragile source of possible growth.

In the crucial healing passage (from page 252, quoted above), Olsen similarly refuses simple stereotypes as she portrays Wes in the struggle among psychological contradictions: "Capable, fumbling; exasperated, patient; demanding, easy; uncomprehending, quick; harsh, gentle; *concerned* with him. *The recognizable human bond*" (252). The apparent contradictions here are not, of course, real contradictions. They are, instead, complex qualities of a man who has been molded by assumptions about how men should act and who is in the process of taking on new tasks that require him to reach beyond those assumptions. They begin to emerge in the early pages of the story, when he insists, "I'll tell you this, though, he's not goin through what me and Sis did: kicked round one place after another, not havin nobody" (240). And they are threaded into his behavior throughout, braiding together the familiar behaviors of his life as a single man in a highly masculinized environment and the developing behaviors of a person defined by his commitment to caring for another. In Wes's behavior throughout the story and in the tracing of Stevie's movement toward adulthood, the apparent contradictions move beyond gender constructions and become the hallmarks of full humanity for both of them: "the coming into being of a caring, more fully human male, and the tracing of it in writing."

All of the story's promptings and embedded values are, of course, interwoven and could be enumerated at far greater length. I will elicit only one more from the interviews, a seventh, though scarcely final, prompting: an inquiry into memory and motherhood, the enduring effects of ordinary daily parenting efforts that are rarely remarked upon. From the story's opening in Stevie's grief for his mother, it is concerned with the physically absent mother and her lingering presence in Stevie's memory. In conversation Olsen describes the relationship of Stevie and his mother as one of "companionship, love, dependence on each other, of those two against an uncaring world." After his mother's death, Stevie continues to draw from his memory of her, "what that dead mother instilled in him." In interview, Olsen goes on, to link her concern for single mothers with the concern for gender-based definitions of behavior: "the masculine attributions of strength, courage, fierceness, daring, will, they have to use every day; their legacy—as in Stevie as he develops" (conversation 5).

Though explicit references to Stevie's mother are few and often painful, her legacy *does* persist throughout the story of his development. She endures in his recurrent fusion of Wes with her: in their shared bodily response to exhaustion, as discussed above, and in Stevie's recognition of their shared facial features as he "looked full on the sleeping face. Face of his mother. *His* face. Family face" (259). She endures in the internal conversations Stevie has with her, especially about being "sponsible" (for example, 259), but also in his feelings of having been deserted by her: "Liar   You promised   and see I'm another place again" (256). But most of all she endures in his learned behavior of giving care as he had received it from her. This caregiving was, of course, integral to his experience of her dying and often returns in his memory as the painful recollection of her death—her bleeding eyes, her bloody quilt, her turning away from him. But it also becomes a resource in his own development, beyond her death and his grieving. Most notably, he has integrated her responses to him into his responses to others: "He had to pile on his coat, Wes's mackinaw, and two towels, patting them carefully around the sleeping form. *There now you'll be warm*, he said aloud, *sleep sweet, sweet dreams* (though he did not know he had said it, nor in whose inflections.)" (259). We, of course, know that he speaks his mother's words, in her inflections, and that it is in large measure her legacy—along with Wes's—that will enable him to become what Olsen foresees for him in the subsequent sections of the novella: "one of those centers of health" (personal communication, summer 1988).

That projection of Stevie is implicit in "Requa I," especially in its most potent refrain and ending phrase: *"stealthily secretly reclaiming"* (265). These strands of the unlimned, which I have temporarily separated as "promptings" that Olsen herself describes in conversation, are not separated in the story but are rather woven and rewoven throughout the text as a shifting and powerfully rendered tapestry of human losses and affirmations. From their interweaving emerges an understanding that far exceeds my critical claims on the story's insights into the harms of circumstances or the healing processes of human development. In much of my analysis I have emphasized grief and loss—both Stevie's personal loss, redoubled by the harms of societal circumstances, and the cultural losses represented by the unlimned, the silenced, the hidden. But implicit throughout has also been the affirmation enacted by portraying these experiences and by identifying the human riches that are woven into Stevie's secret reclaiming: the love and caregiving that he receives from his uncle and his mother, his own love and learning to give care, his resources of memory, his renewed health through meaningful work, his drawing on the resources of the natural world.

Writing in a Mother Tongue

As the third and final strand of my own unravelling of textual fabric and reweaving of critical response, I want now to emphasize what has been implicit throughout: the ways in which distinctive uses of language and form are integral to Olsen's capacity to convey her complex human insights. As it brings to voice a wealth of unlimned experiences, the story also celebrates the capacities of language even to speak of what has been silenced and to be integral to the powers of renewal. Olsen speaks emphatically of the power of language as *sound*, the ways in which "oral, aural" language is a potent part of human understanding. "I think there is a mother tongue," she says, "the language of emotion, a person's first language and sometimes only language. The sounds, the way they're formed go very deep into human reality and also have relation with music."[92] She was not, at that time, speaking directly of "Requa," but her comments on language and on the "mother tongue" have certainly haunted my own thinking about this piece: its immersion in sound, its voicing of the unvoiced, its probing of grief—in a "language of emotion"—its concern with the endurance of the mother in a child's consciousness following her death, its poetry of silence and of music. "Requa" is not explicitly about language in the way that much contemporary literature is, but it *is* about that deeply felt intersection of language and emotion that Olsen evokes with the phrase "mother tongue."

It is, in some sense, through a "mother tongue" that "Requa" is able to put into words experiences that are not verbal, experiences not previously limned. Explaining the same phrase—"mother tongue"—Ursula LeGuin identifies some of her primary concerns, concerns she has in common with Olsen: "It is a language always on the verge of silence and often on the verge of song. It is the language stories are told in. It is the language spoken by all children and most women . . ."[93] LeGuin further elaborates: "Our schools and colleges, institutions of the patriarchy, generally teach us to listen to people in power, men or women speaking the father tongue; and so they teach us not to listen to the mother tongue, to what the powerless say, poor men, women, children" (LeGuin, 151). In "Requa I" Olsen insists that we listen to these voices of the powerless, particularly the child's voice. She gives us experiences that hover on "the verge of silence" in language that regularly verges on music. She draws on the human insights that emerge from emotional life and from the lives of the powerless.

LeGuin also attests to the denials embedded in the contrasting "father tongue," the language of objectivity: "People crave objectivity because to be subjective is to be embodied, to be a body, vulnerable, violable" (Le Guin, 151). This "objectivity" is precisely the language of public definitions I associate with "realism" in my introduction to this volume and that is fully entangled with the assumptions of those in power. Hence, of course, it is one of the primary agents of the silences that Olsen has struggled to break—and that she *does* break. Recall, in this context, the story's opening immersion in subjectivity and its reliance on the sensory responses of the body. Recall, too, the affirmed vulnerability of Wes's sleeping body, the recurrent pain of Stevie's embodied subjectivity. Yes, these embodied experiences do suggest vulnerability; at the same time, they speak of experiences that can be voiced only in their particularity, experiences that hover on the "verge of silence" and bring us to the "verge of song."

The story's title is suggestive of this pattern of silence and music, denial and renewal. Most literally, the story is, of course, named for the town to which Stevie is taken, the town where Olsen herself first encountered the claim of place and the nearly lost lives of "submerged peoples" in that abandoned cemetery. The town *is* an actual place in northern California, a place first settled by the Yurok and named in their language as meaning "at the mouth of the river."[94] Implicitly, then, the title honors the Yurok and their naming of place; implicitly, too, it honors the place itself—in Olsen's phrase, the story becomes a "Hymn to the Earth." But equally, the story is a hymn to work in its poetic evocation of the sounds and rhythms of work processes and its affirmation of the importance of craft in human endeavors. And surrounding and woven into these other meanings is the meaning that readers of English are also likely to hear shadowing the Yurok word— "requiem," or hymn for the repose of the dead—a fitting shadow meaning as we immerse ourselves in the sensory experiences of disorientation and grief that are the provocation for Stevie's story and reach toward the repose that he claims for his mother in his own healing. The story itself interweaves these understandings, these contexts, and becomes an expression of the "mother tongue": its emotion, its poetry, its music, its embodied subjectivity, its affirmation of the powerless.

But the story does not remain purely subjective. Instead it draws on these same powers of language to expand its subjectivity without becoming entangled in the assumptions of the voices of power and "objectivity." It is precisely through its particular linguistic richness that the emotional healing of a working-class boy in complex interaction with his "rough" but caring uncle is able to become an exploration of human needs and human survival, of nature and of work, of love and death, and of the ways that language itself participates in human awareness.

As in Olsen's earlier fiction, one of the ways that this piece both affirms the subjective and expands beyond it is through its narrative voice. For though the voice *is* largely embodied in Stevie's subjectivity, it also opens out from his singular consciousness. Return for a moment to the story's opening, in which the initial rendering of Stevie's dislocation is both highly sensory and highly subjective, tied closely to the particularities of his young life. Even here, however, these qualities are embedded in a complex and distinctive narrative form that highlights Stevie's subjectivity while also reaching beyond it. Repeated phrases— "Moving   sliding.   Having to hold up his head" (for example, 238) or "too sick people" (238)—evoke his exhaustion and his emotional stress and sense of loss. The reliance on participles and fragments and the distinctive use of spatial arrangement, with words isolated on single lines (such as *"forever"* on page 239) and empty spaces between words or paragraphs, emphasizes Stevie's fractured sense of reality. But the absence of quotation marks and the careful use of parentheses and italics to differentiate voices and perspectives serve as reminders that, despite its subjectivity, the story is *not* tied to a single consciousness or framed solely by one character's mental processes. The narrative form, so closely tied to Stevie's unvoiced consciousness, also embraces Wes's distinctive use of language, conveying his own exhaustion as he strains in uncertainty to communicate with his unknown nephew: "Six more hours to go—that's if this heap holds up and we don't get stuck 'hind a load going up a grade. I'll have to put out at work like always tomorrow, and it's sure not any restin we been doin these gone days" (238). And the voice expands beyond even these two consciousnesses to a claim on the silent and ongoing processes of nature: *"(Underneath in the night, yearling salmon slipped through their last fresh waters, making it easy to the salt ocean years.)"* (239). Throughout the story, these strands continue to interweave: the pieces of Stevie's fragmented subjectivity, of Wes's own broken awarenesses, and of the broader perspective tied to the ongoing processes of nature. As they do so, they constantly invoke and resituate the subjectivities of the powerless, the realities of these unvoiced perceptions.

As I suggested in talking about the "mother tongue," the story further expands its claims on language, bridging the subjective and the broadly human, through its similarities to poetry. It is acutely attentive to rhythms and sounds, its "oral, aural" qualities, evident for example in the work rhythms in the language as Wes uses the lathe or as Stevie and Wes work together drawing on multiple skills:

sharping	hauling	sorting	splicing
burring	chipping	grinding	cutting
grooving	drilling	caulking	sawing

the tasks, coaxing
rust gardens (261)

Or consider the whirling sensation in the language when Stevie listens to music: "and round and round and off and on   push on the keys dance   tap   float on the sadness   sleep pushing down clouding and   " (256). The story's structured repetitions also evoke this similarity, as in the careful reiteration of "Moving   sliding. Having to hold up his head" (238) in the story's opening or the reiteration of the crucial healing phrase that also ends the story: *"stealthily secretly reclaiming"* (265). Furthermore, the story evokes poetry in its powerful use of metaphor, most notably its pervasive metaphor of the junkyard, emblematic of what can be reclaimed and hence of Stevie's healing process. The fusion of rust and growth in the passage quoted above—"rust gardens"—draws on this pattern, as does Stevie's task of sorting the junk, attentive to "use-need" and to *"Broken existences that yet continue"* (252). So, too, with Stevie himself as the story traces his growth toward reclamation, his continuation even in the brokenness of his grief.

All of these distinctive features are embedded, woven through the story, never set apart for particular attention. Their effect is both pervasive and powerful. They enable the story to speak even as it speaks of a resistance to cultural values embedded in the language; and they enable Olsen to achieve that final quality of her fiction, an active involvement of the reader in rethinking his or her own life, in reaching toward alternative "life comprehensions." Interestingly, this too is a quality that LeGuin associates with the mother tongue: "The mother tongue, spoken or written, expects an answer. It is a conversation, a word the root of which means 'turning together.' The mother tongue is language not as mere communication but as relation, relationship. It connects. It goes two ways, many ways, an exchange, a network. Its power is not in dividing but in binding, not in distancing but in uniting" (LeGuin, 149).

This, then, is the effect of "Requa I." Not only because it remains to be "finished" as a complete novella but because its very relationship to language invites us into an ongoing conversation, a "turning together." And within its pages it enacts its own turning together, a constant interweaving of its linguistic richness and a constantly developing understanding of human capacities. As it speaks the unspoken dimensions of Stevie's personal healing, it points toward further understandings of human fullness, helping thereby to "change that which is harmful" as it renders visible the unlimned dimensions of human experience.

Conclusion: "Turning Together"—
Reader, Writer, and Narrative Form

The mother tongue, in fact, is the language not only of "Requa I" but of all of Olsen's short fiction. Beginning with "I Stand Here Ironing" and with each subsequent piece, she invites her readers to "turn together" with her in an ongoing conversation. She draws on the "polyphony" of the culture around her, the multiple possibilities of understanding and voice that are embedded in that culture, and she intertwines those in the narrative voices of her fiction. She draws, too, on the oral qualities of these voices, qualities that resist the declarative authority of the "father tongue" and speak instead in a kind of chorus of human possibility: the call-and-response of church service or the surging of family voices in discord and in harmony or the dialogical processes of internal thought in the personal sorting of memory and struggling with past and present. Within that rich complex of language, she has even found ways to give voice to the silent, the suppressed, the unspoken, as she does in Alva's dream vision in "O Yes" or in the many present but unvoiced thoughts of characters in each piece.

In her development of a mother tongue, Olsen also draws on the understandings that emerge through embodied subjectivity, the sensory capacities through which we take in the world around us and by which we are made simultaneously vulnerable and responsive. In the *body* her characters open out from the intersections of physical life and linguistic expression: the narrator-mother's physical movement of ironing and attentive watching, Whitey's scarred flesh and weary step, Carol's faintness and Parry's and Carol's jumping rhythms, Eva's ear for song and the physical inwardness of her being deaf, Stevie's sensory immersion in a new environment not yet susceptible to his conscious apprehension. In all of these, Olsen finds in the language and perceptible insights of the body a further way to resist the assertions of authority, the divisions embedded in the cultural forms that surround her.

The richness and complex capacities of language have always been central to Olsen, never separate from her life comprehensions and her

122

political convictions. Taking her cue from Emily Dickinson—"the Word made Flesh is seldom / And tremblingly partook"—she speaks of "those seldom times when words, using all resources, become living forces that confirm us, change us, transform us. In their luminous beauty and truth enable us to know what we know, feel what we feel, see as we never have before. Catalysts enlarging us, creating new awareness, new perceptions, change making comprehension" ("Word Made Flesh," 1). Through her mother tongue, through her innovations in form, Olsen uses words in this transformative way, finding the capacity to speak the unspeakable, to convey the life comprehensions that prompted her to write fiction in the first place. She has not only described how things "are" for the people around her—enacting the primary goal of realism, as she resisted the conservative forces embedded in traditional realism—she has also and simultaneously conveyed those lives in such a way that she opens circumstances to social change.

Our task as readers is to "turn together" with her, in critical interaction with these powerful stories, to use attentive response to language and form and life comprehension in that same dynamic interaction. Recognizing the conservative force of language and literary form, we can nonetheless participate with Olsen in breaking open our own inclinations toward "conformism" and renewing language's transformative powers. We see, in attentive response to her fiction, alternative understandings of work and community, motherhood and childhood, family life and public events. In our turning together, we join with her in forming new understandings of the "conditions of consciousness and action" (Fox-Genovese, 217) in our own lives, the systems of social relations among which we live: gender, class, race, hierarchies of power. We, too, become a part of the possibilities for renewal that Olsen makes central to her human understandings: *"stealthily   secretly reclaiming"* the life comprehensions that are necessary for fruitful cultural change.

Notes to Part 1

1. Margaret Drabble, "Revelations and Prophecies," *Saturday Review*, 27 May 1978, 54. Drabble attributes this insight to Doris Lessing, whose *Stories* she was reviewing.
2. For example, in "One Out of Twelve: Writers Who Are Women in Our Century," she speaks of how difficult it is "to come to, cleave to, find

the form for one's own life comprehensions." See *Silences* (1978; New York: Delta/Seymour Lawrence, 1979), 27; hereafter cited in the text.

3. See part 2 of this volume, conversation 2, "Hey Sailor What Ship?"; these conversations hereafter cited in the text by number.

4. For more extended biographical information, see the following: Selma Burkom and Margaret Williams, "De-Riddling Tillie Olsen's Writings," *San Jose Studies* 2 (February 1976): 64–83; Erika Duncan, "Coming of Age in the Thirties: A Portrait of Tillie Olsen," *Book Forum* 6, no. 1–2 (1982): 207–22; Elaine Neil Orr, *Tillie Olsen and a Feminist Spiritual Vision* (Jackson: University Press of Mississippi, 1987), 23–37; Mickey Pearlman and Abby H. P. Werlock, *Tillie Olsen* (Boston: Twayne, 1991), 9–36; and Deborah Rosenfelt, "From the Thirties: Tillie Olsen and the Radical Tradition," *Feminist Studies* 7, no. 3 (Fall 1981): 370–406; Orr, Pearlman and Werlock, and Rosenfelt are hereafter cited in the text.

5. Tillie Lerner, "I Want You Women Up North to Know," *Partisan* 1 (March 1934): 4; reprinted in *Feminist Studies* 7 (Fall 1981): 367–69; also reprinted under Tillie Olsen in *Writing Red: An Anthology of American Women Writers, 1930–1940*, ed. Charlotte Nekola and Paula Rabinowitz (New York: Feminist Press, 1987), 179–81. Tillie Lerner, "The Strike," *Partisan Review* 1 (September–October 1934): 3–9; reprinted in *Years of Protest: A Collection of American Writings of the 1930s*, ed. Jack Salzman (New York: Pegasus, 1967), 138–44; also reprinted in *Writing Red*, 245–51. Tillie Lerner, "There Is a Lesson," *Partisan* 1 (April 1934): 4; reprinted in *San Jose Studies* 2 (1976): 70. Tillie Lerner, "Thousand Dollar Vagrant," *New Republic* 80 (29 August 1934): 67–69.

6. See Tillie Lerner, "The Iron Throat," *Partisan Review* 1 (April–May 1934): 3–9; reprinted in *Aphra* 3, no. 2 (Summer 1972).

7. See "A Note about This Book," prefatory note to *Yonnondio: From the Thirties* (1974; New York: Delta/Seymour Lawrence, 1989), vii–viii.

8. When *Tell Me a Riddle* was first published as a collection, the stories were in a different order: "Hey Sailor, What Ship?" "O Yes," "I Stand Here Ironing," "Tell Me a Riddle" (Philadelphia: J. B. Lippincott Company, 1961). It was republished the following year with the stories in the order of their writing (New York: Dell, 1962) and has been reprinted in this form a number of times. I will cite the 1989 edition: *Tell Me a Riddle* (New York: Delta/Seymour Lawrence, 1989); hereafter cited in the text.

9. Cheryl Walker, "Feminist Literary Criticism and the Author," *Critical Inquiry* 16 (Spring 1990): 571. For the formalist rejection of authorial authority, see W. K. Wimsatt, Jr., and Monroe C. Beardsley, "The Intentional Fallacy" (1946), reprinted in W. K. Wimsatt, Jr., *The Verbal Icon: Studies in the Meaning of Poetry* (1954; New York: Noonday Press, 1966), 3–18. For poststructuralist rejection of the author, see especially Michel Foucault, "What Is an Author?" in *Textual Strategies: Perspectives in Post-Structuralist Criticism*, ed. Josué V. Harari

(Ithaca: Cornell University Press), 141–60; and Roland Barthes, "The Death of the Author," *Image, Music, Text*, trans. Stephen Heath (New York: Hill and Wang, 1977), 142–48. See my introduction to part 2 of this volume for an explanation of the interviewing and editing process. Also see Joanne S. Frye, "Tillie Olsen: Probing the Boundaries between Text and Context," *Journal of Narrative and Life History* 3, no. 2–3 (1993): 255–68. Portions of this essay have been integrated into my writing here.

10. Alice Kessler-Harris and Paul Lauter, introduction to Josephine Herbst, *Rope of Gold: A Novel of the Thirties* (Old Westbury, N.Y.: 1984), xiii. I will discuss McCarthyism more fully in subsequent sections.

11. Public lecture at Kenyon College, Gambier, Ohio, March 1982.

12. See especially her work on Rebecca Harding Davis: "A Biographical Interpretation," afterword to *Life in the Iron Mills* (New York: Feminist Press, 1972), 67–174. Reprinted in slightly altered form in *Silences*.

13. Margaret Homans characterizes this assumption as a claim on "transparency between language and experience." See " 'Her Very Own Howl': The Ambiguities of Representation in Recent Women's Fiction," *Signs* 9, no. 2 (Winter 1983): 204. See also Jonathan Culler's characterization of "the first moment" of feminist criticism, when the appeal is "to experience as a given that can ground or justify a reading." See *On Deconstruction: Theory and Criticism after Structuralism* (Ithaca: Cornell University Press, 1982), 51.

14. Lloyd S. Kramer, "Literature, Criticism, and Historical Imagination: The Literary Challenge of Hayden White and Dominick LaCapra," in *The New Cultural History*, ed. Lynn Hunt (Berkeley: University of California Press, 1989), 114. See also Hunt's introduction, which emphasizes "a growing interest in language" among historians (Hunt, 5). Michel Foucault's work has been especially germinal for much of this redefinition of history.

15. Informal remarks at the College of Wooster, Wooster, Ohio, April 1980.

16. Virginia Woolf, "Men and Women," in *Women and Writing*, ed. Michèle Barrett (New York: Harcourt Brace Jovanovich, 1979), 79. Pamela L. Caughie points out that Woolf has actually misquoted Bathsheba, who says, instead, "It is difficult for a woman to define her feelings in language which is chiefly made by men to express theirs." See *Virginia Woolf and Postmodernism: Literature in Quest and Question of Itself* (Urbana: University of Illinois Press, 1991), 24n3.

17. Roger Fowler, *Linguistic Criticism* (Oxford: Oxford University Press, 1986), 19, 34; hereafter cited in the text.

18. Jane Gallop quoted in Alice Jardine, *Gynesis: Configurations of Women and Modernity* (Ithaca: Cornell University Press, 1985), 155. See also Nelly Furman's statement that "Post-structuralist feminism challenges representation itself as already a patriarchal paradigm," in her "The Politics of Language: Beyond the Gender Principle?" in *Making a Difference: Feminist Literary Criticism*,

ed. Gayle Greene and Coppélia Kahn (New York: Methuen, 1985), 76. Susan Stanford Friedman similarly identifies the poststructuralist challenges: "Poststructuralism has made taboo in critical discourse a number of other terms—such as *self, author, work, experience, expression, meaning, authority, origin,* and *reference.* . . . [P]oststructuralists generally share the view that such terms are tainted by their association with what they regard as a bankrupt, defunct, and hopelessly naive humanism. All supposedly operate within a false assumption of the transparency of language, naively unaware of the materiality of language." See "Post/Poststructuralist Feminist Criticism: The Politics of Recuperation and Negotiation," *New Literary History* 22 (1991): 473; hereafter cited in the text. But Friedman's assessment is in the context of making a strong plea for a "post/poststructuralist" feminist engagement, a commitment that I share.

19. The term "general consciousness" is J. Hillis Miller's in *The Form of Victorian Fiction* (1968; Cleveland: Arete Press, 1979), 67. For an exploration of the general understanding of narrative authority as communal, see also Elizabeth Ermath, "Fictional Consensus and Female Casualties," in *The Representation of Women in Fiction,* ed. Carolyn G. Heilbrun and Margaret R. Higonnet (Baltimore: Johns Hopkins University Press, 1983), 1–18; Ermath, *Realism and Consensus in the English Novel* (Princeton: Princeton University Press, 1983), especially 65–92; and Susan Sniader Lanser, *The Narrative Act: Point of View in Prose Fiction* (Princeton: Princeton University Press, 1981), 119–20. (Subsequent references to Ermath are to "Fictional Consensus and Female Casualties" and are hereafter cited in the text.) Lanser has developed a fuller inquiry into relationships among narrative, gender, and authority in *Fictions of Authority: Women Writers and Narrative Voice* (Ithaca: Cornell University Press, 1992).

20. Terry Eagleton, *Criticism and Ideology* (1976; London: Verso, 1980), 81, 144.

21. Personal communication, Soquel, California, summer 1988; hereafter cited in the text. Comments cited as personal communication were part of my original interviews with Olsen in July and August of 1988 but were not included in the final edited version that is printed as part 2 of this volume. See the introduction to part 2 for an explanation of the entire interviewing and editing process.

22. I earlier used these same questions to help frame my investigations of women novelists' use of the first-person narrative voice. See Joanne S. Frye, *Living Stories, Telling Lives: Women and the Novel in Contemporary Experience* (Ann Arbor: University of Michigan Press, 1986), especially 15–16.

23. Cognitive psychology helps to illuminate this point. See, for example, Mary Crawford and Roger Chaffin, "The Reader's Construction of Meaning: Cognitive Research on Gender and Comprehension," in *Gender and Reading: Essays On Readers, Texts, and Contexts,* ed. Elizabeth A. Flynn and Patrocinio P. Schweickart (Baltimore: Johns Hopkins University Press, 1986), 3–30.

24. Aletta Biersack, "Local Knowledge, Local History: Geertz and Beyond," in *The New Cultural History*, 95.

25. Mikhail Bakhtin, *Problems of Dostoevsky's Poetics*, ed. and trans. Caryl Emerson (Minneapolis: University of Minnesota Press, 1984), 6. In the quoted passage Bakhtin is actually speaking specifically of Dostoevsky, but the claim connects with other claims that he makes more generally about the modern novel. In his many investigations of novelistic discourse, he turns repeatedly to the idea that the capacities of language and especially novelistic discourse are multiple, open to the world and change, and dialogical in response to complex and contradictory realities. "Polyphony" and "heteroglossia" are both terms that he uses to identify the quality of many-voicedness that I am attributing to Olsen. I have chosen to use "polyphony" to represent this whole set of concerns.

26. Mikhail Bakhtin, *The Dialogical Imagination: Four Essays*, ed. Michael Holquist, trans. Caryl Emerson and Michael Holquist (Austin: University of Texas Press, 1984), 366. (Subsequent references to Bakhtin are to *The Dialogical Imagination* and are hereafter cited in the text.)

27. Tillie Olsen interviewed by Kay Bonetti in San Francisco, California, March 1981, American Audio Prose Library, cassette tape.

28. Cora Kaplan, introduction to *Tell Me a Riddle* (London: Virago, 1980), n.p.

29. Constance Coiner sees Olsen's recording of marginalized voices in a kind of "heteroglossia"—another Bakhtinian term for multiple voices—as one of her two major innovations in form, the other being the altered relationship among writer, text, and reader. See " 'No One's Private Ground': A Bakhtinian Reading of Tillie Olsen's *Tell Me a Riddle*," *Feminist Studies* 18, no. 2 (Summer 1992): 257–81; hereafter cited in the text. Elaine Orr describes Olsen's innovative form in somewhat different terms but also suggests both political purpose and openness of structure: "The stories . . . recall past events for the purpose of imagining a different future" (Orr, 74); and "the narrative voice denies closure or ending and instead is always opening and reopening. . . . there are no final causes, no necessary plots" (Orr, 77). Mara Faulkner characterizes the distinctiveness of these stories in political terms: "Olsen's unusual range of characters and a triple-layered pattern that combines protest against oppression, celebration of courage and strength, and the heartening possibility of a radically transformed future world." See *Protest and Possibility in the Writing of Tillie Olsen* (Charlottesville: University Press of Virginia, 1993), 14; hereafter cited in the text.

30. "Author Tillie Olsen Wins Rea Award," San Francisco *Chronicle*, 1 April 1994. The full citation from the Dungannon Foundation's press release reads as follows: "With her collection, *Tell Me a Riddle*, Tillie Olsen radically widened the possibilities for American writers of fiction. These stories have the lyric intensity of an Emily Dickinson poem and the scope of a Balzac

novel. She has forced open the language of the short story, insisting that it include the domestic life of women, the passions and anguishes of maternity, the deep, gnarled roots of a long marriage, the hopes and frustrations of immigration, the shining charge of political commitment. Her voice has both challenged and cleared the way for all those who come after her."

For general discussions emphasizing similar formal qualities—but not the thematic concerns—in other modern short fiction, see overviews in Mary Rohrberger and Dan E. Burns, "Short Fiction and the Numinous Realm: Another Attempt at Definition," *Modern Fiction Studies* 28, no. 1 (Spring 1982): 5–12; and Suzanne Ferguson, "Defining the Short Story: Impressionism and Form," *Modern Fiction Studies* 28, no. 1 (Spring 1982): 13–24. Ferguson notes that it is characteristic of contemporary writers to "eschew any kind of plot" (6). Rohrberger and Burns provide a definition of the modern short story as "impressionistic" by such criteria as "emphasis on sensations," "transformation of . . . traditional plot," "increasing reliance on metaphor and metonymy," "rejection of chronological time ordering," and "stylistic economy" (14–15).

31. Teresa de Lauretis, *Alice Doesn't: Feminism, Semiotics, Cinema* (Bloomington: Indiana University Press, 1984), 159. Compare Coiner's statement about Olsen's capacity to display "individual heteroglossia, the fragmenting of voices constituting a self and that self-interdependence with others, . . . one means by which her work offers alternatives to bourgeois individualism" (262).

32. See part 3 for further discussion of reader participation. See also Coiner's similar claim that Olsen expects her readers to be "active readers alert to the connections among a multiplicity of marginalized voices" (259).

33. Elizabeth Fox-Genovese criticizes new historicism as neglecting this intersection: "For the new historicism is tending to restore context without exploring the boundaries between text and context." See "Literary Criticism and the Politics of the New Historicism," in *The New Historicism*, ed. H. A. Veeser (New York: Routledge, 1989), 222. Also in *The New Historicism*, see Louis Montrose's careful assessment of these intersections in what he calls "a new socio-historical criticism," in his essay "Professing the Renaissance: The Poetics and Politics of Culture," 23, and see Catherine Gallagher's distillation of new historical critics' interest in resisting any "fixed hierarchy of cause and effect as they trace the connections among texts, discourses, power, and the constitution of subjectivity," in "Marxism and the New Historicism," 37. Dominick LaCapra's work provides an additional and crucial reminder to balance the opposing views of language associated with new historicism on the one hand and deconstruction on the other; see especially his final chapter, "Intellectual History and Critical Theory," in *Soundings in Critical Theory* (Ithaca: Cornell University Press, 1989).

34. H. Aram Veeser, introduction to *The New Historicism*, xi.

35. Compare Stephen Greenblatt's statement that "cultural analysis must

be opposed on principle to the rigid distinction between that which is within a text and that which lies outside." See "Culture," in *Critical Terms for Literary Study*, ed. Frank Lentricchia and Thomas McLaughlin (Chicago: University of Chicago Press, 1990), 227.

36. Informal remarks at Kenyon College, Gambier, Ohio, March 1982. The dangers of remaining within this line of reasoning are evident in such statements as the following: "The guilt she must have felt at leaving Karla is movingly depicted in the ironing mother's similar thoughts about her daughter Emily" (Pearlman and Werlock, 22). I agree with Olsen that the issue is maternal "anguish" rather than "guilt" (conversation 1) and further think that the confusion of Olsen with her narrator makes it even more difficult to see beyond the culturally constructed assumption that guilt is the issue.

37. Olsen, appendix, "On the Writing of a Story: Tillie Olsen: Help Her to Believe," *Stanford Short Stories: 1956*, ed. Wallace Stegner and Richard Scowcroft (Stanford: Stanford University Press, 1956), 136; hereafter cited in the text as "Writing."

38. Olsen also discusses this incident in "Writing," in which the boy is pseudonymously named "Bob."

39. This, however, is gradually changing, especially in the years since Olsen wrote: "Not many have directly used the material open to them out of motherhood as central source for their work" (*Silences*, 32). See also Olsen's statement about her selections of writing for *Mother to Daughter: Daughter to Mother: A Feminist Press Daybook and Reader*, selected and shaped by Tillie Olsen (Old Westbury N.Y.: Feminist Press, 1984): "Least present is work written by mothers themselves (although each year sees more). . . . That everyday welter, the sense of its troublous context, the voice of the mother herself, are the largest absences in this book. And elsewhere" (275–76). Compare Susan Rubin Suleiman's succinct statement: *"Mothers don't write, they are written."* See her "Writing and Motherhood," in *The (M)other Tongue*, ed. Shirley Nelson Garner, Claire Kuhane, and Madelon Sprengnether (Ithaca: Cornell University Press, 1985), 356.

40. She specifically made this connection in personal conversation in Wooster, Ohio, May 1991.

41. Of significant interest in this correlation is Sara Ruddick's analysis of "Maternal Thinking," in which she explores the kinds of understanding that can be developed specifically through undertaking parental responsibilities. Although this essay has prompted a good deal of controversy—most notably because it risks "essentialism" and because it leaves unexamined some of its embedded assumptions based on class, race, and circumstances—it retains significant interest for its efforts to identify the relationship between ways of thinking and particular practices to which women primarily have been assigned. Note that Ruddick credits Olsen with prompting her analysis: "I first came to the notion of 'maternal thinking' and the virtues of maternal practices through

personal exchange with Tillie Olsen and then through reading her fiction. My debt to her is pervasive." See *Feminist Studies*, 6, no. 2 (Summer 1980): 364. See also Orr's claim, "we have in Tillie Olsen's work a shaping maternal consciousness, a political and spiritual voice arising from mothering realities" (52), and Coiner's claim that "it may have been through the experience of parenting that Olsen learned the limits of authorial control. . . . As a parent one is forced to live intensely 'in relation to,' as the boundary between self and other is constantly negotiated. Such negotiating provides a model in which the ability to listen to constantly changing, heteroglossic voices is prized" (278).

42. Orr sees Emily's pantomime as "a symbol that reexamines the negative imaging of her life. Calling into being an alternate reality, pantomime makes something out of nothing" (83).

43. For an earlier inquiry into motherhood itself as an embedded metaphor in the story, see Frye, " 'I Stand Here Ironing': Motherhood as Experience and Metaphor," *Studies in Short Fiction* 18, no. 3 (Summer 1981): 287–92. This inquiry predates my conversations with Olsen and the resulting probing of boundaries between text and context.

44. See, for example, Faulkner's identification of "three constellations of images, centering on hunger, stone, and flood" (39). Also see her general claim to a *"blight-fruit-possibility paradigm"* (28).

45. Thomas McLaughlin, "Figurative Language," in *Critical Terms for Literary Study*, 84. As McLaughlin says, *metonymy* is a figure of speech based on "associations that develop out of specific contexts . . . such as referring to the king by the phrase 'the crown.' " Unlike metaphor, which relies on deep or mysterious shared meaning, metonymy "relies on connections that build up over time and the associations of usage" (83–84). Thus, ironing in Olsen's story would seem to have a metonymic relationship to women's roles and a metaphoric relationship to harshly defining circumstances. My own argument suggests that the traditional distinction between metaphor and metonymy is inadequate for understanding Olsen's fiction.

46. I share Faulkner's view: "It seems just a little short of miraculous that during those repressive years she was able to write 'I Stand Here Ironing,' 'Hey Sailor, What Ship?' 'O Yes,' and 'Tell Me a Riddle.' . . . [I]n each of these stories Olsen challenges the domestic, social, and political ideologies of the fifties" (26).

47. The information and quotations in this paragraph derive from the first set of conversations that I had with Olsen in Soquel, California, in the summer of 1988.

48. Quoted in Douglas T. Miller and Marion Nowak, *The Fifties: The Way We Really Were* (Garden City, N.Y.: Doubleday and Co., 1977), 406; hereafter cited in the text. For general information about the 1950s, I have found the cultural emphases and the chronology (401–18) in Miller and Nowak especially

helpful in supplementing my own memories and other general sources. Also very helpful are Elaine Tyler May, *Homeward Bound: American Families in the Cold War Era* (New York: Basic Books, 1988), and *Recasting America: Culture and Politics in the Age of Cold War*, ed. Lary May (Chicago: University of Chicago Press, 1989). A more recent—and widely acclaimed—inquiry into the period is David Halberstam, *The Fifties* (New York: Villard Books, 1993). His historical overview identifies similar patterns but tends more to investigate individual personalities rather than to provide general information about the forces at work in a range of people's lives. For specific information about McCarthyism, see Richard M. Fried, *Nightmare in Red: The McCarthy Era in Perspective* (N.Y.: Oxford University Press, 1990).

49. Adrienne Rich, *Blood, Bread, and Poetry* (New York: W. W. Norton and Co., 1986), 179. Also see part 2 of this volume. This apprehension about detention camps was also an important part of the context for another short story, "Seeds" (unpublished), that Olsen was working on during this same time period (personal communication, summer 1988).

50. It is crucial to remember that these generalizations *are* of the dominant ideology and are particularly insufficient for describing the lives of multiple racial and cultural groups and of people of different socioeconomic statuses.

51. Faulkner sees this image as Sisyphian and connects it with a series of Sisyphus images in other Olsen texts (148).

52. Helen McNeil, "Speaking for the Speechless," *Times Literary Supplement*, 14 November 1980.

53. Contrast page 199 of "Hey Sailor, What Ship?" in *New Campus Writing*, *No. 2*, ed. Nolan Miller (New York: G. P. Putnam's Sons, 1957), with page 13 of *Tell Me a Riddle*.

54. Personal communication, summer 1988. Also compare Sandy Boucher, "Tillie Olsen: The Weight of Things Unsaid," *Ms*, September 1974, 26.

55. For background information on Rizal, see Roman Ozaeta, *The Pride of the Malay Race: A Biography of José Rizal*, trans. Rafael Palma (New York: Prentice-Hall, 1949). The poem, "My Last Farewell," in 14 verses, can be found on pages 320–22.

56. Contrast Coiner's view that mimicry here is unsupportive of Whitey's voice and presence, "a microcosm for the dominant culture's behavior in relation to much marginalized discourse" (267).

57. Faulkner also notes the importance of empathy in this section but situates it as a more personal and less historical and cultural concern: "What Helen wants her teenage daughter to see is that Whitey's bravado, rough talk, and expensive gifts mask tenderness and a longing to be part of a family" (74). In general, most critical responses to "Hey Sailor, What Ship?" are marked by neglect of its political concerns.

58. Pearlman and Werlock note, as well, the specific use of color imagery (78).

59. Orr faults the story for its "lack of a central consciousness among characters; we are not certain whose story this is" (94). Pearlman and Werlock indicate general agreement with Orr about this as a difficulty (77). Faulkner, by contrast, identifies it as "another of Olsen's important strategies; along with physical images of unity, it suggests that diverse people can form communities even in a deeply racist society" (102). My own position is similar to Faulkner's, although I identify the strategic importance of this narrative strategy in a somewhat different way.

60. See my explanation of this term in the introduction to this volume and in note 19 above.

61. N. M. Jacobs provides an intriguing gloss on Alva's vision as an account of "the physical and psychological experience of childbirth," in "Olsen's 'O Yes': Alva's Vision as Childbirth Account," *Notes on Contemporary Literature* 16 (January 1986): 7–8.

62. By contrast, Coiner sees this call-and-response structure as a *suppression* of multiplicity: "The univocalizing of heteroglossia is a shared singular escape of people who are trapped in multiple ways. They seem to choose to surrender the heteroglossia of their suffering to the univocal escape of the church/home" (270). In my reading, the church service does not succumb to the pressures of univocality, though I, too, see this as a potential risk here. I also share Coiner's view that Alva's "dream vision," experienced silently, is an important locus of resistance (270–71).

63. Randall Jarrell, "What's the Riddle . . . ," in *The Complete Poems* (New York: Farrar, Straus and Giroux, 1969), 491.

64. See conversation 4 for Olsen's discussion of these biographical sources. For additional background about the Bund and the life of Jewish immigrants in the United States, see Irving Howe, *World of Our Fathers* (New York: Harcourt Brace Jovanovich, 1976). See also Henry J. Tobias, *The Jewish Bund in Russia: From Its Origins to 1905* (Stanford, Calif.: Stanford University Press, 1972), and Charlotte Baum, Paula Hyman, and Sonya Michel, *The Jewish Woman in America* (New York: New American Library, 1976). For a more personal tracing of older immigrants' lives in the last half of the twentieth century, see Barbara Myerhoff, *Number Our Days* (New York: E. P. Dutton, 1978). In her ethnography of the Aliyah Senior Citizens' Center, Myerhoff pays particular attention to stories and language. Particularly poignant in the context of Olsen's affirmation of belief is the accusation that one of Myerhoff's interviewees makes to another (Faegl to Basha): " 'You used to be an internationalist. You used to have beliefs' " (16). In some sense, what Faegl is accusing Basha of is the same potentially cynical attitude from which David must be retrieved at the end of the novella.

65. Al Richmond, *A Long View from the Left: Memoirs of an American Revolutionary* (Boston: Houghton Mifflin Company, 1973), 1; hereafter cited in the text.

66. Tillie Olsen, "Dream-Vision," in *Mother to Daughter, Daughter to Mother*, 261; hereafter cited in the text as "Dream."

67. For an assessment of this age group's Communist Party membership, see Vivian Gornick, *The Romance of American Communism* (New York: Basic Books, 1977); hereafter cited in the text.

68. Duncan, 209. Compare Gornick, "I have found that those Communists who, consciously or unconsciously, said, 'this far I go, and no farther,' live in decent relation to their CP past; whereas, those who were most rigidly orthodox . . . are those who now beat their breasts" (167).

69. Naomi Rubin, "A Riddle of History for the Future," *Sojourner*, July 1983, 4, 18. Olsen's discussion with Rubin also illuminates the richness of Olsen's personal history and includes insights into the Bund as well.

70. I quote the portions of the song that are included in "Tell Me a Riddle." The full song, whose words are by John Addington Symonds (1840–93), has six verses. In the novella, the first verse is quoted in full; the second verse is nearly complete; the final line included in the novella comes from verse 5. For the complete text, see Edith Fowke and Joe Glazer, *Songs of Work and Protest* (New York: Dover Publications, 1973), 174–75.

71. This loss of historical awareness can probably be attributed, in part, to anticommunist rhetoric in the 1950s and again in the 1980s. But note the broader and more historically grounded understanding (although "always" is obviously excessive) that Siberia has a long history as metaphor for exile: "Russia's huge Asiatic hinterland of Siberia has always figured in the Western popular imagination as a limitless frozen wilderness, a place of punishment and exile for the unfortunate victims of Tsarist and Soviet authorities. Dostoevsky languished there for several years and afterwards described it as *The House of the Dead*, while an official government report of 1900 referred to, but dismissed, the concept of Siberia as 'a vast roofless prison.' " See Alan Wood, "Siberian Exile in Tsarist Russia," *History Today*, September 1980, 19.

Note Al Richmond's differentiation of his mother's journey to czarist imprisonment in Russia from his own U.S. imprisonment as a Communist during the McCarthy years: "One morning she saw us being led from the county jail across the street to the federal building, the men in single handcuffs hooked to one chain. This chained procession recalled the final and most cruel leg of the long journey to a Siberian prison. The prison was several hundred miles from the Trans-Siberian Railroad; this distance from the point of detrainment was traversed on foot. This was the *etap*, a physical ordeal. . . . The chain gang was a memory trigger, not a parallel. She was very aware of the contrasts" (339).

For an intriguing historical gloss on Eva's year of exile in Siberia, see Edward L. Niehus and Teresa Jackson, "Polar Stars, Pyramids, and 'Tell Me a Riddle,' " *American Notes and Queries* 24 (January/February 1986): 77–83. They incorporate knowledge of Siberia, astronomy, and late-nineteenth-century pyramidology into a compelling argument for knowing history: "Only by coming to know and understand the past can we possess its heritage, preserving its virtues and avoiding its errors" (83).

72. This is the phrasing in current editions, as it was in the very first published version in 1958. But I am intrigued to note that the line reads slightly differently in a British edition: "Somewhere coherence, transport, meaning, community." See *Tell Me a Riddle* (London: Virago, 1983), 95. The meaning is not so much altered as it is reinforced by the addition of that weighted word in Olsen's lexicon: "community."

73. Pearlman and Werlock use this scene in speculation that Clara is the same character as the narrator in "I Stand Here Ironing" as further evidence of divisions between mothers and daughters: "Typical of all Olsen mother-daughter relations, the mother is 'secret from' the daughter. Clara cannot understand her own mother any more than the ironing mother understands Emily" (Pearlman and Werlock, 108). I do not share the view that secrecy is central to Olsen's portrayal of mother-daughter relations.

74. Tillie Olsen with Julie Olsen Edwards, "Mothers and Daughters," in *Mothers and Daughters, That Special Quality: An Exploration in Photographs* (New York: Aperture Foundation, 1987), n.p.

75. Throughout, my statements about "many readers" derive from reading critical responses and from having conversations with College of Wooster students over a number of years of teaching these stories. My statements about readers are also informed by a reader investigation using "I Stand Here Ironing" as one of its texts. See Maggie Redic, "Constructing Reader Response Theory: Gender, Ideology, and Context," unpublished independent study thesis, Women's Studies, College of Wooster, 19 March 1990. I am grateful to Redic and her advisor, Carolyn Durham, for sharing this work with me.

76. In conversation, Olsen spoke of "the crack" in the novella, "before the cancer element came in" (personal communication, summer 1988). This is where the story shifts from its earlier focus on marital strife to its concern with the dying of "that generation."

77. In informal remarks at the College of Wooster, April 1980, Olsen underlined her claim that "*she* brings him around." Attentive readers notice this exchange as well. See, for example, Faulkner's observation that David and Eva "in some way give birth to each other, their hands umbilical cords, and Jeannie the midwife" (55). See also Coiner's claim that "Olsen aids us in valuing Eva's links to humankind. One of those aids is a resuscitated David with whom we are invited to identify once he has remembered what he had long forgotten" (276).

78. Although my phrasing suggests a certain incongruity of metaphor—weaving or braiding versus fossilizing—the text actually uses both of these to suggest the complex, deep, yet not fixed ways in which meanings persist and

are brought together. Compare Olsen's statement: "There is nothing humankind has developed which is the equal of language to embed, develop ideas and concepts; synthesize, analyse, comprehend; record. Language itself is memory, it is history." See "The Word Made Flesh," Twelfth Annual H. W. Reninger Lecture, prefatory essay to *Critical Thinking, Critical Writing* (Iowa, 1984), 1–8; hereafter cited in text as "Word Made Flesh." In Olsen's understanding of deep history and hope for change, relationships between stones and words and flesh and history and text and fabric are complex, as is also evident in Catharine R. Stimpson's claim on history and hope: "Eva thinks that 'Stone will perish, but the word remain' (p. 90). The text will then serve, not only as history, but as answer to those who might ask, 'But what is to be done?' They are to perpetuate the hope and to redeem the defeats." See "Tillie Olsen: Witness as Servant," *Polit* (Fall 1977): 10.

79. Compare Orr's identification of "piecing" or quilting as a central metaphor in Olsen's work (176–81).

80. Michael A. Peterman makes this line central to his comparison of Olsen with Margaret Laurence: " 'All That Happens, One Must Try to Understand': The Kindredness of Tillie Olsen's 'Tell Me a Riddle' and Margaret Laurence's *The Stone Angel*," in *Margaret Laurence: An Appreciation*, ed. Christl Verduyn (Peterborough, Canada: Broadview Press, 1988), 70–81. Compare Helen's plea to Jeannie in "Hey Sailor, What Ship?": "Jeannie, I care you should understand" (34).

81. A number of critics note the central role of music in the novella. See, for example, Orr, 114; Werlock and Pearlman, 110; and Sally H. Johnson, "Silence and Song: The Structure and Imagery of Tillie Olsen's 'Tell Me a Riddle,' " in *Tillie Olsen Week: The Writer and Society*, 21–26 March 1983, sponsored by Augustana College, Rock Island, Ill., et al.

82. See Olsen's statement about her readers: "the common work that we do together": "Tillie Olsen: From a Public Dialogue between Olsen and Marilyn Yalom, Stanford Center for Research on Women, Nov. 5, 1980, and Subsequently," in *Women Writers of the West Coast: Speaking of Their Lives and Careers*, ed. Marilyn Yalom (Stanford: Capra Press, 1983), 64; hereafter cited in the text as Yalom dialogue.

83. I use here the edition published as "Requa I" to indicate that Olsen sees this as the first part of a longer piece. See "Requa I," *The Best American Short Stories of 1971*, ed. Martha Foley and David Burnett (Boston: Houghton Mifflin, 1971); hereafter cited in the text. When I mean to suggest the ongoing work on the more extended novella—as yet unpublished—I will call it "Requa."

84. Olsen in a 1974 talk at Emerson College, Boston, quoted in Rosenfelt (404).

85. The first critical attention to "Requa I" noted this emergence from

silence. See Blanche H. Gelfant, "After Long Silence: Tillie Olsen's 'Requa,' " *Studies in American Fiction* 12, no. 1 (1984): 61–69; hereafter cited in the text.

86. Orr elaborates on this passage, connecting it to Stevie's memories, saying, "Eyes become Stevie's link with his past" (125). As with most of Olsen's metaphorical insights, the eyes here seem to bridge metaphor and metonymy, as they are also a crucial feature of his material environment, new to him as a rural one.

87. See conversation 5. See also Gelfant's earlier assertion, still in Olsen's mind: "Tillie Olsen intends the landlady, Mrs. Edler, to play a larger part in Stevie's life in the version of 'Requa' she hopes to complete. Wes, apparently, will die, and Mrs. Edler will carry on his role as 'mother' " (69). Although Olsen will openly discuss subsequent sections of "Requa," she is understandably reluctant to include those projections in printed interviews since the writing is still ongoing.

88. Note that the inscription on the lamb tombstone is nearly identical to one Olsen includes in *Mother to Daughter* (100):

MILENA WILETT
1 yr. old

Thy Mother strives in patient trust
Her bleeding heart to bow,
For safe in God, the Good, the Just
Her baby's sleeping now

Fort Bragg, California

Olsen has indicated that she takes an active interest in tombstone reading, in seeing the human histories traced in cemeteries (personal communication, summer, 1988).

89. Compare "The terrible thing about class in our society is that it sets up a contest for dignity." See Richard Sennett and Jonathan Cobb, *The Hidden Injuries of Class* (1972; New York: Random House, 1973), 147; hereafter cited in the text.

90. In my reading, the real power of the language here comes from the honoring of the tasks and tools at hand rather than from the similarity to Shakespeare that Faulkner notes, although Faulkner's observation is to the point: "In this brilliant recombination, the making of poetry and everyday, skilled labor are bound together as manifestations of human intelligence. Both Shakespeare and technological waste become pieces of junk that need to be and can be reclaimed and retooled by 'human mastery, human skill' " (129–30).

91. Faulkner's general claim about Olsen's fiction is pertinent here: "In all of these families, the meanings of mothering and fathering blur, shift, and

become one meaning" (79). See also Orr's statement about "Requa I": "In this last fiction, Olsen transforms male according to female and in so doing universalizes a feminist maternal spirituality, a vision of need and desire spring from the memory of a lost mother . . . " (Orr, 122).

92. Personal communication, summer 1988. See also observations to this effect in the dialogue with Yalom: "Olsen thinks of herself as 'an oral/aural writer' "; Olsen herself says, "I use the 'mother tongue' primarily, the language of the deepest, purest emotion, language that does not come primarily out of books, but the language of first thought, emotion" (63).

93. Ursula K. LeGuin, "Bryn Mawr Commencement Address," 1986, in *Dancing at the Edge of the World: Thoughts on Words, Women, Places* (New York: Harper and Row, 1989), 150; hereafter cited in the text.

94. Critics have misattributed Yurok meanings to the name. Gelfant says that it means "broken in body and spirit" (62). Orr says, " 'Requa,' or 'Rekwoi,' is an Indian name for a holy place, Olsen has said, where dances are performed to keep the floods away" (121). Both meanings are apt and may inadvertently distort observations that Olsen has made about the power that Requa has had in her own life. Nonetheless, Olsen herself does not at present claim a specific Yurok translation, and the Yurok dictionary provides the simple place label as its meaning. See R. H. Robins, *The Yurok Language: Grammar, Texts, Lexicon* (Berkeley: University of California Press, 1958), 242.

Part 2

THE WRITER

Roots, Sources, and Circumstances: Tillie Olsen in Conversation with Joanne Frye

An examination of the critical work on Tillie Olsen reveals that she is unusually open to interaction with readers and with other writers: her personal remarks in individual conversation or public comment are often cited as the source for critical insights or inspiration for further thought. But extended interviews about the roots and sources of her fiction are not readily available.[1] To explore these concerns at length, I spent three days in wide-ranging conversation with her over a period of several weeks in July and August of 1988. I shared with her in advance a series of questions that were prominent in my own thinking. She then used these questions and the interaction that developed between us as the basis for hours of associative probing of her own personal history and the circumstances within which her fiction developed.

The preface to *Silences* provided my dominant concern in posing questions: "This book," she wrote, "is . . . concerned with the relationship of circumstances—including class, color, sex; the times, climate into which one is born—to the creation of literature."[2] The centrality of *circumstances*, then, became the near-refrain for all of our conversations.

Olsen's responses here resonate with three themes that she explores in *Silences*. First, as I pointed out in my biographical sketch in part 1, her life as a woman is evident as pervasive circumstance for her fiction, and her "life comprehensions" are intertwined with her experiences "as writer, as insatiable reader, as feminist-humanist, as woman" (*Silences*, 118). Second, her thought processes follow from the living of a rich and complex life and the coming to writing after many years: "The cost of 'discontinuity' (that pattern still imposed on women) is such a weight of things unsaid, an accumulation of material so great, that everything starts up something else in me; what should take weeks, takes me sometimes months to write; what should take months, takes years" (*Silences*, 39). In her fiction, this "cost" is clearly also part of the value, as it yields the compression and the complexity of form. In the conversations that follow, the talk, though not compressed like the fiction, is similarly rich, complex, and intertwined, nourished by this value of accumulated material. What sometimes looks like digression always comes back to the central strand; indeed, everything *does* "start up" something else, but always as a part of an evolving connectedness of issues. Finally, her commitment to the lives of those people rarely present in literature pervades her thoughts here on human capacity for growth, as it pervades her fiction.

What cannot be evident in a written transcription is the emotional power of these commitments and self-definitions: the timbre of actual voice and the human empathy in face and gesture. What is also not fully evident in this edited transcript is the wealth of interconnection with other writers and with historical circumstances. Our conversations began, for example, with her extended thoughts on writer Moa Martinson and included references to more than 30 different writers as diverse as Cora Sandell, Isaac Babel, Olive Schreiner, Milovan Djilas, Sue Miller, James Baldwin, Jean Rhys, and Henry James. Each insight seemed also to evoke a factual connection to the particulars of history. I felt myself to be in conversation not only with a writer of powerful perception and linguistic gifts but also with a person living in an interconnected awareness of literary and historical circumstance.

I was moved and exhilarated and exhausted by these conversations, as I believe Tillie Olsen was as well. Neither of us had ever undertaken a process quite like this before. But from those shared hours I came to a far richer understanding of both Olsen's fiction and the complex and dynamic process by which human experiences and insights can be shaped in language, in literary form.

What are the circumstances that shape each of the short stories—or "pieces," as she prefers to call them? From what life experiences do they arise and to what life concerns do they respond?

From tapes of these conversations, I constructed a typescript, tracing roots and sources, identifying the power of circumstances. I rearranged her comments and edited them extensively to distill and highlight the wealth of understanding she had shared with me in conversation. I also interjected my own comments—and identified them as mine— wherever that seemed necessary for clarity or emphasis. In that first typescript, except for minor adjustments necessary for bringing sentences together, I retained Olsen's phrasing—the rhythms of her speech and the distinctive currents of her wide-ranging thought. I then shared my typescript with Olsen in the spring of 1990, when we again spent several days together going over her earlier words, re-editing for greater concision and clarity, talking together about meanings and language. Following our second set of conversations, she did an additional edit for clarity in written form, working in that process still to retain the oral quality and the initial sense of process and openness. Finally, in the summer of 1994, she did one last review of the written form of our conversations, adjusting phrases and details while again retaining the thrust of the original content, as well as the commitment to the conversational form that is evident in both phrasing and punctuation.

The interviews as printed here are, then, the distillation of an intensive effort to probe—in multiple conversations—those roots, sources, and circumstances for the short fiction. I am immensely grateful for the care and time and energy that Tillie Olsen committed to these conversations.

1: "I Stand Here Ironing"

JF: *You've identified in* Silences *the general circumstances that led to "I Stand Here Ironing." How do you think those circumstances affected its form?*

The very circumstance that much of it was written and rewritten and rewritten on the ironing board late at night, as I have said more than once. The very timbre, rhythm of the piece, the back and forth movement as the iron itself moves; the late night uninterrupted quiet; the rare time "to remember, to sift, to weigh, to total." Then the visual: whatever garment it is, "helpless before the iron" contrasting with the human content of what pre-occupies the mother—what, at the very end, becomes the mother's cry: "help her to know that (as a human being) she is more than this dress on the ironing board, helpless before the iron."

For me, always, the form comes primarily out of what it is I am trying to get said in the best way I can say it. But even that is dependent on what my capacities are at the time, my personal situation, and my actual circumstances, both material and personal: that is, the writing time available to me; what is happening in my work and family life, and in the larger environment, in society. The fact is that when I was writing this, circumstanced motherhood was not then mine.

I wrote in *Silences* about "comprehensions possible out of motherhood

. . . the very nature, needs, illimitable potentiality of the human be-ing—and the everyday means by which these are (enabled or) distorted, discouraged, limited." Unformulated, without realizing it, in "I Stand Here Ironing" I was trying to write of both; make both visible, undeni-able.

What began to emerge (again unformulated) in the specific telling, was the roots, the why of those too often damaging "everyday means,"—including the situation of a mother in that society: the insti-tutions and the people who have determining power. "She was a mira-cle to me, but when she was eight months old I had to leave her with someone to whom she was no miracle at all." *Had to.* "Even if I had known, what difference would it have made? It was the only way we could be together." *The only way.* Lines from the piece itself.

I have seen so many questions for students at the end of anthology reprints of "I Stand Here Ironing"; so many of them about the "guilt" of the mother, so few of them about society and its institutions. Only one concerns itself with the nuclear threat.

By 1954, the time I began to struggle with "Ironing," there was an enormous difference between that young mother of one small child in the 1930s when I was writing *Yonnondio* and the forty-two year old mother of four—the eldest twenty-two, the youngest six. It was a difference even more than the sum of all that I had lived, experienced, in the intervening years; a cataclysmic element for myself and for all the world—the explosion of the first nuclear bomb. Oh, the complex of factors which enter into the writing of one piece. But to return to "I Stand Here Writing" [this slip of the tongue seemed so fitting that it went unnoted by either of us at the time]—that element, that fuel, was the realization after Hiroshima that I had in some way to try to write again and to write on the side of life against death. The mother's—in the larger terms, the caring person's—sense of how precious young life, *all* life, is—the dearness and transitory nature of life—the desire to protect, remove threat, harm, had acquired an intensity near obsession because of this new possibility to end all life on earth. Years passed, however, before I was able to write of this—the first piece I considered publishable after I rebegan to write.

There were two immediate changes in my circumstances that made the writing of this story possible. Although I really had no more time than I had had before and certainly no less responsibility nor immersion and fascination with my children, I had a comparative peace inside me—instead of being torn apart all the time by what was happening with my children when I was away working. The first circumstance that changed for me and enabled me was that down the street moved a new neighbor—someone who had a baby just six weeks younger than my youngest—Laurie, the first baby I'd had full time to be home with. When at six months, I had to go back to part-time work, I now had a friend who also had to work part-time. And, in a time-honored way, we traded off; my children had a home with her when I wasn't there, and her children had a home when she could not be there. With the inner turmoil gone, I was able for the first time to have enough of me left over for writing, even if still most of the time it was late at night.

But I didn't start out to write "Ironing." I tried to write another mother story, based on a dear friend, an old comrade in arms from work in the thirties and forties, my Warehouse days, a single mother. When she came to San Francisco, it was without immediate family; we became her family. But there are the problems of raising a child, when you are a young mother and working. Her son now was in junior high, and a very dear kid, but he was picked up one night with other boys in a car in the wrong neighborhood—San Francisco's working class Mission district. They, innocent time, had been drinking, *beer*. One of the boys had a record. My friend was ordered to appear in juvenile court and prove to their satisfaction that she was a good mother, that she had the right to keep Freddy. The night before, we were actually up nearly all that night—and all that time I was ironing too—trying to figure out how she could establish that she was a good mother. The boy had, without realizing the damage it would do, let on that she had what was in those days called "a boyfriend," a seaman, who stayed overnight with them when he was in port. Therefore, by standards of the day she was "immoral"—an early version of Sue Miller's *The Good Mother*. That night we relived his life and hers; gagged at the difference between the way that you're judged from the outside and the true reality. I wanted to write those realities in a way to *inform* the kind of people who had the power to take away one's child.

I tried and tried to write that story, and I couldn't make it right. I ended up with my own "I Stand Here Ironing" and "all that life that is outside of me, beyond me."

The other change in circumstance I've already referred to—an earthquake change: my youngest in grade school; my eldest grown, living her own life (that time of motherhood-daughterhood over for the two of us); in-between a sub-teener, a teenager; then my own age (many of my friends grandmothers already)—and eighteen–nineteen years of mothering. There was a consciousness, comprehension, perspective, I could not have come to before.

And guilt was beginning to be what mothers were over and over being told they were experiencing when matters were not right with one's child, in one's child's life. The need to write against this crept into the piece. The use of the word "guilt" to define the actual anguish, the justifiable anguish, the legitimate anguish which has never been legitimized—an anguish too often sourced in harms to one's children and to oneself arising in that agonizing having to raise children in a society not concerned with, even hostile to, human flowering; the damning and paralyzing effect on women when they're told that what they are feeling is *guilt*. One is guilty only for what one oneself is responsible for. But if the situation is that it's the terrible schools; the poor child care; the competitive putdown world; if it's exhaustion; if you can't be there when needed and there's nobody else to care, then the anguish, anger, even powerlessness is a *reality* reaction. And to a situation common with others. About which something *can* be done.

I feel that one of the reasons "I Stand Here Ironing" is still being taught and read is because it was written *without* guilt. It was specific about situations and specific about oneself, including the wisdom that "came too late." It concerns itself with more than personal circumstances. It's meshed into the context of life.

JF: *You mentioned Hiroshima—and I've heard you speak passionately about the threat of nuclear war. Would you elaborate on how that deeply felt knowledge was a source for this story?*

Well, the place where the mother breaks down, you remember, is when, after living over all that compounds nineteen years of her daughter's life, she hears her daughter say, and "quite lightly": "in a couple of years when we'll all be atom-dead it won't matter a bit."

Unbearable, that acceptance; unbearable, the unknowingness of, therefore the giving way to the forces that make for criminal, premature, unnatural death. Unbearable, that the young were not armed with the knowledge of our willed human history, our genius to resist, to act for life, our power to change.

I think back again to that morning of Hiroshima—like the morning in "I Stand Here Ironing"—getting the kids to child care on time and their lunches packed, a common morning in many a home these days, morning after morning, that near hysteria. Nevertheless, all had gone comparatively well and my little one-year-old was in my arms with that wonderful feeling of the warm body surrendered against you, and I ran down the stairs, humming a lullaby my mother used to sing. There was a store downstairs—there still is a store downstairs from 903 Castro—and I read the headlines, read the story, and knew that death had entered the world in a way never had it been before, that at that moment I and all living things on earth—memory and the past and our future—the earth itself had entered a time when all might be no more. And, as I said at the beginning, I knew I had to write on the side of life, that this was central. And then I had to drop off Kathie at that evil place that was harming her and go off to work. And years later . . . "I Stand Here Ironing."

JF: *I'm interested in your use of the mother's voice in this story, especially given your recognition in* Silences *that mothers are so rarely present in literature.*

Less and less true in our time, happily. I think now that probably that direct voice of the mother was very important. I did not realize then that this was the first time the direct voice of the mother herself appeared in literature.

JF: *Did you have a particular addressee in mind as the mother's "audience"— the person to whom the monologue was addressed?*

It doesn't matter to whom the monologue was addressed. That's for the reader to imagine.

JF: *What about your sense of the reader? Was there something that you particularly wanted the reader to understand?*

Only everything—all I've spoken of here, and not spoken of.

I know painfully well what I wasn't able to make clear, the meaning of that cry, that summons of the last sentence: *"Help her to know that she is more than this dress on the ironing board,"* (she is of the human species whose nature it is NOT to be) *"helpless before the iron."* I tried and tried. . . . Wait! I put it into words at last years later; a state-wide gathering of essay-winning students about Emily's age: Iowa's 1984 "Critical Inquirers." [Rummages through files, reads.]

> Human will, courage, capacity to change what degrades, harms, limits, is inherent. That is the nature of our human species. Again

147

and again we have evidenced the capacity and will to change what degrades, harms, limits; create lives and societies ever more in accordance with human needs and potentialities.

Once slavery covered most of the ancient earth. Once. Once feudalism, the serf and caste systems, colonialism, prevailed. Once. Not forever. They were done away with not by great men but by numerous nameless "everyday" human beings who presumably could not have known what freedom or human rights were, never having experienced them. Few could read or write.

Once we sacrificed other human beings to propitiate invisible powers, spirits, Gods. Once we accepted the divine right of Pharaohs, kings, emperors, czars, feudal lords, masters. Once we believed that famine, disease, the eighteen hour a day seven-day work week, the subordination of women, slavery serfdom, the caste system, as the natural order of things, not to be questioned. Once. Yet the divine right of kings became the rights of man, the belief that all men (not yet slaves and/ or women) are created with certain inalienable rights.[3]

So long a passage, and yet there is more. In 1948, in the name of all humankind, in the passion to not let reoccur what resulted in World War II with its blood and suffering and horror and millions of deaths, and first atomic bomb use; in order to safeguard, perpetuate life; and to act against ills, injustices, inequalities still harming human beings [long breath]—the United Nations in its Universal Declaration of Human Rights not only restated the human rights which had been won (or only proclaimed) the centuries before, went beyond to the next great step for Humanity: Yes, an end to the scourge of war; but never yet expressed, *it defined human needs, human capacities, potentialities—as Human Rights. It specified the means*, the economic, cultural, educational, social means necessary *to their fulfillment—as Human Rights.* (Trampled under by the Cold War, which I believe never had to be.)

I couldn't help all that pouring out. I wish I could incorporate all this knowledge of the past, this newer vision, almost reality, of our future, into every reading, every talk I give. The need has intensified, not lessened in these times, in this our world. Somehow to say it *was* central to the whole piece, why I finally created the mother standing there ironing, Emily coming in with her light graceful step, the dress helpless before the iron. But I failed in saying what I tried so to say. Yes, the context had, has not been developed for that comprehension.

The context was not, is not, there for the Emilys or for most carers for human life. This bone and blood knowledge that humans have faced, solved and transcended so many agonizing problems, horrors (in our personal lives as well) is hope, strength, armor that we, as our human species has done in the past, can face, solve, transcend what we must today.

But you see, I was struggling in my own way with the same problem that led Virginia Woolf to the form she developed and then abandoned in her *Pargiters:* how can you say what is not generally accepted with unmistakable force and clarity, when the context has not been established? You cannot, in the form of *The Waves*, write against prevailing, entrenched ideas and institutions. That can happen only after a movement has articulated different perceptions, truths. You have to write in the powerful factual form of *Three Guineas* or before that, more deferentially, *A Room of One's Own*. I like to believe I could have written a better "I Stand Here Ironing" if it had been later on, in other circumstances. I still think of it as a beginning, a re-beginning, work.

I don't see that "Ironing" has been of clear use to illuminate our possibilities and our strengths, but it has certainly been a healing story. It has had singular use in our time especially, because daughters (and sons) who are raised in times of despising and blaming of mothers have over and over again, on reading it, understood something of what trying to raise a child means—often given a copy to their mothers. And I will never forget, for instance, the time I read at U. Mass. Boston, the new campus, and sitting in the front row were women in their cafeteria uniforms. They'd arranged for time off to come because the daughter of one of them had been given "I Stand Here Ironing" to read in one of the community colleges around there, and she xeroxed it and sent it to her mother—then came home that week end to "really talk" with her mother—the first time in years that they'd broken through the estrangement between them. And the mother passed that story around to her co-workers, mothers, and they all came. Readers will say to me, often, "*I* was that mother"—or they'll say, "I was Emily" or "I was that younger sister." To me, true literary honors.

2: "Hey Sailor, What Ship?"

JF: *The remaining three pieces in* Tell Me a Riddle *are more closely linked together and suggest a more experimental narrative form, especially in the use of multiple points of view.*

As you have assessed, these other pieces were really pieces, in that there was a book I was going to write, a full-length book, and I didn't have the time. So these are literally pieces. But this writing was also part of my coming back as a writer, and, like everything but "O Yes," had to be taken up, interrupted, put down, taken up, interrupted, put down, taken up, interrupted, put down.

I was certainly not trying for a more experimental form or multiple points of view. The first time I heard the expression "multiple points of view"—and it was in regard to "Hey Sailor"—was at Stanford. I hadn't been reading criticism, analysis. The fact is that both what I was trying to say in this and my capacities to say it had developed to the point where I could write in that way. I *was* further along as a writer. And that development was true with each succeeding piece.

JF: *"Hey Sailor, What Ship?" is the only piece in* Tell Me a Riddle *that is not centered in specifically female experience. And yet it seems to me to be very much grounded in the experiences of family life. How do you think your own family circumstances at the time helped to shape your understanding here?*

In a way, this *is* centered in specifically female experience—I would argue with you. With the exception of Lennie, that seafarer is lensed through the eyes of four differently-aged female members of a family—and within that family home.

This followed "I Stand Here Ironing" and my own kids were older. I learned from them that children of different ages perceive differently. Many of us who are mothers see this: in the way children grow; in what has impact and meaning for them; in what brings them larger life including experiences outside the family; in how the pressures of one's peer group and the way society views individuals shapes more and more their response to experience.

Jeannie is the oldest. The change in her between the Jeannie in "Hey Sailor" and the Jeannie in "Tell Me a Riddle" expresses what I feel those of us who have been part of movements and those of us who have been privileged to see human growth over a period of time have seen: that what may be true at one age or one period may change into deeper comprehensions, caring, later.

(By the way, what I had to say about growth is, of course, what is not taken into consideration enough, pegging people to where they are now, instead of acting towards them with that reality sense that people can and do change.)

Again, "Yields possible out of circumstanced motherhood."

Helen urges Jeannie "to understand." Seemingly, Jeannie is deaf to what she says. But a deposit remains, as you see in the Jeannie of the later pieces. After all, Jeannie, as I wrote her, was growing through a time in which there was little in the outer soil to confirm her regard for Whitey or to yield the later kinds of comprehensions she was already evidencing in "O Yes," comprehensions that teach the opposite of contempt: understanding, caring understanding—and, as Helen says in "O Yes," that "caring (which) asks doing." In the background of the book, of course, was the fact there had been already two caring generations—the grandparents, Eva and David, and Helen's generation.

JF: *In addition to comprehensions rooted in family life, a clear knowledge of sailors' lives seems to be an important source for "Hey Sailor."*

For me—that girl—woman from landlocked Omaha who came to San Francisco—the seamen and the refugees were an essential part of what was my special luck, privilege, as a human being and as a writer. They brought a wider world; they brought the news; they also brought me literature. Some were great readers—you have time on board ship—it was on board ship that they were able to become readers. During the Spanish Civil War, many of them joined the Lincoln Brigade to fight against Franco with his Hitler-Mussolini backed forces, and many died there. I learned about the real situation in the Philippines and about José Rizal, heard El Ultimo Adiós, from Filipino seamen. From seamen I learned the truth about what was happening in Central America, Chile, the Banana Republics, so much of the world.

I guess another autobiographical element in "Hey Sailor" was the fact that my own children grew up around seamen and other single men and sometimes single women, who did not have family life except pretty much around us. With the men it was very poignant, especially the Filipino men. When my kids were growing up, Filipino women were not allowed in the U.S. Others of the seamen were immigrants, refugees, or came from inland families. Some of the letters or spoken responses I've had to "Hey Sailor" have to do with such men: how for children especially they were the gift-givers, the adventurers, the wider world. But what came evident to me in that time—whether there were or were not strong family bonds—is how deep the hunger for family life, for being around children went; and beyond that for roots, for community.

151

That was a very, very rich period and maybe I'll never be able to do it justice now. But my kids, who grew up in that time, were fortunate.

I have to add how unfortunate it was that I called the central character "Whitey"—in the later Civil Rights struggle time it became a term of contempt for white people. I could as well have called him Blackie or Curlie or High or any one of the other nicknames common among seafarers. The choice of that name also made it difficult for two real Whiteys, who read the piece, to separate themselves out from the fictional one.

Autobiographically speaking, the "Whiteys" were the only men I knew then who were truly helpful and thoughtful when it came to housework, or looking after the children for a while—with utmost respect for and delight in children.

JF: *Many readers focus on the alcoholism as central to their understanding of Whitey. How do you see its presence here?*

Yes, he has become a helpless alcoholic, but what to me is central is how he came to be so—what losses, betrayals, separations were *not* because he was drinking. Why is it that alcoholism, though there are genetic preconditions, is associated with certain kinds of life, occupations, periods, societies? We have had in our lifetime some very important historical lessons around addictions. There was a time when millions of Chinese were drug addicts. That ceased to be after the Chinese revolution—ceased to be, in a generation. In our own country, in a decade, we became the largest drug users in the world. How does that happen? What does it tell us?

JF: *I'm interested in the way your responses repeatedly intertwine the personal and the political, the recognitions from family life and from your life outside the family, including your activism.*

So were they intertwined in my life. So many human beings in my life (remember I have lived seventy-seven years) were experienced by me not only in their personal life, but also in their work, neighborhood, activity setting—and, of essential importance, as public events profoundly affected their personal beings. Depression, prosperity; war, peace; movements for social justice, the Vietnam war convulsion, or periods of quiescence, indifference; public policies to promote the common good—superb education, health, a decent standard of living, opportunity—or its opposite, such as we have lived the last decade; the time into which one comes into one's youthhood, the 30s, 40s, 50s, 60s, 70s, 80s—these are inseparable from the shaping of a person and what happens in their personal life. And I've left out the color of one's skin, and one's sex that also determine so much.

JF: *What you were saying about seamen—in fact, the whole of "Hey Sailor"— seems to suggest a special relationship that can exist between men and children.*

It can and does exist, in varying degree, but o what obstacles—so much of past and present ways of being, so much societal impedes it, reinforces harmful, ignorant attitudes, practices. We still have not established a context for how human infants—especially the boy child—are too often misshapen into beings who do harm to others.

The one place in this where you see the Jeannie that may yet be, is where she traces the scar on Whitey's face and the tenderness and regard and understanding with which she speaks to him.

JF: *The piece invokes an entire fabric of historical context, even though it never specifically describes historical circumstances. What circumstances were particularly important to your own thinking at the time?*

The harm—I'm using that word again—happening with human beings in that time. What was going on with many, many in that "McCarthy" period wasn't being recorded. Anguish over "our forfeited garden of Eden"; "the death of the brotherhood," of friendships; the destruction of the Whiteys. Various details—obscure, I'm afraid, in this. Seamen McCarthied off the waterfront. Or, as this "Whitey"—if he did finally get to ship—restricted to certain ports, and then often denied the right to get off the ship. He couldn't get off in Korea, in Pusan, because of the Korean war and the question about his "loyalty" because he had been active in a Left union.

The successful—with a few exceptions—doing in of good unions built on the principle that "An injury to one is any injury to all"— John Donne's "no man is an island" expressed their own way. Yes, when most working people in our country and in European countries were illiterate, they nonetheless had consummate ability to express complex truths in a few direct simple words.

Well—that "lost garden"—not really lost—such as Whitey's generosity—that wonderful sharing and it wasn't only seamen, of course; it was the practice of a larger community: sharing, part of what I call creative realism, how you use your resources, and beyond that, caring for a common good. This is in "O Yes," too: the doing in of community—Helen wanting that place of strength, strength from an understanding community.

JF: *The whole question of "lost brotherhood" is central to "Hey Sailor," and I can see that sense of lost community that you've just described. And yet it doesn't feel totally lost to me.*

Within a person's lifetime it can be lost; great struggles can be lost. But the tenacity, the will to create it, is there, time after time after time.

It is also true, incidentally, that certain ways of making a living have largely vanished because of technological change, and with them the beings who got their livings in that way—so in that sense it's lost. Many of the "Left-led" unions did go under. One of the characteristics of the unions that were under attack was a true sense of brotherhood and a true idealism. The mottoes of the craft unions in the last century also tell you something about the idealism of the time that was inherent in "brotherhood," in calling each other brothers and sisters. In our own lifetime, since this was written—in the fifties decade in which this was written—a new "beloved community" was coming into being in the Civil Rights movement. We have also seen it in the student movement and, in its way, among the soldiers in Vietnam; we see it now around AIDS.

JF: *The dedication interests me. Who was Jack Eggan? What was his connection to the "lost brotherhood"?*

His real name was Julius and we named our daughter Julie after him. He was known as "the Clipper," as in Clipper ships, because he had deliberately sailed the last of the masted ships. I have a photograph of him with his bashed-in nose, taken when he was a kid. I realize now how young he was when I knew him. At the age of seventeen (he lied about his age), he became the welterweight champion of the Navy. He remains to me the single most dramatic "transformation" of a human being that, in a personal sense, I have witnessed—the kind of legendary growth that became visible to us all with, say, a Fannie Lou Hamer or a Malcolm X.

Except for his love and passionate protectiveness for his younger brother—they both were orphanage kids—he had grown up in what he called, accurately or not, a "beast" life, someone who exerted power by the use of his fists. He left the Navy at eighteen to make a living as an ordinary seaman, and in the hopes of ensuring a foster home and schooling for his brother. This was at the time that organization was beginning on the ships. Almost immediately he became a leader. He was what is called a natural leader; even much, much older seamen looked up to him. He joined the Young Communist League, as many like him did, was sent off to school and became an avid reader, a starved reader, a thinker, an informed and true lover of literature. He was one of those people who confirmed what from my childhood on I had been taught to believe: that there was great potentiality in human beings, given circumstances, and that movements for change were blossoming circumstances.

It was very touching, his awkwardness in the beginning around children, because he had in the beginning, unlike many of the others, not been raised in a family, around small children.

When he said that about his "beast" life, he didn't see that his sense of romance about sailing ships and his deciding to ship out was part of his restless seeking for the most adventurous full life open to him. He was one of those many many seamen who volunteered for the International Brigades—one of the most resourceful, depended upon, and brave of them and was killed in the retreat across the Ebro. He remains very living with me—I wish he could have lived on.

JF: *What about the story's reference to Pedro? I assume that's the port of San Pedro. Did something specific happen there?*

No, that too is obscure. When I wrote this I wasn't even thinking of being published and therefore of making my references clear. I was concerned with writing about the Whiteys, the Blackies, the Curlies. Most of the seamen who were not permitted to sail because of the McCarthy years were drydocked in San Pedro, as were the seamen who were given temporary and limited clearance and had long waits for ships. This was where they could at least sometimes get lumber ships going up and down the coast, or "banana boats" going down to Central or South America.

Too late for a little explanatory footnote.

JF: *Yet it does communicate, without footnotes. And it's very powerful.*

Thank you. "Deeck and his room where he [Whitey] can yell or sing or pound and Deeck will look on without reproach or pity or anguish"—

155

which, of course—and I only realized it years later—is somewhat like what Helen sees in church. But Whitey does go back, and Helen and Lennie, partly because of those tasks of everyday life and the children and also the different forms of movements that don't offer quite that kind of community—as with so many others at the time, are beginning to lead much more individual lives: "inside, each in his slab of house . . ."

Anyhow, I was writing better than in "I Stand Here Ironing," so I say in defense of it. And the phrase "Hey Sailor, what ship?" is very beautiful. It's how some of the seamen would greet each other. And the Whiteys, some of them, used it uptown, too, when they met you. I heard once, José, softly greet Blackie Myers, another seaman, a legendary one: "Hey, Marinero, what ship?" Music, poetry, a question that persists, that became to me a way of phrasing to myself that question about the place, the direction, of human lives I was encountering.

3: "O Yes"

JF: *I'd like to talk about the circumstances of your writing "O Yes." Perhaps we can start with the 1950s and your creative writing fellowship at Stanford University.*

Stanford first. And can we please quote this part from a piece I wrote recently for Stanford about myself and that time?

> I did not come to our writing class that late September day in 1955 as the others came. I was a quarter of a century older. I had not had college. I came from that common everyday work, mother, eight-hour-daily job, survival (and yes, activist) world seldom the substance of literature.
>
> I came heavy freighted with a lifetime of ever-accumulating material, the sense of unwritten lives which cried to be written. I came from a twenty-year silence "when the simplest circumstances for creation did not exist . . . Nevertheless there was conscious storing, snatched reading, beginnings of writing, and always the secret rootlets of reconnaissance."
>
> I came as stranger; of the excluded. I came as the exiled homesick come home—*my* home, where literature, writers, writing had centrality, had being. I came to Dick and Ann Scowcroft, the Mirrielees sisters, my to-be first and dearest writer friend, Hannah Green; to the hovering presence of Stegner (then on leave), and to unnamed

others who embodied that centrality—and remain living sustenance to this day.

I came to circumstanced time.[4]

The fifties was the time of a so-called "silent generation." There's a certain resemblance to what is superficially said about the eighties as a time of me-firstisms—inactivity, uninvolvement in social concerns. I stress the word superficially. But the fifties had a special setting. It was frighteningly close to the terror of the McCarthy years, and actually began still in the McCarthy period. What had happened in Nazi Germany was only a few years past, so the nightmare consciousness of it—and the indications that it could happen here—were tormentingly heavy for many of us. We knew that the detention camps used to intern Japanese Americans had been secretly readied for those of us considered unAmerican Americans by the McCarthys. When, for instance, I learnt I had to have recommendations to submit with my Stanford application in 1955, I was terrified. As I myself was in FBI files, anyone I asked might be implicated—"guilt by association"—might also, if the worst happened, end up in a concentration camp.

So the McCarthy period is also part of the personal background which, although not specifically in "O Yes," had partly to do with my deciding to write of two youngsters who were Black and white instead of two white youngsters. I greeted the fifties' Civil Rights movement, then in its first stages, with great hope and joy. Here was the first real break against the fear and the prevalent feeling that one must not involve oneself in activity against the powers-that-be. And in that privileged, all-white, Stanford world, I wanted to write more than ever about race, racism, as well as class; the need for community; the selection process; separation; create young human beings and their elders in the crucible of this. And—dwelling more and more in the realm of written language, much of it consummately used (I'm quoting the Stanford piece again), I could evidence "the *other* consummate ways language is, has been used: the older, more universal oral/aural speech by human beings denied the written form" (64).

JF: *"O Yes" is dedicated to "Margaret Heaton, who always taught." In what way was she a part of your thinking about this piece?*

Margaret was an English teacher. There were several other people I wish now I had also dedicated it to but her death was so fresh at the time. She was white, and she taught at the most prestigious high school—*the* academic high school in San Francisco—where she was the most sought after English teacher. She was very conscious of the workings of racism, worked actively against it, and was in charge of a summer workshop, called, in the language of the time, Human Relations; really about racism. I went for those six weeks, one of four people selected by the city-wide PTA. It was 1950. I came to love Margaret very much.

Margaret had been formed in the time of the thirties and I think perhaps she had been one of the people who drifted in and out of the Communist Party at one time, as had at least a million Americans in the mid-thirties. But that whole ideology of "Black and white, unite and fight" which we used to not only proclaim but try to live—the whole focus on the situation of Black people in this country and the side-by-side association one was fortunate to have with others of every human hue, as well, was one of the great dividends, the great yields out of that particular movement. It had remained as a lifetime commitment with her.

I took Margaret to a service at a Black church where for a small while, I sang in one of their choirs. The tendrils, the roots for "O Yes" go so far back, as did my singing in that choir. I grew up in a partly Black neighborhood. Around the corner was the Calvary Baptist Church and I very early fell in love with the music I heard and when I was nine or ten I began to come on Sundays both to listen and to sing. That was where I heard for the first time Alva's "dream vision" which I was to hear in other forms years later in two other churches. There were "musical teas," at which long, long rhyming poems would be recited from memory or "prose" recitations like this one of Alva's. We have come to know something of the great eloquence of many Black preachers, but these women—so many of whom were illiterate or near-illiterate—also had that eloquence.

In San Francisco, in the late forties, early fifties, I would sometimes go on Sundays to church with a friend, one of the few Black women in our neighborhood. I took it for granted that going to the same schools, being neighbors, her children and my children would also be friends, as she and I were. Part of what also fed "O Yes" was seeing what happened to those kids when they reached junior high. Separation again.

But to get back to Margaret Heaton. She came with me one Sunday morning. She herself went to a Fellowship of Reconciliation, multicultural, church. She had never been to the kind of Baptist church most Black people attended. She had never heard that music. She had never heard such sermons. She had never been exposed to all that intensity. Well, she fainted. Some of it, of course, was physical reaction—the sheer battering of those great waves of sound. But the largest part was the exposure to the intensity, the beauty of expression, the extremity of emotion. By now, everyone has some familiarity with that intensity, that gospel sound, for it came to be incorporated into commercial music. It began to come in first with rhythm and blues, then rock and roll, but really was introduced to USA America at large by Aretha Franklin and the other daughters, sometimes sons, who had grown up hearing and singing this music which came out of real extremity, purity of emotion in a religious sense, although now associated commercially with other content.

There is another semi-autobiographical root and that is the experiences of my third daughter, Kathie, who, as in the story, had gone from grade school with her friend to a junior high, where the friendship became so changed. She came with us also to church. But she didn't faint, although she too was frightened, deeply affected by what took place. It was Margaret who fainted.

I realized— understood in the writing of this—another important factor, for these stories are so much, so deeply out of the fifties: the human hunger for community, the desperate need "for a place of strength . . . where loving hands waited to support and understand." Like a lot of teachers, Margaret Heaton had terrible decisions of principle to make about when to speak up, when to act, when to stand up for others, how much to endanger herself. When the loyalty oath was established as law, people like Margaret, who had fought to see that our country lived up to the ideals we proclaim, were the vulnerable ones—and those who were associated with them.

In thinking about the fifties, people think in terms of Arthur Miller and Lillian Hellman and the Hollywood Ten, but the truth that has been obscured is that hundreds and thousands of people lost their livelihoods, their standing in society, and were at terrible risk of imprisonment. Again—another lesson in my lifetime of what and who history focuses on and who and what get left out.

Well, whatever Margaret's associations had been, we never talked about it. I never asked her, for obvious reasons. She decided, after a great deal of torment and soul-searching, that she would sign the loyalty oath because if she refused to she would no longer be in a position where she had influence and could be effective. She guessed, what did happen, that the teachers who stood on principle and refused to sign this unconstitutional requirement would be fired and, in most instances, unable to teach, isolated, and sometimes their lives wrecked; completely changed. She did continue, as did many, in every way she could, to act.

Many human beings in the fifties felt terribly alone, particularly caring, conscientious people like Margaret, for all the fact that they had friends and people who loved them. They saw how quickly people were being isolated, excommunicated, condemned; and that does something to the human fabric, to trust. Children, including my own, were also terribly scarred in this period. Yet it was surprising the people who stood by you, just as it was surprising the friends who, in fear, did not. It does not enter into "O Yes," but separation in *this* terrible sense was certainly a characteristic of that time.

Yes, all the *Tell Me a Riddle* pieces are deeply wrenched out of the fifties. I didn't write about Margaret or Katherine and her family or my own Kathie except in the way that you take from here and you take from there and you don't tell everyone's truth or a single individual's truth—but it is a compound.

JF: *"O Yes" seems to resist any simple claims about religion, particularly in the lives of oppressed people. What are your thoughts on religion here?*

Again, it had to do with that special time, not only the hunger of people for a place where they feel they belong and are treated with dignity but the special character of Black churches and the other churches that *are* people's solace, source of community, source of strength and keep alive the human spirit of resistance, of deeply felt song, of joy. What was the basic institution that made the Civil Rights movement, the human rights movement possible? Where was its major fortress? The churches, the Black churches. Where did you see the strength to carry on that struggle? Think of those mostly nameless women, most of them still unrecorded, although if you watch *Eyes on the Prize*, you see their faces.

I'm trying to remember the way Marx finished his famous sentence that people usually only know half of the quote—religion is the opium of the people and the only consolation they have in a heartless world.[5] Opium—a drug. What use do drugs have for those who rule? Whatever weakens, whatever distracts, makes one lose one's sense of reality, weakens one as a human being. But the religion that I was writing of was the religion that was people's solace, and again source of strength, of human resistance.

I was the daughter of socialist atheists who understood and who tried to understand but were unalterably opposed to the opium and the divisive kinds of religion. Like Blake, they believed, "Thou art a man; God is not more / Thine own humanity learn to adore."[6]

JF: *Race and racism are obviously very important to "O Yes." What other personal circumstances helped to shape this concern?*

"O Yes" was the one piece I wrote completely from beginning to end in the eight freed months of the Stanford Fellowship. The struggle against racism, the evidences of the workings of it, have been a part of my life from the beginning, growing up in the neighborhood in which I did, and with my Socialist parent background. I think of the time when I was very young, the caravan that was set up to go down to Oklahoma where there had been terrible, terrible race riots in Tulsa and a large part of the Black community was burnt to the ground. My dad was one of those who organized the caravan to rebuild some of those houses.

This too was a time of terrible reaction in the United States. It seems only some historians and those who lived through it know about the Palmer Raid period around the end of World War I, another concealed chapter in American history. All over this country there were the so-called race riots, putting the "black man"—in quotes—"back in his place." I remember the burning of one after he was lynched in Omaha. I was nine and it was done in our neighborhood, our partly Black neighborhood. I remember standing on the fringe, smelling burning human flesh, almost paralyzed with horror, and still in nightmares I see some of those terrible distorted faces.

During the Civil Rights movement, so many Black youngsters' lives were changed and some of our best writers came to voice: Toni Cade Bambara, Alice Walker, Nikki Giovanni. (Then I would have said Negro or colored out of respect—you didn't use the term Black.) But Parry herself is pre–Civil Rights time. I hope and think I wrote her in a way so that you could envision her in the later Civil Rights time. Some of the people you might have heard at the Democratic convention were a little bit younger Parrys or from-the-South Parrys.

My two eldest children had natural relationships with Black children because part of their lives had to do with neighborhood, union and movement friendships and activities, and we lived in San Francisco's Fillmore and Mission mixed working class districts. A lot of multi-racial possibility was structured in in the thirties and part of the forties, times of the Margaret Heatons in the schools too. But by that period of the mid-fifties, when Kathie entered junior high, the sorting process was becoming dominant with its competitiveness, judging, tracking—and conscious or unconscious racism—part of that whole period of reaction. I have never gotten over having to live through knowing wonderful kids, as bright as my kids or brighter—or some of them not as bright but needing special help—and seeing what happened with most of them because they were denied enabling circumstances. As for Alva and Helen, that relationship was also created out of lived realities, the luck of various natural relationships when you work with people on the job and carry on common battles and live together and do your shopping and other things together and help each other and are in each other's homes, and are human beings with, to each other for all the fact that your friends are subject to humiliations and insults and circumstances which you are not subject to. Say, the whole way Parry was treated getting books and assignments for Carol—which would never have happened to a white Carol.

As I said in the Stanford piece:

> I was again migrating from one world into another—and in more than the twice-a-week commute to Stanford. It had been so with me, unarticulated, in my youthhood, when I crossed the tracks to Omaha's academic high school. It was so now with me, as it was now happening in my children's lives. I was freshly experiencing, re-experiencing that terrible agony, harm, of having to live in a class/sex/race separating, circumscribed time, when those among whom we are born, live, work, those with whom we are most deeply bonded, cannot journey along with us into that other world of books, of more enabling circumstances for use, development of their innate capacities. (64)

Perhaps it might have been better to have written an "O Yes" about the forced separation between two same-skinned youngsters, still so unwritten of. The shaping character of class is not understood in our country. Often, too, what has its common roots in the circumstances of one's being working class, scornfully termed "lower class," is mistaken as being rooted in racism if one is a person of color. Humiliation, shamings—what someone called "hidden injuries of class"—poor education, the contempt the world seems to hold about one's people and one's self as failures, losers. How strong having to be ashamed is in the shaping of people. That, too, was part of the makings of "O Yes"—the reaction against shame, that "mute cry of violated dignity."

Last of all, in that time of "pervasive cynical belief that actions with others against wrong were personally suspect, would only end in more grievous wrong" (64), that time of fear to act—and coincidentally, significantly, the first happenings of a new wave of freedom movements—was the deep cry in me to also express the need to care, to act, and that "caring asks doing."

JF: *What are your own experiences of the tension that Jeannie defines as "rise . . . but don't get separated"?*

I've already spoken of this, written of it in the quoted Stanford piece. But to add: in one of my "utterances," quoting Eugene Debs, "when I rise, I do not want to rise out of my class, but with it"—I added only three words: "Nevertheless, he rose." Yes, he remained a fighter, every fiber of his being was for his class, nevertheless, he "rose." He sought out the company of those with whom he could talk books, art, music, all that part of culture which had been the province of educated privilege, by and large, and in those forms had been denied his class.

I very early tried to make part of my life this culture which had been the province primarily of privilege. So I, all my life and increasingly so, was in that sense trying to rise but not get separated.

Time after time, my sense of solidarity has been primary in making decisions about the direction of my life and work. Writing of our class, of color, of cities, yet living separated, is not sufficient for me. Yes, the tension, the contrast, continues—here with my very own neighbors, the lives of so many of my friends, yes, and of my own children and blood-kin. (But I live with, among, needing-to-be-made-visible realities. I am not separated.)

Living through several decades when it has been possible for the first time for an increasingly significant number of first generations of working people to "rise," I have seen (lived)—over and over again—what you term tension, "the split heart." Time after time, directly, indirectly, or as we begin to have film, literature, art, theory out of this first generation—I have seen that blood struggle and the coercions to what's known as "pass." It's outlined in the last part of *Silences* (263–64).

Educated people are told all the time that they are middle class but in actuality most are working class. They, or their people just before them, have won some of what was previously the prerogatives of the privileged. But for most who are salaried it's still true that "they have nothing to sell but their labor power." Most of those who teach in academe are in community and state colleges, serving those who will be (many already are) working people. And the only power they have is the working class power to negotiate together or sometimes withdraw their labor power—that's the meaning of the phenomenon in our time of teachers or nurses, public workers, going on strike.

Yet rise or not, Parry forever is part of Carol, as is Alva. And they have lived what inequality of circumstance is. Consciously or not, they know: I might have been she; she might have been I.

JF: *How did your experience of motherhood help to shape your understandings in "O Yes"?*

It was inherent in all I wrote and have said about "O Yes." First: "caring asks doing." You really only know a society, what kind of a society it is, who it benefits, who it harms, how the harm happens, when you have to do with life from the beginning and live how it is shaped and misshaped, when you learn what power you have and don't have, how much more power the outside world has. One has to "mourn the illusion of the embrace."

It's hard to hold onto motherhood truths and understandings against the outside realities that determine so much about what is going to happen with your children.

JF: *The idea of* caring *seems to be not only a pervasive theme in your writing but also a crucial link between your experience of motherhood and your involvement in movements.*

And in my relationships. Yes.

4: "Tell Me a Riddle"

JF: *Let's talk first about the dedication. Who were Seevya and Genya?*

Seevya Dinkin was her name, born in 1885, scarcely four feet, eight inches tall. Buried in "Tell Me a Riddle," that visual evidence of generational history: "Stranger grandsons, tall above the little gnome grandmother, the little spry grandfather,"—the difference enabling, or denying, circumstance for growth can make. Still in the Depression years, having to stretch her pennies, in the wake of renting me a room, Seevya embraced me into her teeming household: instruction, dazzlement, human theatre; music, talk, a stream of various people— and two marvelous girl-children, her daughters. I'd come back to San Francisco in '36 alone, having had to leave Karla with family in Faribault and in Omaha and part of the luck in my life was that she took me in.

Some nights the living room floor of her crowded flat would be carpeted with hungry, unable-to-find work youngsters who knew they could flop there for the night, wash up, feel welcome,—and be sure of at least one meal the next day, sharing the family breakfast: Seevya's hot oatmeal with raisins. Most of them were sea-going guys, waiting the long long wait between ships; over the succeeding years some of them became part of the need to write and the "Hey Sailor," "Requa," too. And it was at Seevya's I first met Harold "Mink" Johnson, a master story teller to whom credit belongs for some of the stories my fictional Whitey tells.

Seevya was one of those who made me love and respect—almost to the point of awe—the leap over centuries that that revolutionary generation had to make (and not only in Eastern Europe, and among Jews). That amazing leap, especially for girls,—from centuries of illiteracy, ignorance of the larger world, lives from an early age of the hardest work, a future as bearers of many children—to new ways of being, believing, acting. Then once in revolutionary circles, the world of literacy, of culture opening up for them, hungrily devouring all they could get their hands on, falling permanently in love with literature, classical music, history, knowledge. In her last years, little Seevya was proud president of the Petaluma Shakespeare Society. David's wit in "Tell Me a Riddle"—not the bite—is like Seevya's. Seevya's caring asked—and got—doing—and fostering—and nudging beyond where one was, to where one could come to be. Her death became part of my consciousness of the perishing of that generation, and the need, the urgency, to write of them.

Genya is Genya Gorelick. You may read of her in the first chapter of Al Richmond's *A Long View from the Left*[7]—his great mother. She was and has remained to me one of the most learned and beautiful human beings I have ever met. She, like Seevya, came from that terrible childhood, girlhood, into that same movement in czarist Russia.

165

Still as a girl, a young woman, she became a famous orator and a national leader of the Bund. The manner of the dying of the old woman in "Tell Me a Riddle" was the manner of Genya's dying. On her lips— in between the most labored breaths, in a gossamer voice, in five languages—came song, memorized phrases, poetry. They were—as in the epigraphs heading up chapters in Du Bois's classic *Souls of Black Folk*—wisdoms, aspirations, expressions from the best of the world human heritage, including that from one's own origin. Yes, in five languages so that there was much I could not understand, languages besides her native Yiddish and Russian she had learnt to read and somewhat speak during her six years in czarist prisons, five of them in Siberian exile, sometimes in solitary confinement. She had made the trek with other prisoners, on foot, in chains, all those thousands of miles across Russia and across Siberia.

Once released, she emigrated, first to England, then to our country. But in 1917, when the Russian Revolution began, she took her three-year-old son and went back. Only to be imprisoned again—this time by the Germans (it was still World War I) when their troops occupied her town. Al, her little boy, came into prison with her. In the next few years, he almost died—during the time when Polish troops "liberated" their town, then again during the civil war with its hunger and typhus epidemic. Genya often had to leave him with others, for she was deeply involved in the bringing to birth of what she believed was a new era in the liberation of humanity. She was one of the most eloquent voices and brilliant organizers in that chaotic time.

By the early twenties, her disagreement with much that was happening in the newly-born U.S.S.R. was so great, that she made the anguishing decision to return to our country, and to obscurity. Al, her son, whom I knew over fifty years, as with Genya, is one of the human beings I have loved, learnt from, and honored most throughout my life.

The passing of that generation, catalyzed by my own mother's death, did become wellsprings of "Tell Me a Riddle." But what I began to write, was something else.

JF: *What were your intentions when you started?*

In the beginning I was interested in what drives older people apart after being together for many, many years. That was a comparatively new phenomenon then: marriage breaking up so late in life. I was also interested in what keeps people together in spite of the tearing and

166

harmful discord between them. How much was bonds, in both senses of the word, how much the compulsions of society?

For centuries and in nearly all "cultures," there had been characteristic separations between men and women, sometimes termed the division of labor, although in actuality, what Olive Schreiner wrote was true: "Within our bodies we bore the race. Through us it was shaped, fed and clothed. . . . Labour more toilsome and unending than that of man was ours. . . . No work was too hard, no labour too strenuous to exclude us."[8] And men, even terribly exploited men, had freedoms, powers that women did not have. In a different way than in my *Yonnondio*, this much older, re-beginning writer could write about the workings of this division in a vanishing generation, yet so close to centuries of previous generations in this regard.

Another phenomenon, only then evidencing itself with the increasing lifespan, was the torment around how and where to live in one's old age (and this was before Medicare; and Social Security still comparatively new). My father, with other members of the Socialist Party and the Workmen's Circle, sought to establish a place where they could live out their old age in an affordable community of shared vision, life experiences, activity. Both my parents were active in raising funds and designing plans for such a "Home," which did come into being in Media, PA. My father went to live there some years after my mother's death.

Then came those four deaths within a year. And not only those deaths: others, such as the mother of a seafarer very dear to me, a carpenter's wife, mother of ten, obscure, she who'd been a leading poet as a girl in her native Iceland; and others of that generation still alive, born U.S.A.ians, and émigrés from other parts of the world of various origins, human hues,—but all committed to the achievement of that particular vision expressed in "These Things Shall Be," and other of the words, phrases, on the lips of that dying woman. So heritage became part of it, the *meaning* of that heritage for us. I felt a special urgency, a special need to write of it because of my revulsion to what was happening in the late forties, the fifties,—the betrayal of that vision, that hope, the abandonment of the Universal Declaration of Human Rights by what I saw as regressive forces, policies of those in power again in my own country—and elsewhere.

I began "Tell Me a Riddle" in early 1956, the last few months I was at Stanford, towards the end of that year of writing resurrection for me. Wait, let me read from something I wrote for the catalog of an

167

exhibit of Stanford writers' manuscripts, part of Stanford's centennial celebration:

> arterial closeness to death and dyings of four of the human beings ineradicably dearest to me: my mother, my father-in-law Avrum, Seevya, and Genya. All four of that generation whose vision, legacy of belief—in one human race, in infinite human potentiality which never yet had had circumstances to blossom, in the ever-recurring movement of humanity against what degrades and maims—I tried to embed in that novella. (*First Drafts*, *Last Drafts*, 63–64)

And the dyings had roused in me consciousness of death in a way I had not had before; when that older generation was gone, if still I were here, I and my generation were next. I wanted, needed to through writing, with all I could summon, *live* dying, *live* the facing to death, the leaving of life,—that journey. As for my own mother, I could not write of *her* way of dying; I could only write personal utterances; she is not Eva; but o she is profoundly present on every page of "Tell Me a Riddle."

JF: *What circumstances then changed for you? And how did "Tell Me a Riddle" change?*

I had begun to win back what I may have had at one time when I was working on parts of *Yonnondio*—facility. I did write all of "O Yes" in that period at Stanford, those not quite eight months. True, I still had, as I say in *Silences*, a full extended family life and responsibilities, yet I also wrote the earliest draft of the first part of "Tell Me a Riddle" before I had to put it aside.

In my 1962 talk, "Silences," I spoke of that most harmful time when I had to leave writing at the full, to return to the world of work, "someone else's work." Nevertheless, from time to time, I took up, put down, took up, put down the rest of "Tell Me a Riddle." In this period, I was also sometimes hospitalized—the harm had entered my body. When it became clear that I was not going to be able to make the particular kind of full time needed to create a long-length piece, I began to do what I could, when I could. I tried to embed all I could in the piece as it turned out to be. I had always intended to go on with Jeannie, with that family, though none of this was really on paper, except in notes here or there; I'm not a writer who sits down with everything worked out. Now I had three generations to write of.

I'd become a published writer in this time: "I Stand Here Ironing" was picked up for *Best American Short Stories* by that great and by me beloved friend of the story, Martha Foley. Also, "O Yes," then entitled "Baptism," was published in *Prairie Schooner* and "Hey Sailor" in Nolan Miller's widely read anthology, *New Campus Writing #2*.[9] Thus readers who would never have come to me in the original publications were now able to read me. Nobody wanted to publish "O Yes," absolutely nobody; nobody wanted to publish "Hey Sailor," except, finally, these two. They were not what was being written in that period.

Well, the circumstances of writing very much affected its form.

JF: *The question of belief is central to the story. How was this question a part of your thinking about the fifties and about those of "that generation" of whom you've been speaking?*

Certainly so much of what was happening in the late forties and the fifties was again a test of belief versus cynicism. "I Stand Here Ironing," which was originally called "Help Her to Believe," was also about belief, as, in a way, was "O Yes"—*"caring asks doing. It is a long baptism into the seas of humankind, my daughter. Better immersion than to live untouched."* The times were making it essential for me to reiterate it as embodied in those who once had been—or, like that old woman— remained believers.

The fifties. The prominence then of *The God that Failed*—very different from other reminiscences which were being written mostly in Europe by those who had also left the Communist Party or renounced its leadership—but never renounced their past and the hopes and beliefs that it embodied. Most of those who remained—as with myself— "believers," never came to writing it at all.

Among those hopes, beliefs, and actions had been that war must not be any more, that human life was sacred, that this was the central task and that human beings of whatever color, nationality, or sex—all comprising one human race—had certain universal needs and rights. In our thirties movement, we had tried to keep World War II from happening. We had fought the rise of Nazism and the continuation of totalitarianism and colonialism wherever we knew of it. We had in our own country—in a time when, in Roosevelt's words, "one third of the nation were ill-fed, ill-clothed, ill-housed"—fought to establish Social Security, unemployment benefits, union rights to fight for "an American standard of living." Along with the reaction, the McCarthyism, the Cold War which began at that time, there was a contending spirit in the fifties that remained in continuity with the movement of the thirties and forties. Perhaps those beliefs were best expressed in the 1948 Universal Declaration of Human Rights, (I keep referring back to it) subscribed to by every country then in existence, and also in the later UNESCO Declaration of the Rights of the Child.

Remember that after the monstrous blood-letting, the murder of millions in World War II, which could have been prevented, there *was* a "family of man" period of hope, of belief, of conviction in regard to what the future should be. "Never again let this be"; eliminate "the scourge of war," usher in true living-out of human rights, and go beyond rights stated in our 1776 American revolution, the 1789 French revolution; spell out economic, educational, other rights and means to a fully human life.

So much positive and hopeful was happening in our country: the GI Bill, for instance; the previously landless for generations being enabled to buy homes; the previously considered ineligible for higher education being enabled to return to school; this country really putting its money into education and establishing free or minimal cost state and community colleges—no burden of huge student loans then. For the first time numbers of us who did not come from educated, privileged families were enabled to come to education, that precondition for a fully human life. There was much focus on "human relations," "tolerance," genteel words for exploring and fighting racism, bigotry.

Yet all this was already beginning to be done under by the Cold War: not only the economy turning more and more to armaments, to supporting occupying garrisons all over the world, but also the beginning of the campaign against the gains of the thirties moving towards a society where human needs, human rights, the common welfare, would be pre–eminent. Any activity of human beings with other human beings to make such changes, to do something about wrongs, was not only dangerous (the McCarthy era was already beginning), but one's motivations were not out of conviction, but a way of evading personal problems, or satisfying ego, or worse,—naive baseless idealism. Better, safer, not to act. As Melville wrote of the abolitionists: "Indolence is the child of heaven/ And energy the child of hell./ The good man pouring from his pitcher clear/ But brims the poisoned well."[10] Yeats was also often quoted, as still he is: "The best lack all conviction, / While the worst are full of passionate intensity."[11] Orwell, in his *1984*, predicted the future as "a boot stamping in man's face forever."

Throughout my lifetime this indictment of activism, this teaching of despair.

Again, one of the reasons why I fastened on this generation of believers to write about was that it was in this time when it seemed as if the next great advance for humanity was in the process of happening, away from what had so harmed and divided humanity in the past—in this *very* time, all these other forces became manifest to return people to the worst of our past. This older generation—the Evas, the Davids, had grown up, been misshapen by that terrible past—they knew it and had lived it. It's a lack somewhat in "Tell Me a Riddle" as I wrote it that it's hard for most to understand Eva's "Race, human; Religion, none." But when Eva—who learned that on hospital records she was recorded as "Race, white; Religion, Jewish"—cries out, "At once go and make them change. Tell them to write: Race, human; Religion, none"—it was because in her native czarist Russia, as in some of the world now, religion and repressive state were one and deliberately bred bigotries and hatreds and sometimes bloodletting between peoples, as did apartheid separations of people into races and nationalities. Now in that terrible time of the fifties, these harmful forces were again being bred, fostered, exacerbated.

Their generation had tried to free themselves from those terrible ghettos of the past, the bigotries, superstitions, divisions, fears, ignorances; the old ways of being. Against the "monstrous shapes of what had happened in their lifetime"—they still believed that "these things shall be."

JF: *The song, "These Things Shall Be," seems very much a part of that belief in change.*

Yes. And it expresses the essence of the aspirations, the hopes, the beliefs in the future. It is an old Socialist hymn that comes out of an old religious hymn, and I learned it as a child from the Socialist Sunday School hymn book; in our time it has been adopted as a United Nations hymn and is sung by school children in some countries on Universal Human Rights Day. "These things shall be, a loftier race"—meaning one human race, not higher race in the Nietzschean or Nazi sense—"then e'er the world hath known shall rise / with flame of freedom in their souls / and light of knowledge in their eyes." How passionately that "flame of freedom" and "light of knowledge" must have been sung.

171

They shall be gentle, brave and strong
to spill no drop of blood, but dare all . . .
on earth and fire and sea and air

JF: *How do you see the place of religion in the thinking of Eva's revolutionary generation?*

"To spill no drop of blood." That hope, that belief in humanity, that this will come to be. Yet the Evas' world was one where because of religious hatreds, blood was shed over and over again. As in our world today—Muslims, Christians, Jews, Shiites, Sikhs, Hindus. In her youth, as in much of the world now, the church and the repressive state were one, and deliberately bred such hatreds, bigotries, as a way of dividing, of ruling; of channeling shame, deprivation, and wrong against those of another religion. National group was set against national group, "race" against "race"—again as in our world now.

Woven into religion was the belief that what is happening is ordained, one's fate; or one is being punished for sins, perhaps sins committed in a previous life. Justice would be done in afterlife; in Judaic belief, one must wait for the Messiah. Eva and her generation all over the world lived the effects of religions of this kind, not only as that solace in a cruel time, but also as the perpetuator of divisions, of a caste-class system, of ignorance and superstitions, of humiliations for women—a monstrous brake on the genius of humanity: the will to change what is wrong.

In the same section where Eva says, "Race, human; Religion, none," she also says, "To smash all ghettos that divide us—not to go back, not to go back"; ghettos of clan against clan, tribe against tribe, "ethnic group" against "ethnic group," and skin color against skin color.

Late in his life, my Dad, in the course of telling how hard and anguishing was this break with the deeply held beliefs of one's people, beliefs clung to for centuries; how it was that his young self and the other young selves came to their radical beliefs, could bear to cause—and experience—such pain, said: "We could not wait for a Messiah to bring a beautiful future. We realized that we ourselves, acting together, must be the Messiah."

They were so conscious, too, of how much the beliefs and practices of the orthodox religions had to do with the situations of women. Yes, and the Evas did believe that we are one human race and that we must recognize it and begin to live in that way. Born human now, as in

172

centuries past, we still are, as my mother said, "crucified into a sex, a color, a walk of life, a nationality.[12]

JF: *What enabled that generation to begin to see beyond sexual divisions?*

What I've said before was the soil for this: human included women. In our own family we had that evidence of the difference breaking with harmful traditions, practices, beliefs of the past can make in a movement for human freedom. My father was the only son in a family of girls. My dearest aunt, my father's oldest sister, died in her mid-nineties, except for her name not able to read or write—something I only learned her last few years of life. O the contrast between her and her younger sisters; they fortunate enough to be born at a time when there was a revolutionary movement in their city—in their case the Socialist-Jewish Bundists, in my mother's case Tolstoyans—who broke with tradition and as a matter of belief in innate capacity, taught illiterate girls how to read, write; opened up the world of culture and thought to them. They, the younger sisters, became intellectuals, omnivorous readers, one a learned philosopher, one an economics (?) professor in the Soviet Union. The aunt, to whom I owe so much for the ways she taught, appreciated, and loved me, for all her astounding memory, wit, gift for inimitable language; her powers of observation, for "putting two and two or a hundred two together"; her insights, empathy, lovely ways of handling life and bringing out the best in everyone—this aunt had "only" the "book of life" out of which to learn her wisdom—practice *and* theory. Revolutionary study circles read Bebels, Engels, on the family, on the "subjection" of women; discussed this as reflected in their own lives, lives of others; tried to advance women into leadership. But there is a difference between "seeing beyond sexual divisions" and changing; there have to be *societal* changes making it possible to live differently, as Hardy's Jude and Sue, as many a feminist has or is learning.

Scenes in "Riddle." Eva of that generation, her consciousness of the little granddaughter, the little grandson, in the process of being "crucified" into a sex—"Dody hunching over in pretend-cooking" while Richard ("Watch me, Grandma") is "snaking up the tree, hanging exultant, free." The cry within Eva—"Climb too, Dody, climb and look"—seeing the little ones already acting out according to old, old circumscribed and in certain periods of human history probably somewhat necessary ways of being and doing. Now, society could solve performing these necessary tasks of life by other means. Nancy, too— Paul's wife. It was Paul who loved his mother, but it was his wife he expected to take her to the doctor, do other such tasks.

My Eva, as I tried to write her, was not as some have interpreted her—perhaps because of preconceptions and hungers for validation some women in our time feel—she was not a frustrated career woman, a woman embittered because she did not have time for herself, wanted "never again to '*have*' to move to the rhythms of others." In dying, her anguish was not for her woman's life, gone into (loved) children and tasks, but about what was central in our time. That "still, century after century," the failure to make the changes that would enable human potentiality to flower, the torment as to whether or not humanity would be able to do away with the nuclear threat of extinction, the other threats of war, injustice, reaction, ghettoization, the barbarities of the past still so present. She "accepted," I say accepted in quotes, what her woman's working-class life had been. Indeed, she saw herself in the context of her own generation, including her own generation of women.

JF: *I believe you quoted a Randall Jarrell poem in connection with the title of this piece when you were at the College of Wooster.*

I quoted Randall Jarrell at Wooster but that was a fragment of a poem never published in his lifetime, only after his death, in 1965, years after I'd finished this—a wonderful way to answer questions about the title:

> "What's the riddle that they ask you
> When you're young and you say, 'I don't know,'
> But that later on you will know—
> The riddle that they ask you
> When you're old and you say, 'I don't know,'
> And that's the answer?"
>
> "I don't know."[13]

"Tell Me a Riddle" was not the best title. I wish ever more I had called it "These Things Shall Be" but it does also have to do with the riddles of life we grope for the answers to, or whether the answer we come to *is* the right answer. It has something to do, too, I suppose, with the passion with which kids ask riddles, that lovely passion they just seethe with. There's a lot to riddles, speaking of what's out of motherhood.

JF: *Will you say something about the narrative voice here?*

I didn't think of a narrative voice. I just struggled, as usual, with what I was trying to say, to get as much of it said as right as possible. There were so many problems. I had to keep reminding the reader that Eva was deaf, almost blind—and most of all that she was dying. "The great ear pressed inside her . . . the sweat . . . the long shudder seizing" are not only the body response to profoundly emotional happenings,— they are the workings of the cancer, growing. So did passages come into being, or came enriched by this need.

So much work too in the deepening, the thickening of the narrative after they leave Hannah's: the first-time plane ride; the crucial, the determining sky, the vulnerable earth, however I said it. Vivi's crowded house: what the feel of a baby evokes, to "it's for Disaster, Grandma"; rocks; spilling memories; the airport farewell and the "eyes which look back at her with the eyes of others before them." Jeannie; the sea; sands. Mrs. Mays; the singing and faces of the old. Then—what transpires in the poor room "like a coffin." Eva's anguished questions to David—not about herself, not about herself—and reading on his face that she was dying.

All along, beginning at Hannah's, the ever heightening consciousness of the significance, the meaning, of what was happening around her, and remembered from the past—the new experiences also evoking, drawing on what had been. Now with her *conscious* knowing of her coming death,—thought, recollection, association, were being summoned into being as never before. Not for comprehension alone, but to deepen, enlarge, each perishing moment. I already was having to leave out so much, yet somehow, nevertheless, retain the essence, the import?—what Virginia Woolf called "making one thing stand for two hundred." The problems of such selection.

The new awarenesses: the poignancy, evanescence, continuities of life (the spent waves feeding the new). What Jeannie brings, evokes. Everything intensified, illumined—and illuminated by what had been. And the cancer growing,—robbing flesh, voice.

How, out of the memories which boil up and her conscious recollectings (no, not as a memoried wraith); how, out of the newnesses, the freshnesses of the immensely conscious Nows (more intense even than

175

in her long-ago morning of childhood's first time experiencings);—how, out of the compound of both, make for my Eva at last: "coherence, transport, meaning."

And remember: David, Jeannie, the children: the need to encompass the ways they were responding to, involved in, the stages of her dying (as I who created them all was also living it). Most of all, David, *their* relations:—what experiencings, what questions, what attainings, what self-knowledge, he came to in living her dying. In dying she gave him back the sense of his life.

So the many many strands I was struggling with made the particular narrative voice. Never mind that I could not say all I wished. Never mind that I could not attain language commensurate to the beauty of her farewells to life, the immensity (that word again) of conscious dying, of meeting death. Something remains. And Eva's dear personal ceasing ("for the dying take with them their dead when they die") did become also the dying of one lived portion of that very special generation with its beliefs and comprehensions. How to encompass that too, had shaped the narrative. And the reading aloud of what I was writing over and over until it came right to my ear.

5: "Requa I"

Note: Our conversation about "Requa" had a distinctive character because of the context of both time and place. We had this conversation as we were sitting in Tillie Olsen's working space, surrounded by what she refers to as the "makings" of the piece: notebooks, scraps of paper with notes on them, maps, family photos, small regional brochures, historical photos. We centered our conversation on the piece that was published as "Requa I," but, even more than the pieces in Tell Me a Riddle, *this is truly a piece of something larger. The larger piece—a "novella" that develops out of this first part—was what she was, in fact, typing up during the period in which we were having our conversations. Thus her comments here are much more immediately a part of ongoing work, as yet unpublished.*

JF: *The publication of "Requa I" came nearly a decade after the publication of* Tell Me a Riddle. *What were the circumstances for your work on this piece?*

Again, context of the time, strands of this and that, an accumulation of years. The immediate impulse: we were camping up north, on the Smith River, which is the last huge river on the California side of the

Oregon border. We were camped up here [pointing on the map]; it was 1959. Purely by accident, hiking up along the river on a trail we thought might lead us to the mouth, we followed this road trying to get down to the river and instead we came to this little off-path and stumbled onto this sweat-house, pretty much in ruins then. Up above it were these two upright markers. This one, Captain Spott, died October 20, 1911, born 1811, native of Requa. At his side, a little round stone for Pegah, his wife. Climbing up further behind, we saw a lot of bones, a few skulls, also a few upended grave markers just lying there. Already a spell was cast.

From there we went up and up, knowing nothing about the places we were passing and that this was where the old Indian village of Rekwoi (Requa) had been. When we finally reached the top with its panoramic view of the forests, the river mouth, and up and down the coast—as in this photo—we felt awe. Awe—that almost universal human response to mountain tops, to high beautiful places—which for so many ancient peoples made them sacred.

We again camped up on the Smith River several years later, and purely by accident, shopping in Crescent City, passed by this modest house on a corner with its little sign—Del Norte Historical Society— went in and met Ruth Roberts, volunteer curator, true historian, and true friend—and champion—of the Yurok natives. It was from her we learnt who Captain Spott was, heard for the first time of Robert and Alice Spott. This is Robert Spott here in this photo; this, his sister Alice. Their faces are also in Theodora Kroeber's *Almost Ancestors*, Theodora Kroeber, author of *Ishi, Last of the Yahi*, wife of the anthropologist who with his partner, Lowie, wrote what is still considered the definitive book on the California Indian. It is partly dedicated to Robert Spott. And here, in Theodora Kroeber's *The Inland Whale*, a book largely informed and inspired by him, are some of the Yurok tales he shared with her. Neither Alice nor Robert—forgive the first names— are in my "Requa" directly. Nor is Ruth Roberts. But their vision and the course of their lives informs it, as does the place itself. Roberts said of Spott that he had the greatness in him to be president of the United States. Instead, except that he was the eloquent head of his Yurok people, he lived an obscure workingman's life, all manner of Jack-of-all-trade jobs, including working as a carpenter for the Kroebers at one time. He was also a veteran of World War I. Mrs. Edler does have something of Ruth Roberts in her, including her involvement in a real-life fight to keep a Yurok cemetery from being ploughed under.

She told us that the not-yet-reburied bones and skull that we had seen the first day above the sweat-house, were the aftermath of the losing of that battle. That battle is a part of the background of "Requa."

I kept making occasional notes, returning to the place. It was nineteen sixty-eight–nine I began the actual writing it—just before I went to Amherst.

JF: *What sorts of things did you record in your notebooks?*

I see a note: "not to forget the impulse"—one of various other impulses—"toward the vanished, those in the way of 'destiny,' those in the way of those in power—and facing extinction." The various beauty of that country—here is one of so many jottings—"colossus redwoods and so far below them, tiny white flowers with threadlike stems, partners in growth with the redwoods since prehistoric times, glowing with a soft strange phosphorescent light seen nowhere else on earth." (In a way "Requa" is my "Hymn to the Earth.") So many respondings to Nature, on the history of that region; on the Native Californians; the two hundred different languages that California tribes spoke. Most of the notings are the workings-out of what will become "Requa": the setting itself, Stevie, Wes, the boarding house, Mrs. Edler, the junk-yard—all that.

By the way, religion is in this too [looking through papers]. And death. And mourning, "raising oneself from the dead."

I see I say, "I write this not as a scholar. Larger truths embodied in the real Robert and Alice Spott as in the created Stevie. Truth that all of us who live as part of or come from submerged peoples know, capacities expressed in whatever ways they could be, but latent—lost there, untraced."

These are old notes, too, very old notes among the very first ones— "City boy into nature. Life so fragile in him. That summer rooting him back into life. The dead mother. She (that means Mrs. Edler), repository of pioneer feeling. The single uncle, rough. The living dead. Robert Spott. Hundred year old mahogany woman. The man with the shot out eye. The pull to death. Life low in him." Makings.

So many thirties notes. The migrations. The Bonus Marchers when desperate World War I Vets camped in D.C. while petitioning Congress for their Bonus. MacArthur ordered them fired upon, their makeshift shelters burned. The Depression time. The Depression is in here all the way through, how it was lived in and by people.

178

JF: *What other sources might you point to, particularly for the distinctive use of language?*

There are so many, many sources. The time I began this was a time of fear of and contempt for technology, the opposite of Walt Whitman's recognizing it as the "technological sublime." Regardless its terrible history of misuse, the exploitation of it for profit, with the consequent criminal damage to the environment and numberless human lives; its development for mass murder war—technology when used for good is, and has been, our great means for freeing humankind from the kinds of work-task, survival existences which still consume the bulk of most lives. Imagine the enormous, joyous benefits to society with the fully flowered use of human capacities in the ways denied before. The advances in science, the arts, medicine, all fields of knowledge and human endeavor, which have been made in just this century by those daughters and sons of denied people—are only an indication of what can be.

Well, along with these thoughts, that challenge, for a while I worked in the office of a junkyard, every manner of tool and equipment junked there. A revelation place for me where the human genius for invention, the creation of ever-better tools for various tasks, and of language to describe them, was manifest. Waste shoddiness, built-in obsolescence, here and there too.

It is immodest to say, but the sections of "Requa" describing these tasks, these tools, have the precision, the rhythm, the sound, of true poetry. If I read it aloud to you, you'd hear—but words in the service of everyday work, of tools, are not accorded such recognition.

I live in a period where many kinds of tools, the basis for civilization, some originating and developed over centuries,—as many kinds of skills—are leaving the world forever—because of new processes. So I was also recording, trying to fix into "art," that vanishing which had not been recorded into literature. And in its *natural* context, not as "found" poetry or exotica, or to establish authenticity, but to write those tasks with the rhythm surrounding their movement, the palpable feel of what is being handled and the surroundings in which they are being used; as for the tools, to try to set their names in some way so that their inherent poetry, the very sound, comes as real as if heard in the ear. . . . I've envied the hundred-handed god—talk about human needs and aspiration embodied in godlike form!—I've also envied the one that has eyes all around its head, but o what it would be to have a hundred ears—with ear stoppers when needed.

"Requa," even more than work I have already published, needs to be heard aloud, as well as read.

JF: *Let me ask a different kind of question. "Requa I" was published as a short story. How is it related to the larger work, the whole "Requa"?*

Well, I didn't want it to be published so. I kept saying, this is part of something longer; this is just the first part and everything in it has to do with what is to follow. This was understood by *Iowa Review* who first published it. But Martha Foley loved it so, asked for it for her annual *Best American Stories* volume that year. I told you she dedicated that volume to me and she almost never dedicated a volume. So we agreed to call it "Requa I," meaning *part* one. I still didn't know then exactly how long it was going to be. They publish a hundred pages now as a novel, and also publish story sequences as a novel, giving the lie to that artificial separation in fiction.

It goes on from that first part. What happens with Stevie remains central.

JF: *Did you make any special effort to develop a sympathetic response to Wes?*

No. What you call sympathetic response comes from what is inherent in the nature of the Wes's, as I came to know and understand them, and in what transpires between Stevie and him.

The Wes's. Seemingly, he's a bastard to his nephew, right? Rough, put-down behavior, beats him. Well, at the same time, he's teaching Stevie skills; he *cares* about equipping him to function in this world. He's taken responsibility for him. He's, quoting him, "doing the best he knows how" in his life of necessity, of limitation; of hard capable work and little compensation, little respect.

How hard the Wes's have to work. Human tiredness, human exhaustion. I was writing of that too in *Yonnondio*—Anna in her stupor of exhaustion and Mazie startling her awake, as Stevie startles Wes out of his helpless, exhausted doze, at last getting to sit down after his ten hour work day.

I've known many Wes's. They are the fathers, grandfathers, sometimes brothers, husbands of many of us: limited, bigoted, and often racist, often in most ways sexist. But also there is so much to respect and, yes, value them for. Their undervalued, necessary skills without which the world could not function. Skills, work, we suddenly discover as essential after, say, an earthquake, any kind of calamity,—or certainly during a work-stoppage. . . . And we do not have enough of a sense of their lives—including the class realities; how they came to be as they are; the "hidden injuries of class" which work on them: contempt for them as losers, their work as "shitwork"—and how their human need to assert outraged dignity shapes so much of their being.

JF: *I'd like to pick up on the question of class and ask you to elaborate on how this concern shaped your thinking about "Requa."*

Not only "Requa"—it has shaped what I am as well as all I've written. I've just said some of the ways, in talking about Wes, talking about work. For years I've said that if you fed into a computer for analysis, every page of what is taught in literature classes, perhaps—a guess— 3 to 5% would be about everyday, necessary work, including the work of teaching, of nursing, of mothering. It is almost totally absent, the *content*, the life, of this work, which has and still does take up most of human lives. And when "lower class" (I hate that term) people do appear, seldom have they been written of in their full dimension. They are most often faceless servants, slaves, working people. Or they're "Them"—"colorful characters," caricatures really, grotesques, low I.Q., abnormals, incestuous (with no context),—a lower order, not fully human like "us." This is changing as the newer voices, daughters and sons of every color, raised up working class, write. So I suppose according full humanity is part of the welter out of which "Requa" was shaped. The Stevie's—that working-class kid. The Wes's. The Yee's. The others.

JF: *How do you see Stevie developing as he grows up?*

Chronologically, except for two end pages, what follows concerns only the next four more months of Stevie's life. But the seeds, the shape, the presage—I can't find the right word—of what he will become are in the so far published part.

JF: *You seem to be also exploring notions of masculinity.*

Exploring, yes. Drawing on the past. Reflecting. Observing. Delineating. Most of this exploring is in the rest of "Requa," although much is already in that published part. Including the ways of forming; of resisting; what is already formed; including motherless Stevie, now in an almost stereotypical "man's world"; including Wes, so little in his life to prepare him for becoming solely responsible for a young human being. As I hope, believe, that inherently we are one human race—the coming into being of a caring, more fully human male, and the tracing of it in writing is very important to me.

I must add that the time I began and was writing "Requa," was also the late 60s, 70s time when what you called the "notions," the strictures, of masculinity were being challenged. It was preceded by the open homosexuality of some of the then much-publicized beats; the daring-to-be long-haired hippie males' rejection of their fathers' ways and lives; the love-not-war gentle "flower children"; the young men in the anti–Vietnam War protests who refused the centuries-old tradition of going to war and killing being the supreme test and proof of one's manhood; all along, the actions of tens of thousands in the civil, freedom–rights movement in the South,—every week, images of their nonviolent resistance to the brutality and violence rained against them, their moral, physical, will, strength, courage, endurance—a new vision of "manliness" (and womanliness); and, of course, the questionings and consciousness birthed by the new feminism. Validation again to me of my lifelong hope, beliefs.

JF: *Did your recurrent concern with the circumstances of motherhood enter into your work on "Requa"?*

Yes. As I've just said about Wes, and Stevie—son of a mother, having to work away from him and raise him alone, sometimes out of necessity put him in institutions—the companionship, love, dependence on each other, of those two against an uncaring world,—as "Requa" develops, I try to make more and more evident what that dead mother instilled in him. And later—though I must not talk about the unpublished—there is another "single" mother, left with her brood and having to manage somehow after her man runs out on them—to go with the bonus army it turns out. O those single, unhelped mothers. I never get over their lot—the dimensions of their task; the masculine attributions of strength, courage, fierceness, daring, will, they have to use every day; their legacy—as in Stevie as he develops. And the other mothering—what our society assigns mostly as the responsibility of mothers—that taken on by others who care—as Yee, as Mrs. Ed, again as Wes with (lucky in this regard) Stevie.

Yes. Needless to say, I didn't sit down and write, "motherhood is part of what I want in this."

JF: *What kind of reader do you have in mind?*

I don't have a reader in mind. I hope and work for a reader who will enter into what I am trying to get said—someone who will open themselves up to what I have written, and if I have written it well enough will be validated or changed by my comprehension,—and will have some sense of the care I put into the writing of it.

Notes to Part 2

1. Two somewhat more extended interviews are available: Tillie Olsen interviewed by Kay Bonetti in San Francisco, California, March 1981, American Audio Prose Library, cassette tape; and Naomi Rubin, "A Riddle of History for the Future," *Sojourner* 8, 11 (July 1983): 4,18.

2. Tillie Olsen, *Silences* (1978; New York: Delta/Seymour Lawrence, 1979), xi; hereafter cited in the text.

3. The paragraphs quoted here occur in a slightly different order in the published version of the talk. See Tillie Olsen, "The Word Made Flesh," prefatory essay to *Critical Thinking, Critical Writing* (Iowa, 1984), 6.

4. Tillie Olsen, personal statement included in "Tillie Olsen," in *First Drafts, Last Drafts: Forty Years of the Creative Writing Program at Stanford University*, prepared by William McPheron with the assistance of Amor Towles (Stanford: Stanford University Libraries, 1989), 63; hereafter cited in the text.

5. "Religion is the sigh of the oppressed creature, the feeling of a heartless world, and the soul of soulless circumstances. It is the opium of the people." See Karl Marx, "Towards a Critique of Hegel's *Philosophy of Right:* Introduction" (1844), in *Karl Marx: Selected Writings*, ed. David McLellan (Oxford: Oxford University Press, 1977), 64.

6. See William Blake, "The Everlasting Gospel," 11.75–76. Exact wording varies.

7. See Al Richmond, *A Long View from the Left: Memories of an American Revolutionary* (Boston: Houghton Mifflin Company, 1973).

8. Olive Schreiner, *Women and Labour*; see *Silences*, 26.

9. All of these were published in 1957.

10. See Herman Melville, "Fragments of a Lost Gnostic Poem of the Twelfth Century."

11. See William Butler Yeats, "The Second Coming."

12. See Tillie Olsen, "Dream-Vision," in *Mother to Daughter: Daughter to Mother: A Feminist Press Daybook and Reader*, selected and shaped by Tillie Olsen (Old Westbury, N.Y.: Feminist Press, 1984), 263.

13. Randall Jarrell, "What's the Riddle . . ." [1965], in *The Complete Poems* (New York: Farrar, Straus and Giroux, 1969), 491.

Part 3

THE CRITICS

Critical Voices in Historical Context

Probing critical practice and developing a definition of "a new socio-historical criticism," Louis A. Montrose asserts that "not only the poet but also the critic exists in history."[1] I have spent much of this book investigating the historical interactions that have shaped Tillie Olsen's short fiction. It is only fitting in this final section that I mark out as well some of the historical interactions that influence the critical response to that same fiction: only thus can I hope to reopen my own analysis to the ongoing interaction between text and world.

At the time that the pieces in *Tell Me a Riddle* were published, first individually—1956, 1957, 1960—and then as a volume in 1961 and in their present order in 1962, critical practice in this country was resistant to the kinds of claims about history, politics, feminist understanding, and personal experience that I have made central here. Lary May, a historian of the 1950s, describes the broad set of assumptions at work during this period: "humanists increasingly studied text without context, social scientists context without text, making it impossible to see the mutual interaction between art and society, history and ideology."[2] Writing in 1966 in more specific response to the discipline of literary study, Louise Rosenblatt describes a similar isolation of literary object: "the current, almost hypnotically repeated emphasis on 'the work itself' as distinct from author and reader."[3] Also at work during this period was the shifting set of expectations about short stories as genre. Judith Arcana points out: "By 1950, . . . American critics had begun to divide story writers into two broad categories: those who (basically) maintained the traditional form and those who (mostly) experimented with it."[4]

Such views and expectations—that life and art must be kept separate and that stories were either traditional or experimental—were not congruent with Olsen's understanding of her work; although she decidedly valued the expressive capacities of language and the art of fiction, she saw her work as centered not so much in technique as in human insight and experience. Nonetheless, the period's primary emphasis on form was almost certain to shape the first responses to her published fiction. One reviewer saw the stories as "perfectly realized works of art."[5]

Another attributed to her "an almost miraculous rendering of the interrupted rhythms of thought and speech patterns, with expert economy, with effective counter-pointing of past and present, with judicious use of traditional and contemporary narrative methods or devices."[6] A third said that the characters are "as delicately done as a perfect fugue,"[7] and a fourth cited an "economy of language" so stern that Olsen "can spend no word that is not the right one."[8] A fifth, in condescending praise, claimed that the stories "depend on her own experience, and that experience seems to be narrow. But . . . it is also one that she has felt deeply and pondered and imaginatively absorbed." This reviewer ended by calling the title novella "a remarkable piece of work" and expressing the hope that Olsen "may now move ahead to fiction in which everything depends on the powers of invention."[9]

I find this review of particular interest because it was written by Irving Howe, a critic well known for his interest not only in form but in politics, a critic who was praised in a 1993 essay honoring him, following his death, as "the perfect representative of 'the New York intellectuals'—those brilliant critics of politics and culture" and to whom was attributed a love of "beauty" over "estheticism": "Irving's greatest thrill was high art that felt democratic."[10] And yet in writing in 1961 of Olsen's fiction, he, too, participated in the hierarchies of the period, honoring "invention" over "experience" and condescending unashamedly to the particularities of female experience, though explicitly honoring the experiential connections to "the Jewish trade unions or communal organizations" (Howe, 22). It is particularly intriguing that Howe felt he could recognize "experience" on the basis of knowing that Olsen "is a woman in her forties who has raised a family and then returned to her earlier ambition to write short stories" (Howe, 22)—surely a serious reduction of the complex life and history that Olsen brought to her writing and drew on in shaping the embedded histories of her characters.

My point, however, is not to rebuke Howe for an uncritical acceptance of these prevailing hierarchies—male over female, invention over experience, the text itself as needing to be separated from the context—but to situate his critical voice at the time of *Tell Me a Riddle*'s publication. The primary emphasis in essentially all of the reviews was on "the work itself," the art and the control of language, and with some understanding of how the chosen form related to then-current trends in fiction writing; in praising these stories, even when they wished to move beyond the implicit hierarchies, the reviewers laid primary emphasis on Olsen's gifts with language and form, remarking especially on her stylistic compression, her "ear" for the sounds of language, and the emotional power of her characters' lives. When the category of "experience" came into play, it was largely as something to be purged.

A notable exception occurred in the *Time* review, "Radicals and Working Stiffs," which went on from its "perfect fugue" into an unusual reference not only to experience but also to political concerns: "Nebraska-born Tillie Olsen, whose father was for 30 years state secretary of the Socialist Party, writes with compassionate knowledge of the radical immigrants and the working stiffs who fought the big industrial battles of the early 20th century" (101). A less obvious departure also occurred in Dorothy Parker's review, which spoke not only of the "economy of language" but also of the distinctive power of the stories as it derives from human emotions, not just literary skill: "her tales are far more powerfully moving, dig far deeper in the memory than do the reams of exercises in lyrical style that clutter the bookshops" (66).

But each of the reviews, even in their more exceptional claims, was necessarily informed by the particular discourse of the period; the claims, on the whole, were either explicitly resistant to trends or congruent with them. It is not surprising, then, that the first essay on Olsen published in an academic journal, *Studies in Short Fiction* in 1963, moved from an opening emphasis on human emotion—"anguish"[11]—and a brief overview of plot to a second section on the stories' universality and their exceptional "skill and power" (25). The author, William Van O'Connor, insisted, with the times, that the stories must be universal, decidedly not "just" female or specifically political in context: "The stories push away from the individual and the unique, toward the world of Everyman" (24). Similarly, he insisted that their primary value lies in this crafted universality.

I have paid detailed attention to these early responses because they are so suggestive of the actual context within which the stories were written. Though I will not give as much detailed attention to subsequent changes in context for readers, I do want to suggest that these changes were also crucial for ways of thinking about the stories. Following the initial response to the publication of *Tell Me a Riddle*, the 1960s brought little critical attention to Olsen's work. This period, of course, saw the rise of several kinds of political activism—most notably the increasingly visible civil rights movement, the student movement, the antiwar movement, and the resurgent interest in several versions of

socialist and leftist politics, which threaded through these other movements—but did not bring an automatic attention to the kinds of fiction
that Olsen had written and published in the 1950s and early 1960s.
The political concerns that *are* so deeply embedded in her short fiction
did not immediately provoke a written response even from those critics
and readers who were becoming increasingly committed to the politics
of social change that became so important through the 1960s and into
the 1970s. Hence the relative unavailability of her work and the relative
lack of critical response.

What did, then, prompt a renewed attention was a heightened feminist consciousness and the increased activity of the women's movement
in the late 1960s and early 1970s. There was a renewed interest in
reading women writers and in reading *for* insights into gendered experience, with the consequent development of women's studies programs,
including a larger number of classes for which fiction such as Olsen's
would have particular bearing. Teachers were seeking out texts that
raised questions about dimensions of women's lives that had been
previously obscured, and readers were more likely to approach literary
texts with their interests already attentive to such questions. Interestingly, the 1970s also brought an increased interest in the short story
as form (see Arcana, 182). Hence it is not surprising that *Tell Me a
Riddle*, which had been out of print for several years, was reissued in
paperback in the early 1970s, nor is it surprising that one of the reviewers of this new edition laid explicit claim to concerns that were unmen-
tioned in the earlier set of reviews; writing in the *Nation* in 1972,
Elizabeth Fisher said, "Tillie Olsen is not only a great writer, she is
a feminist artist."[12]

From these concerns with feminist thought, with women's experiences, and with classroom instruction readers and critics developed a
greater willingness, throughout the 1970s and 1980s, to affirm experiential issues in response to Olsen's fiction—an emphasis that, though
silenced or submerged in early reviews, was almost certainly important
to most readers throughout their histories of response. In 1974 Sandy
Boucher wrote eloquently of the personal and cultural context that
shaped her approach to Olsen's work, beginning with her first meeting
her in 1965: "Her politics scared me, especially her feminism, because
I was so frightened of seeing myself in what she said."[13] At the time
of writing the essay Boucher claimed a very different context for herself
and gave thoughtful and personal form to describing an Olsen reading
in San Francisco and to Olsen's remarks afterward. Boucher cited not

only the power of the fiction but also the power of Olsen's presence and her personal engagement with feminist and teaching concerns: "For some years now Tillie has been actively engaged in teaching, a labor of love centered around the reclaiming of work by women writers. . . . She has encouraged the republication of some of the works which were at first available to her students only in copies Xeroxed from out-of-print editions" (29).

Thus Olsen herself was both agent and focus of a growing network of shared texts and insights that developed through the growing feminist movement and the emergent women's studies programs of the 1970s. Many early references to the stories in *Tell Me a Riddle* appeared in introductions to anthologies or in personal essays like Boucher's. They spoke especially of her work for the Feminist Press in bringing "lost" fiction by women back into print, her work as visiting faculty at a number of colleges and universities, her lovingly circulated "reading list" of texts out of women's lives, her essays and lectures exemplified by "One Out of Twelve: Writers Who Are Women in Our Century," which became a centerpiece for *Silences*. The network moved out from personal references as readers and teachers shared photocopies of that essay before it became more easily available with the publication of *Silences* in 1978 and called attention to the power of the stories in *Tell Me a Riddle*. Along with the publication of *Yonnondio* in 1974 and the reissue of *Tell Me a Riddle* in 1971, the publication of *Silences* in 1978 helped to move feminist discussion of literature from underground networks into a more visible presence in critical discourse.

Some of the earlier response to Olsen's fiction during this period, then, came directly out of the critics' wish to give public voice to their own experience with the fiction, to share in writing what they had previously shared in conversation within that informal network. Writing shortly before the publication of *Silences*, Linda Heinlein Kirschner called *Tell Me a Riddle* an "underground classic," just beginning to have a wider audience. Her chosen forum—a 1976 issue of *English Journal*—says something about her motivation: to convey to other English teachers the insight this fiction has into parent/child relationships. She argued from classroom experience that "I Stand Here Ironing" is "a story that speaks effectively to high school students."[14] In a 1980 essay titled "Tillie Olsen: Storyteller of Working America," Sally Cunneen began by situating herself as a teacher and went on as well to lay claim to her own personal response: "feeding on them [the stories] as I do."[15] Like most of Olsen's readers, both Kirschner and Cunneen spoke of a personal interest in the fiction that preceded their academic interest; like an increasing number of Olsen's published critics after the reissue of the paperback edition, they both merge personal concerns with their written criticism.

From the 1970s into the present, the critical response to Olsen has retained this central concern with experiential connections on the part of the critic. Though it is not often claimed as significant in the published criticism in literary journals, teaching, of course, is an obvious point of connection for many who write about literary texts. Nancy Huse, for instance, discusses both her own and her students' responses to "O Yes." Her discussion draws effectively on a set of intersecting reader concerns elicited in the classroom and pursued, as well, in the particularities of her own reading: racism, maternal care, human separations. Teaching both prompts and focuses the response for her, as for many of Olsen's critics and readers.[16]

Other critical voices also reveal their experiential interests in response to the stories. Vicki Sommer, for example, writes as a social worker who finds in Olsen's work "a clear understanding of how environmental forces shape the lives of human beings and how the individual can to some degree shape and mold the environment."[17] Julia E. Connelly writes as a doctor, making an explicit case for the usefulness of "Tell Me a Riddle"—and of Tolstoy's *The Death of Ivan Ilych*—in providing physicians with guidance in understanding the fuller personhood of a cancer patient: "The stories of ill persons contribute knowledge to our less easily knowable patients."[18] Robert Coles, in *The Call of Stories: Teaching and the Moral Imagination*, not only draws on his own extensive practice in child psychiatry but also and more explicitly lays claim to his wide range of teaching experiences in medical schools and other diverse graduate programs.[19] Throughout his investigation of "teaching and the moral imagination," he honors students of all ages, in public high schools as well as professional schools, and he honors teachers such as his wife who have worked with students in difficult circumstances. In this context he makes, as well, explicit connections to medical practice and work in other community agencies, finding in Olsen's fiction ways to help people respond to crises of health, alcoholism, poverty, racism, and family strife. Implicit in all of these responses through work life are the ways in which the critics and the stories seem to be in similar pursuit of human knowledge, through careful inquiry into the stories' experiential insights.

One strand of the resurgent interest in Olsen during the 1970s and

1980s took the form of a focused concern with motherhood. As she has said in *Silences*, literature has suffered from the loss of "the comprehensions possible out of motherhood"[20]; in Susan Suleiman's phrasing, "Mothers don't write, they are written."[21] This feminist attention to Olsen's work led readers such as Annie Gottlieb, in *Mother Jones* in 1976, to claim the particular value of texts like Olsen's for opening up genuine dialogue between two sisters, one a mother and the other childless: "My sister and I owe our dialog to a few women who have found the courage and determination—and the *time*—to write with honesty and art about their experience as mothers in American society. These women have been freed to speak their often painful truth by the communal support of the Women's Movement, which in turn has drawn inspiration from the work of a few pioneers—foremost among them Tillie Olsen." Speaking of Olsen's stories and novel, she says, "they testify poignantly to what it means to be a woman, a mother and a seeking, beleaguered self, under 20th-century patriarchy."[22] Gottlieb's comments make explicit both the importance that the feminist context had for her own reading and the urgency of her own personal response to the fiction.

Pieces published since the 1970s pursue the concern with experiential understanding from multiple perspectives. Annette Bennington McElhiney explores the pervasive concern with women's lives in Olsen's fiction in a 1977 essay significantly titled "Alternative Responses to Life in Tillie Olsen's Work."[23] Specific concerns with the experience of motherhood as integral to many women's lives prompted such essays as my own " 'I Stand Here Ironing': Motherhood as Experience and Metaphor" in 1981 and Helen Pike Bauer's " 'A Child of Anxious, Not Proud, Love': Mother and Daughter in Tillie Olsen's 'I Stand Here Ironing' " in 1989.[24] Although both essays focus closely on textual concerns, both also claim and affirm the centrality of female experience; speaking of the narrator-mother, Bauer makes her womanhood central: "the facts of her woman's life, its emotional as well as economic exigencies and constraints, provide the context" (35).

Bridging two areas of experiential concern, Bonnie Lyons situates the fiction more explicitly in Olsen's experiential context: "Tillie Olsen: The Writer as a Jewish Woman." Lyons opens this 1986 essay with a direct claim on experiential promptings: "That Tillie Olsen's work is radically perfectibilistic in spirit and vision is obvious to most of her readers. Less obvious is that the two principal sources of that vision derive directly from her experience as a Jew and as a woman."[25]

Her analysis pursues these two experiential patterns as they are threaded through the fiction. A similar claim on the roots of vision in experience exposes even more directly a clear reason why many of us as critics have focused on the notion of experience: because we are looking for connections to our own lives, insights into our own experiences. John Clayton, thus, shapes his inquiry into Olsen's Jewishness in terms of his own Jewishness: "I care because if Olsen and [Grace] Paley are not Jewish writers, then how am *I*?" He goes on to affirm his "own heritage as a radical, secular, humanist Jew"[26] and to see this same heritage in the fiction of both Olsen and Paley.

Throughout the 1970s and 1980s, critical response to Olsen continued to weave together a complex set of experiential concerns: biographical, feminist, political. As the earliest exploration of biographical materials, a 1976 essay by Selma Burkom and Margaret Williams provided crucial information and prompting for subsequent explorations. They begin with a personal narrative of Olsen's appearance at a Virginia Woolf symposium, but go on to investigate the interrelatedness of Olsen's "daily life" with her biographical history, her personal presence, and her fictional texts. Interestingly, also as the earliest such exploration, the essay seems defensive about political concerns, insistent on Olsen's "humanism"[27] and on the priority of her "genuine poetic skill" over any "propagandistic assertions" (69).

Subsequent biographical inquiries are less abashed in investigating Olsen's political history and convictions. Both Deborah Rosenfelt in 1981 and Erika Duncan in 1982 focus on Olsen's roots in the 1930s, particularly her political involvements with the Communist party. Rosenfelt's probing of historical contradictions in Olsen's political background—a tradition she labels "socialist feminist"[28]—is framed by both her own driving concerns and her investigations of Olsen's: "This paper, then, is part of an ongoing dialogue about issues that matter very much to both Tillie Olsen and myself: the relationship of writing to political commitment; the 'circumstances'—a favorite Olsen word—of class and sex and their effect on sustained creative activity, literary or political; and the strengths and weaknesses of the radical cultural tradition in this country" (Rosenfelt, 373).

An open claim on politics—feminist and/or socialist—and a direct assertion of biographical sources—Jewishness, femaleness, work life, family life—seem to have been most forthcoming in work published in the late 1970s and early 1980s.[29] More recent work has not denied political or experiential concerns, but it has necessarily taken into account further changes in critical assumptions. The very concept of "experience"—as I noted in my own first section here—has become suspect, and the complexities of how language intersects with politics and experience have become themselves the object of inquiry.

But even in recent sustained inquiry into Olsen's work, some of which focuses explicitly on textual analysis, the power of experiential and political concerns in shaping the inquiry is acknowledged. Most notable in recent work are the first book-length analyses concerned solely with Olsen and her work—Elaine Neil Orr's *Tillie Olsen and a Feminist Spiritual Vision* (1987), Mickey Pearlman and Abby H.P. Werlock's *Tillie Olsen* (1991), and Mara Faulkner's *Protest and Possibility in the Writing of Tillie Olsen* (1993)—and Constance Coiner's essay " 'No one's Private Ground': A Bakhtinian Reading of Tillie Olsen's *Tell Me a Riddle*," published in 1992 in *Feminist Studies*.[30] Among these, Coiner's analysis is most openly concerned with politics; she claims, for example, a shared "commitment to social change" and is particularly concerned with "Olsen's sociopolitical vision" (281). But her work is most concerned with a complex assessment of intersecting concerns in response to the texts themselves. So too with Elaine Orr's and Mara Faulkner's books: Orr's analysis is explicitly feminist and undergirded by biographical information and Faulkner's looks "at Olsen's works nested in each other and in her life and surrounded by ever-widening historical, social, and political contexts" (Faulkner, 12). Both, too, along with the Pearlman and Werlock book, primarily analyze language and form. Faulkner is particularly interesting in this regard, for though she claims "a historical perspective" (Faulkner, 10) and identifies political concerns, her book's greatest strengths are its investigations of metaphor and of thematic contradictions; she does not, in fact, do much concrete historical situating of her textual investigations.

In various ways, then, this most recent work takes the step implied in Rosenblatt's 1966 challenge: to reenter both author and reader into the understandings of "the work itself" (Rosenblatt, 277). It does so in the context of contemporary concerns with the instabilities of language, the uncertainties of "experience," and the impossibilities of historical and biographical "truths." But it persists in the attempt to work through these complex intersections and to situate the "works themselves" among these intersections.

Tillie Olsen and the Common Reader

As I have suggested, Tillie Olsen's work received only informal and irregular critical attention for a number of years. The recent publication of the three book-length studies—as well as the publication of Kay Hoyle Nelson and Nancy Huse's collection, *The Critical Response to Tillie Olsen*, published in 1994—suggests a change in the kind of critical attention that her work is receiving. But this change does not necessarily imply a significant change in her readership. Like critics, of course, other readers are always situated in history, shaped in part by the assumptions and values of their own historical contexts. And their reading is inevitably shaped by such material factors as the availability of texts and the frequency with which texts are taught or cited. Still, Olsen's readers have persisted in responding to her fiction in complex ways, through their own personal contexts, throughout the shifts in critical assumptions that I have outlined above. And it is these readers—in Virginia Woolf's phrase, these *common* readers—who have granted Olsen's work its most compelling recognition.

These readers, though "common," are not "ordinary" in their responses, as they have sought out her work and responded to it through their own concerns, regardless of current critical directives. They rarely seem to read simply for the plot or the immediate interest. Nor do they ignore the verbal complexities of Olsen's fiction. Instead, they seem to respond in all their particularity, from the immediacy of their own specific contexts, to the yearnings Olsen expresses as part of her definition of the reader she wants to have: "I hope and work for a reader who will enter into what I am trying to get said—someone who will open themselves up to what I have written, who will comprehend it, who will be validated or changed by my comprehensions, and who will have some sense of the care I put into the writing of it."[31] The bridge phrase here is the wish for a reader "who will comprehend it"— who will, in other words, understand it fully and well and appreciate the "care" that shapes the writing, but who will also, in some sense, *be comprehended by it*, taken into it wholly and hence "validated" or "changed" by Olsen's own comprehensions.

These readers appear in many contexts, as part of a network existing often outside the usual processes of critical acclaim, even during more recent periods of public critical attention. To enter this network, they sometimes rely—as they do for discovering many writers—on the agency of classrooms and anthologies: in fact, both "I Stand Here Ironing" and "Tell Me a Riddle" have been widely anthologized and are often taught in both women's studies classes and literature classes. But readers also form this network themselves through less institution-alized means of sharing: in families, in hospital rooms, on airplanes or trains—over cups of coffee and over the telephone.

I have been such a reader; I have personally known many other such readers. Often they are mothers and daughters who have shared their reading experiences as ways of sharing in deeper personal intimacy—college-aged daughters who have phoned their mothers with the excite-ment of exchange and of being able to teach their mothers something new; middle-aged mothers who have given the book as gift to their own mothers and shared a treasured reading with daughters who are in the process of coming of age. But not just mothers and daughters—these readers are also brothers and sisters, pleased at having found a voice that can speak of life experiences for which they haven't found a voice themselves; they are lovers who are trying to develop their own distinctive repertory of shared experiences, shared texts; they are working people in pursuit of stories from their own lives. They *are* common readers, comprehending their lives in and through these sto-ries.

As suggested by my initial overview of published criticism, much of this work is more concerned with "common readers" than with other critics: high-school students trying to address the painful process of conversing in the midst of racism as they work towards integrated schools in the 1960s; social workers who have found these stories crucial in their understanding of clients; doctors and medical students who are struggling to understand the differing lives of their patients in clinics or on their deathbeds; cancer patients who are trying to understand their own mortality; adolescent children who are living with their parents' alcoholism; sisters who are learning to converse across the differences of childlessness and motherhood; writers and teachers claiming the stories as resources for their own lives and work.

I have heard Olsen herself cite her readers' responses, describing vividly the reactions of sailors who have phoned her and said, "Where's Whitey?" knowing from their own reading experiences that she under-

197

stood some essential dimension of their lives.[32] I have heard her tell of the row of women in cafeteria uniforms who had come to hear her read because of her story's impact in a transformative healing between one mother and daughter (see conversation 1). Olsen says, "readers will say to me, often, '*I* was that mother'—or they'll say 'I was Emily' or 'I was that younger sister.' These to me are the true literary honors."[33] I too hear readers grant these "literary honors" when they say to me that they now see their mothers—or their grandparents or their siblings or their uncles or themselves—with fresh insight. In comprehending the stories, these readers have also been comprehended by them and hence have come to comprehend their own lives.

This common reader that Olsen's texts require must, then, be thoughtful about language and written expression but also about his or her own life and its living. This reader must be ready to expend effort and fully engage in the reading process itself. This reader responds to the respectfulness that Olsen makes integral to her writing:

> There is something else that I learned early, and everything in my life reinforced: don't have contempt for people, don't have contempt for your readers, trust them, they are intelligent, they have lived as profoundly as you have. Maybe they haven't articulated what you the writer have, but they'll fill it in with their own lives, they'll write it along with you. You do not have to spell it out for them. You do not have to tell them everything. You do not have to, in that particular kind of protective way, bring them into your imagined world. They will bring to it their full beings, they'll give your writing a dimension it may not really have on the page, and I assure you I am not as good a writer as some of you may think I am. It is you and what you bring to it . . . the common work that we do together . . . all this is part of the making of style.[34]

In her own statements and in the attention that readers have accorded her work, Olsen's readers *are* both "common" and committed to the "life comprehensions" that her textual comprehensions require: they yearn for her insights into those lives that are not yet fully present in literary forms and they respond with the attention to language and life that her writing expects.

Her respect for her readers, her recognition that readers do bring themselves as "full beings" to a text, her acknowledgment that reading and writing are a partnership—these qualities in Olsen's work are integral to readers' claims that she is as "good a writer" as many of us think she is. Occasionally this openness to lives and expectations has seemed to become authorization of sloppy reading. Pearlman and Werlock rightly point with dismay to the errors that seem to pepper much of the published work on Olsen: misreading of facts, false attribution of causality, inaccurate designation of place (xi–xii). I agree that these errors can be troubling, but I do not share Pearlman's and Werlock's assessment of their source. For one thing, I think that this sort of sloppiness is common—still nonetheless distressing—in early responses to contemporary writers in general. Beyond that, I want to dispute the claim that the errors follow from the " 'unfinished' quality of Olsen's writing," which "leads to a damaging syndrome not previously noted—critics frequently adding to or subtracting from the stories. Olsen's admirers, many of whom are writers and critics, seem to be interpreting her fiction as saying more than it does, and consciously or unconsciously they fill in the gaps, essentially rewriting the stories" (Pearlman and Werlock, xi). Like Olsen, I believe, instead, that it is integral to her work that readers *will* "fill it in with their own lives, they'll write it along with you." Even though I want to call attention to and even "correct" genuine errors and miswritings—misquotations, misstatements of fact such as Jane Van Buren's unsupported claim that Eva and Jeannie have both had an abortion and that Eva has lost a child in Korea[35]—I do not want to do so at the expense of rejecting the kinds of active reader involvement that Olsen's stories require.

Like many of Olsen's critics—and like Olsen herself, as indicated in the statement I quoted above—I am convinced that much of the richness of her writing does come from its openness to interaction with readers, its expectation that readers will bring their lives to the text and take the text back into their lives. Indeed, many of Olsen's most careful critics—those that avoid errors of fact and false attributions of event or causality—make her fragmentariness a central value to their critical work. Shelley Fisher Fishkin's comment on *Silences* is pertinent to the associative form of the fiction as well: "In the blank spaces between the fragments, the reader is given permission to pause, to think, to insert her own response, to recall her own experience, to listen to her own voice."[36] Constance Coiner, writing about the stories in *Tell Me a Riddle*, takes as her epigraph Terry Eagleton's statement about "turning authors, readers and spectators into collaborators" (257). She then goes on to consider at length the "reworking of relationships among writer, text, and reader" (273) that forms a part of Olsen's democratizing and political strategies—"structures and strategies that require readers to contribute to the emergence of heteroglossic meaning. . . . [W]e are not given free rein as readers, but we are asked to act responsibly as members of a complex human community" (274). Similarly, Elaine Orr, in her analysis of "Requa," speaks of the centrality of readers' responses—"the story may await not so much Olsen's finishing of it as readers' response" (121)—and affirms Olsen's fragmentary style: "One of the great paradoxes of Olsen's texts is the sympathy their incompleteness evokes in her readers. . . . Olsen's words to us are brief, her style fragmentary, almost hesitant, her writing like a voice searching for itself and listening as much as—even more than—speaking" (135).

I note that my structure and approach have led me to speak of "critics" as if they were different from "readers," as if we were not all both critics and readers. I will allow the loose distinction to remain—that critics are those who write professionally of texts and language—but I want to return to the notion that every critic of Olsen is also a common reader of Olsen, a reader drawn to this fiction through his or her own passions and convictions and life history. I think of my own first essay on Olsen—the piece on "I Stand Here Ironing" written as I struggled with my experience as a single mother, though written with a distance I took to be necessary to a "critic." I think of Deborah Rosenfelt's powerful investigation of Olsen's roots in the American Left of the 1930s, written in part out of her own passionate commitment to movements for social change. I think of Elaine Orr's *Tillie Olsen and a Feminist Spiritual Vision*—the first book-length study of Olsen—in the preface of which she situates her first reading of Olsen's fiction "in the confluence of several important events: an academic introduction into the ways language and story both reflect and create our reality; a discovery of feminist criticism; and the birth of my own child" (ix). The book itself, prompted by a passion for spiritual understandings (quite different from my own interests and driving passions) and a recognition of women's daily experiences, is careful in its scholarship and thoughtful in its critical responses—the work of a critic and a situated, impassioned reader. I think, too, of Pearlman and Werlock, who—despite their distrust of what they see as "a mistaken or misguided tendency to publish only laudatory or eulogizing criticism" (xii)—also pursue their own careful study in the context of their experiences as women, writing, in part, from "a jumbled sense of awe, excitement, and trepidation" (ix). Mara Faulkner, who also retains a certain distance in much of her analysis, nonetheless situates her reading very personally in her preface. She cites her enriched understanding of her parents "thanks to Tillie Olsen" (vii), and she expresses her gratitude to her Benedictine community "for helping me understand what community means—an understanding that is crucial to my life, of course, but also to a careful reading of Tillie Olsen's work" (viii). These are just a sampling of critical responses—quite different from each other, but in my view all careful and thoughtful—each driven by identifiable passions and convictions and life histories.

I think, too, of Robert Coles—not an academic literary critic but an important published commentator on Olsen's work—whose 1975 review of the reissued *Tell Me a Riddle*, has helped to define its place in American literature: "Everything she has written has become almost immediately a classic."[37] More recently Coles has also drawn together his own reading of the fiction with that of many common readers in *The Call of Stories*. In both of these responses to her work, it seems to me that he is acting simultaneously as an impassioned reader and a "critic": his choice of profession as child psychiatrist was clearly predicated on his desire to change the conditions of children's lives; his response to Olsen's fiction is similarly grounded in *her* commitment to social change, as well as his attentive valuing of her choices in language and form. His work as critic, like the more traditional critical work I have cited, is driven by identifiable passions and convictions and life histories.

In many ways, Olsen's critics and readers are enacting a kind of reading that takes place among most common readers. As Louise Rosenblatt has insisted throughout her years of important work on the act of reading—even during periods when formalist approaches to literary texts dominated among academics—"the reader can read only out of past experience and present interests" (283). Often, however, Olsen's readers are doing so with a particular passion wrought from the knowledge that her stories are speaking of lives that are silenced in many literary forms. Thus, her readers are especially likely to identify lives as women, as children, and as working people, as feminists and as political activists among their most active points of engagement with the stories. And it is not surprising that their reading approach is congruent with the approach more often used by feminist literary critics than by any other group of critics with whom I am familiar. Sandra Gilbert's

relatively early explanation of feminist criticism as distinguishing between the critic and the reader suggests just those features that Olsen
has pursued in her readers:

> The Critic, after all, sounds like someone who has so *mastered* his
> reading that he [*sic*] can *criticize* it, both in the ordinary (evaluative)
> and the extraordinary (analytic) sense of the term. . . .
>   The Reader, on the other hand, is hot and human—and therefore
> somehow imperfect. Afflicted by texts, she or he struggles to under-
> stand them, accepts or resists secret messages, gropes toward sub-
> merged meanings, struggles with glyphs and graphs, codes and
> ciphers. For as a representative (rather than a regnant) intellect,
> the Reader sees that texts are everywhere. Enclosed in contexts,
> embarrassed by pretexts, the reader devours poems, inhales syntax,
> exhales codes, and is in fact assaulted by so many and such various
> messages that she or he may eventually come to feel that they are
> inscribed on her or his skin.[38]

Gilbert goes on to say, "For most scholars of literature by women . . .
research [is] a kind of re-search for their own lives" (854). So too
for most readers—men and women and children—of Olsen's stories,
regardless of "scholarly" credentials: in our reading we are "re-search-
ing" for our own and others' lives, reading as "hot and human" readers
within our own contexts, pursuing syntax and codes and messages but
feeling ourselves fully implicated in our reading.

This human engagement—which some have claimed comes more
readily for women readers[39] and which many continue to see as central
to feminist analysis[40]—is again in many ways a feature of all reading,
more readily pursued and affirmed by Olsen's readers. Although there
are very few empirical investigations into the act of reading, the available research tends to show that *all* readers read from within and draw
upon their own particular contexts. In their study of the cognitive
processes involved in reading, Mary Crawford and Roger Chaffin make
the point succinctly: "Studies of the effects of background on comprehension and memory are few, but their conclusions unequivocal and
unsurprising: background does make a difference."[41] They also describe the processes by which readers' expectations—the schemata we
use to interpret and respond to what we see, what we read, what we
claim to understand—are an active and integral part of our reading
experiences:

> The studies described in this section reveal that comprehension and memory are active processes in which the external message and the internal knowledge structures of the understander interact in complex ways. Understanding a text is not simply a matter of unpacking a parcel and taking out a fixed set of information; memory is not a wax tablet on which experiences stamp their impressions. . . . The process of building a meaning, a representation, is frequently accompanied by alterations and distortions that are imposed by the nature of the schemata used to encode the information. Such alterations are not a sad failing to which humans are prone in moments of weakness, they are the essence of comprehension; they reflect the operation of schemata. Furthermore, it is schemata that allow the understander to go beyond the ideas overtly expressed by providing the elaboration, explanation, and interconnections that we call *understanding.* (10–11)

The problem, then, with focusing on the "errors" that we might identify in readings of Olsen's fiction is that we are likely to be denying the very "essence of comprehension." We are *not* merely "unpacking a parcel"; we are actively drawing together our own "knowledge structures" and the possibilities inherent in the written text with which we are engaged.

For reading Olsen's fiction, this whole process is particularly complex. This is in part because of the unusual density of the fiction itself, that compression to which so many of the reviewers, critics, and readers refer. Distinctive in themselves, especially in their compression as *short* fiction, Olsen's texts also share in the linguistic complexities of much twentieth-century fiction. As Wolfgang Iser points out, modernist fiction—and, I would add, postmodernist fiction as well, despite other differences—is much more likely to suspend *"good continuation,"* to be shaped by gaps or "blanks" in the text and thus to lead readers constantly to form and abandon perceptual images in an ongoing process.[42] Such gaps and complexities actively require the reader to *construct* a reading rather than merely be led through one.

Consider, for example, the active involvement required to draw out and reconstruct the complex history of Eva in "Tell Me a Riddle": as impoverished girl in the Russian village of Olshana, as likely victim of the pogroms to which Jewish peoples were subjected, as orator of the 1905 revolution, as prisoner in solitary confinement—and then as immigrant wife and mother, raising seven children and struggling against the constraints of class and gender. This history—like the history of Whitey in his days of active union organizing and leftist resistance or the history of Emily and her mother fighting poverty during the Depression or the history of Alva's and Helen's friendship and the cultural constraints of racism or that of Stevie at his mother's deathbed and in his grief—is not offered to us as linear and straightforward. Nor are such summaries sufficient to describe the histories we actively work to construct during our readings. What they can remind us of is precisely how nonlinear these texts are and how much they do rely on a suspension of *"good continuation"* and hence on an unusually high level of reader effort. The response of a 16-year-old high school boy exemplifies both the difficulty and the value of Olsen's stylistic complexities: " 'I found it hard to read her at first. The teacher had to explain a lot, the way she writes. But once you catch on—well, you get caught. She has this way of getting you to stop and think, and the story is so packed, you can't put it out of your head so easily' " (Coles 1989, 53).

Iser further correlates the experience of reading nonlinear texts with the experience of indeterminacy in human living: "This experience corresponds to the openness of the world, and so the serial variations constantly turn definitive, current, and given world views into mere possibilities of how the world can be experienced" (211). This response, too, seems to be borne out by readers' responses to Olsen's fiction. The students that Robert Coles describes in racially complicated circumstances are especially suggestive of how this interaction with the world might take place. For example, one black student— male and in the eleventh grade in Atlanta during the early 1960s— responded to "I Stand Here Ironing" by making "a point of letting us know that 'never before' had he so identified with people in a 'white family.' . . . [F]or a while this sturdy and athletic young man worried on that score: 'I thought to myself: what are you doing, getting yourself into her head? But I couldn't stop it from happening' " (Coles 1989, 50). The story prompted powerful memories of his childhood, provoking a further sense of interaction with the world in which he was living, and then opened onto a personal emotional response: " ' That's what happened to me when I read the story for the first time: I started crying, and I didn't know why' " (50).

I do not wish to be claiming that this particular reader's response is the response of all readers of Olsen's fiction. But I do think that it illustrates powerfully the capacity of her complex renderings of human experiences to open onto readers' experiences and even, at times, to help readers to bridge their felt differences from other people. This reader, in his anxiety that he had somehow allowed himself to "get into [a white girl's] head" and in his subsequent acknowledgment of emotional release, seems to me to be attesting to the story's capacity to transform his sense of the world in which he lived, a world in which he is explicitly forbidden entrance into a white girl's head, a world in which he is told that he has no commonalities with a white girl. Yet the story has enabled him to bridge those differences. Coles goes on to affirm the representativeness of this bridging: "Such moments of resonance across racial and sexual lines kept arising as my wife went through the essays she received from her students . . ." (Coles 1989, 50).

In my own teaching, I too have found African-American students to be especially responsive to the circumstances of "I Stand Here Ironing." Indeed, I have had several students, both black and white, initially take the story to be "about" an African-American mother and daughter. I was interested in this "error," but not terribly surprised by it. The emphasis on how appearance is culturally constructed has, in recent years, been especially central to African Americans, dismayed as is the story's narrator by the expectations that a girl "should look a chubby blonde replica of Shirley Temple."[43] And if a particular student had recently read Toni Morrison's *The Bluest Eye*, in which Shirley Temple is a painfully present icon of racially constructed notions of beauty, he or she might be especially attentive to seeing this contrast in a racial context. Furthermore, a higher proportion of African-American readers will be experientially attuned to the way in which economic constraints are particularly harsh in single-parent families and to the way in which a single mother will nonetheless provide for her family. Because these understandings are embedded in complex linguistic formations, with gaps and confusions and omissions, we *are* more likely to "make mistakes" of detail in our memories—to draw upon the knowledge structures we have developed in our own living. As Crawford and Chaffin say, "the schema fills in missing information, and later the memory trace may not distinguish" (5).

On a less complicated level, I recall with some chagrin that in my first essay on Olsen, I simply asserted that the mother's thought processes are prompted by a phone call from a school counselor.[44] My own particular schema—constructed almost certainly from memories of how public schools function and what sorts of interactions seemed to me most likely—had filled in the unnamed prompting for the mother's monologue. I confess to a sense of relief when I eventually discovered that, indeed, Olsen's preliminary planning for the story indicates that she, too, had in mind a phone call from a counselor[45]; but such a discovery is not really pertinent. What is more pertinent is Olsen's current disavowal that "it doesn't matter"—which was her response when I asked her what she had in mind. Indeed, it *doesn't* matter, so long as the reader's schemata for memory and information do not *falsify* other necessary understandings embedded in the story.

Students, for example, who have on first reading speculated that the "you" might be the missing father of the story—and I have talked with students about such preliminary speculation—*do* need to return to the story and seek out the references that situate the "you" as someone from Emily's current school environment, someone "official" and wanting to be "helpful," but not really a part of Emily's more complex personal context. To test such possible interpretive conflicts we need to return to the rich verbal constructs that are the stories themselves, because each story has a distinctive life to which we owe our most careful "comprehension." But we never can totally separate those verbal constructs from our readings of them—nor should we really wish to do so. Reading, by its very definition, is an *active* interaction between that text, what Crawford and Chaffin call "the external message," and our own situatedness, "the internal knowledge structures of the understander."

More significant knowledge structures that we readers bring to these stories, then, will be those that derive from our particular "hot and human" interests, which draw us to the stories: our lives as women and children and working people; our commitments as feminists and as political activists. As I have said, these are the lives and commitments that many readers identify as central to their initial interest in Olsen's fiction. It is, in fact, entirely possible that those students who projected the "you" as the absent father did so out of just such human concerns: for example, an experiential schema that yearned for the presence of the missing father, having noted that he early disappeared and left no trace. I did not, in fact, ask them if this schema derived from an experiential response. Nor do I know for certain the experiential schemata that may have led students to hypothesize an African-American family in the story. But I do know that my own driven concern with the story derived from a powerful need to find textual resources by which I might understand the economic and societal constraints that operate on the care a mother can give to her children, particularly when she is single. I know, too, that this experiential need gave greater resonance to my understanding of the "they" who enact the constraints within the story—and greater attunement to the underlying and pervasive love that the mother expresses for Emily. My written response was surely shaped by my own critical assumptions at the moment of writing; my reading response was equally surely shaped by my own life engagements at the moment of reading.

Finally, I want to emphasize a dimension of our situatedness that has been implicit in the reading experiences and "distortions" that I have been discussing: the doubleness of the interaction between text and reader. Mikhail Bakhtin describes this as a general feature of reader involvement: "The work and the world represented in it enter the real world and enrich it, and the real world enters the work and its world as part of the process of its creation, as well as part of its subsequent life, in a continual renewing of the work through the creative perception of listeners and readers."[46] That is, the reader brings to the text a whole range of human experiences and expectations that help to fill in the gaps, that Olsen's stories even invite us to use to fill in the gaps. But the interaction also suggests that we take the understandings of the text back to our living. One of Robert Coles's medical students spoke of the ongoing and interactive effect of reading literature such as Olsen's: "You can't forget the stories, and you think of them not only here, when you're talking about them, but in your car or when you're walking, or when you're out there doing your work. . . . Sometimes, the story I read merges with the situation I'm in . . . and it all becomes part of me" (Coles 1989, 182). So, too, with most of Olsen's readers: we bring our lives to the stories; we take the stories into our lives.

Most potently with Olsen's fiction, we take the stories to our lives as new consciousesses of human experience. We see not only the past understandings that are integral to the stories, not only the present empathies that are developed through our attentive reading. We see as well the possibilities for generating new understandings and alternative futures. As Cora Kaplan says of "I Stand Here Ironing," "The story points to what is beyond it, to a future altered by its reading, lived by the reader" (Kaplan, n.p.). Similarly, I have had students tell me that the story drew them into it in such a way that they felt a responsibility to engage in changing the social circumstances that it traces. In all of Olsen's fiction, the reader is drawn toward such commitments and toward the reciprocity required of an actively engaged human subject.

From these understandings, developed through thoughtful and responsive reading, Tillie Olsen's readers, then, become a part of that larger community that Patrocinio Schweickart suggests that feminist critics seek: "to connect not only with the author of the original text, but also with a community of readers."[47] As we develop our sense of a reading community, we renew as well our sense of participation in our own immediate historical realities, our own interactions with a range of human communities. Not by messages from the texts but by alertness to them, we realize in our own contexts the harms done to human beings and the struggles against those harms. In our own time when, as Olsen says, "the vision of full humanhood is battered, scorned, deemed 'unrealistic,' "[48] we can—as attentive readers—nonetheless identify ways to participate in our own claims on "hope" and "belief," our own struggles toward fruitful social change. This renewed sense of our own participation is the real impact of our reading partnership with Tillie Olsen.

Notes to Part 3

1. Louis Montrose, "Professing the Renaissance: The Poetics and Politics of Culture," in *The New Historicism*, ed. H. A. Veeser (New York: Routledge, 1989), 24.

2. Lary May, introduction to *Recasting America: Culture and Politics in the Age of Cold War*, ed. Lary May (Chicago: University of Chicago Press, 1989), 9. Compare Dominick LaCapra's warning about positivism and formalism: "one reducing texts or artifacts to their narrowly constative dimension as documents in the reconstitution of 'contexts' or 'social realities,' while the other becomes fixated on the internal play of the performative dimension of texts isolated from the 'external' (or externalized) contexts of their writing, reception, and critical reading." See *Soundings in Critical Theory* (Ithaca: Cornell University Press, 1989), 17. Vincent B. Leitch's historical analysis of twentieth-century American criticism suggests that, although "the New Criticism was over by the late 1950s as an innovative and original School," it nonetheless "served for growing numbers of academic critics and scholars as 'normal criticism' or simply as 'criticism' for a period extending well beyond that. See *American Literary Criticism from the Thirties to the Eighties* (New York: Columbia University Press, 1988), 25.

3. Louise M. Rosenblatt, "Coda: A Performing Art," in her *Literature as Exploration* (New York: Modern Language Association, 1968), 277; hereafter cited in the text.

4. Judith Arcana, *Grace Paley's Life Stories: A Literary Biography* (Urbana: University of Illinois Press, 1993), 184; hereafter cited in the text.

5. Richard M. Elman, review of *Tell Me a Riddle, Commonweal*, 8 December 1961, 295. For an overview of early critical reception, see Abigail Martin, *Tillie Olsen*, Boise State University Western Writers Series, no. 65 (Boise, Idaho: Boise State University), 30–31.

6. William Peden, "Dilemmas of Day-to-Day Living," *New York Times Book Review*, 12 November 1961, 54.

7. "Radicals and Working Stiffs," review of *Tell Me a Riddle, Time*, 27 October 1961, 101; hereafter cited in the text.

8. Dorothy Parker, review of *Tell Me a Riddle, Esquire*, June 1962, 65.

9. Irving Howe, "Stories: New, Old, and Sometimes Good," *New Republic*, 13 November 1961, 22; hereafter cited in the text.

10. Leon Wieseltier, "Remembering Irving Howe (1920–93)," *New York Times Book Review*, 23 May 1993, 31.

11. William Van O'Connor, "The Short Stories of Tillie Olsen," *Studies in Short Fiction* 1 (Fall 1963): 21; hereafter cited in the text.

12. Elizabeth Fisher, "The Passion of Tillie Olsen," *Nation* 10 (April 1972): 472.

13. Sandy Boucher, "Tillie Olsen: The Weight of Things Unsaid," *Ms*, September 1974, 26; hereafter cited in the text.

14. Linda Heinlein Kirschner, "I Stand Here Ironing, by Tillie Olsen," *English Journal* 65, no. 1 (January 1976): 59.

15. Sally Cunneen, "Tillie Olsen: Storyteller of Working America," *Christian Century*, 21 May 1980, 570.

16. Nancy Huse, "Re-reading Tillie Olsen's 'O Yes,' " in *The Critical Response to Tillie Olsen*, ed. Kay Hoyle Nelson and Nancy Huse (New York: Greenwood Press, 1994), 196–205.

17. Vicki L. Sommer, "The Writings of Tillie Olsen: A Social Work Perspective," in *Tillie Olsen Week: The Writer and Society, 21–26 March 1983*, sponsored by Augustana College, Rock Island, Ill., et al., 75.

18. Julia E. Connelly, "The Whole Story," in *Fictive Ills: Literary Perspectives on Wounds and Diseases*, vol. 9. of *Literature and Medicine*, ed. Peter W. Graham and Elizabeth Sewell (Baltimore: Johns Hopkins University Press, 1990), 151.

19. Robert Coles, *The Call of Stories: Teaching and the Moral Imagination* (Boston: Houghton Mifflin Company, 1989), passim; hereafter cited in the text.

20. Tillie Olsen, *Silences* (1978; New York: Delta/Seymour Lawrence, 1979), 202, compare 32; hereafter cited in the text.

21. Susan Rubin Suleiman, "Writing and Motherhood" in *The (M)other Tongue*, ed. Shirley Nelson Garner, Claire Kuhane, and Madelon Sprengnether (Ithaca: Cornell University Press, 1985), 356.

22. Annie Gottlieb, "Feminists Look at Motherhood," *Mother Jones*, November 1976, 51.

23. Annette Bennington McElhiney, "Alternative Responses to Life in Tillie Olsen's Work," *Frontiers* 2 (Spring 1977): 76–91.

24. Joanne S. Frye, " 'I Stand Here Ironing': Motherhood as Experience and Metaphor," *Studies in Short Fiction* 18 (Summer 1981): 287–92; hereafter cited in the text. Helen Pike Bauer, " 'A Child of Anxious, Not Proud, Love': Mother and Daughter in Tillie Olsen's 'I Stand Here Ironing,' " in *Mother Puzzles: Daughters and Mothers in Contemporary American Literature*, ed. Mickey Pearlman (Westport, Conn.: Greenwood Publishing, 1989), 35–40; hereafter cited in the text.

25. Bonnie Lyons, "Tillie Olsen: The Writer as a Jewish Woman," *Studies in American Jewish Literature* 5 (1986): 89.

26. John Clayton, "Grace Paley and Tillie Olsen: Radical Jewish Humanists," *Response: A Contemporary Jewish Review* 46 (1984): 37.

27. Selma Burkom and Margaret Williams, "De-Riddling Tillie Olsen's Writings," *San José Studies* 2 (February 1976): 65; hereafter cited in the text. Compare in the same period Ellen Cronan Rose's insistence on Olsen's art as distinct from her politics, on her humanism rather than her feminism. See "Limning: Or Why Tillie Writes," *Hollins Critic* 13, no. 2 (April 1976): 1–13.

28. Deborah Rosenfelt, "From the Thirties: Tillie Olsen and the Radical Tradition," *Feminist Studies* 7, no. 3 (Fall 1981): 372; hereafter cited in the text. Erika Duncan, "Coming of Age in the Thirties: A Portrait of Tillie Olsen," *Book Forum* 6, no. 1–2 (1982): 207–22.

29. Compare also Catharine R. Stimpson, "Tillie Olsen: Witness as Servant," *Polit: A Journal for Literature and Politics* 1 (Fall 1977): 1–12, and Cora Kaplan, introduction to *Tell Me a Riddle* (London: Virago, 1980); hereafter cited in the text.

30. Elaine Neil Orr, *Tillie Olsen and a Feminist Spiritual Vision* (Jackson: University Press of Mississippi,) 1987; Mickey Pearlman and Abby H. P. Werlock, *Tillie Olsen* (Boston: Twayne Publishers, 1991; Mara Faulkner, *Protest and Possibility in the Writing of Tillie Olsen* (Charlottesville: University Press of Virginia, 1993); Constance Coiner, " 'No One's Private Ground': A Bakhtinian Reading of Tillie Olsen's *Tell Me a Riddle*," *Feminist Studies* 18, no.2 (Summer 1992): 257–81. Each of these sources hereafter cited in the text.

31. See in part 2 of this volume conversation 5; conversations hereafter cited in the text.

32. Personal communication, Soquel, California, summer 1988. See also Boucher: "Tillie tells us how, after the story was published, men would call her on the phone to ask, 'Where's Whitey?' They knew him. He was them" (28).

33. See conversation 1. Compare Olsen's statement in an interview with Linda Park-Fuller: "it is the greatest tribute to the writer . . . when the people

who read you either really respond to it with the life of their reading or when, even more, they want to give it life in a different medium, in their own medium. . . . The greatest of all prizes, the greatest tribute, the greatest awards are the ones that the reader or performer gives." See "An Interview with Tillie Olsen," *Literature in Performance* 4 (November 1983): 77.

34. "Tillie Olsen: From a Public Dialogue between Olsen and Marilyn Yalom, Stanford Center for Research on Women, Nov. 5, 1980 and Subsequently," in *Women Writers of the West Coast: Speaking of Their Lives and Careers*, ed. Marilyn Yalom (Stanford: Capra Press, 1983), 64.

35. Jane Silverman Van Buren, *The Modernist Madonna: Semiotics of the Maternal Metaphor* (Bloomington: Indiana University Press, 1989), 166. Compare with Pearlman and Werlock, who also cite the false attribution of the two abortions as evidence of misreading (xii).

36. Shelley Fisher Fishkin, "The Borderlands of Culture: Writing by W. E. B. DuBois, James Agee, Tillie Olsen, and Gloria Anzaldua," in *Literary Journalism in the Twentieth Century*, ed. Norman Sims (New York: Oxford University Press, 1990), 160. Compare with Elizabeth Meese, "Deconstructing the Sexual Politic: Virginia Woolf and Tillie Olsen," in *Crossing the Double-Cross* (Chapel Hill: University of North Carolina Press, 1986); she speaks of "open invitations to the reader to participate in the text's creation" (112) and affirms Olsen's choice of form in *Silences:* "She then calls upon the reader to write the text—no longer her text, but occasioned by it and by the voices speaking through it" (110).

37. Robert Coles, "Tell Me a Riddle by Tillie Olsen," *New Republic*, 6 December 1975, 30

38. Sandra M. Gilbert, "Life Studies, or, Speech after Long Silence. Feminist Critics Today," *College English* 40, no. 8 (April 1979) : 853; hereafter cited in the text.

39. See the introduction to *Gender and Reading: Essays on Readers, Texts, and Contexts*, ed. Elizabeth A. Flynn and Patrocinio P. Schweickart (Baltimore: Johns Hopkins University Press, 1986), xxviii.

40. See, for example, Nancy K. Miller, *Getting Personal: Feminist Occasions and Other Autobiographical Acts* (New York: Routledge, 1991).

41. Mary Crawford and Roger Chaffin, "The Reader's Construction of Meaning: Cognitive Research on Gender and Comprehension," in *Gender and Reading*, 11; hereafter cited in the text.

42. Wolfgang Iser, *The Act of Reading: A Theory of Aesthetic Response* (1978; Baltimore: Johns Hopkins University Press, 1980), 186; hereafter cited in the text.

43. Tillie Olsen, *Tell Me a Riddle*, (1961/1962; New York: Delta/Seymour Lawrence, 1989), 7.

44. Pearlman and Werlock point this out (see 139n4).

Part 3

45. Tillie Olsen, "On the Writing of a Story: Tillie Olsen: Help Her to Believe," appendix to *Stanford Short Stories: 1956*, ed. Wallace Stegner and Richard Scowcroft (Stanford: Stanford University Press, 1956), 135.

46. Mikhail Bakhtin, *The Dialogical Imagination: Four Essays*, ed. Michael Holquist, trans. Caryl Emerson and Michael Holquist (Austin: University of Texas Press, 1984), 254.

47. Patrocinio Schweickart, "Reading Ourselves: Toward a Feminist Theory of Reading," in *Gender and Reading*, 56.

48. Tillie Olsen, "The '30s: A Vision of Fear and Hope," *Newsweek*, 3 January 1994, 27.

Chronology

1906–1907   Ida Beber and Samuel Lerner immigrate from Russia following the 1905 revolution.

1912 or 1913   Tillie Lerner born 14 January, second of six children, to Ida (Beber) Lerner and Samuel Lerner, Omaha, Nebraska.

1918   Moves with family from Nebraska farm to Omaha.

1925   Crosses tracks to enter Omaha Central High School, the city's academic high school.

1928   Leaves school to work full-time at various unskilled jobs, including pork trimmer in packinghouses.

1931   Joins Young Communist League (YCL); works in and tries to organize packinghouse workers in Kansas City.

1931–1932   Jailed in Kansas City for seven weeks for leafletting at packinghouse; never brought to trial. Develops pleurisy and incipient tuberculosis.

1932   Moves to Faribault, Minnesota. Daughter Karla born. Begins work on *Yonnondio*.

1933   Moves to California, working in Venice and Stockton, and eventually settling in San Francisco. Meets Jack Olsen, YCL comrade. In years following, works as hotel maid and linen checker, waitress, laundry worker, solderer of battery wires, jar capper.

1934   Continues active in YCL during the San Francisco Maritime Strike and the General Strike of 1934. Publishes poems: "I Want You Women Up North to Know" and "There Is a Lesson." Publishes essays: "The Strike" and "Thousand Dollar Vagrant." Publishes first fiction, "Iron Throat," in *Partisan Review*; this later becomes the first chapter of *Yonnondio*.

1936   Lives with Jack Olsen.

1937 Feature writer for *People's World.*

1938 Daughter Julie born.

1943 Marries Jack Olsen. Daughter Kathie born. Central in PTA's establishment of first public child care center in San Francisco.

1940s Writes occasional column for *People's World.* Serves as president of the California CIO's Women's Auxiliary and directs northern California CIO war relief. Serves as president of McKinley PTA. Writes reports and leaflets; edits PTA newsletter; active in community activities.

1948 Daughter Laurie born.

1955–1956 Receives Stanford Creative Writing Fellowship and attends Stanford University.

1956 "Help Her to Believe" appears in *Pacific Spectator.* Mother dies.

1957 "Help Her to Believe" reprinted as "I Stand Here Ironing" in *Best American Short Stories.* "Baptism" (later "O Yes") appears in *Prairie Schooner.* "Hey Sailor, What Ship?" appears in *New Campus Writing No. 2.*

1959 Receives Ford Foundation Grant in Literature.

1960 "Tell Me a Riddle" appears in *New World Writing No. 16.*

1961 "Tell Me a Riddle" receives first prize O. Henry Award for Best Story of the Year. First book, *Tell Me a Riddle,* collection of four pieces of short fiction. In its 29 December 1961 issue, *Time* names *Tell Me a Riddle* one of the 10 best books of the year.

1962–1964 Fellow at Radcliffe Institute.

1965 "Silences in Literature," talk given at Radcliffe in 1962, appears in *Harper's Magazine*; part of ongoing involvement in the women's movement.

1965 Makes home in St. Francis Square, cooperative housing "dedicated to the ideal that all races, religions, and beliefs can live together in harmony."

1967 National Endowment for the Arts, Grant in Literature.

1969–1970   Professor and writer-in-residence at Amherst College. In subsequent years serves as professor, lecturer, writer-in-residence at Stanford University; Massachusetts Institute of Technology; University of Massachusetts, Boston; University of California, San Diego; University of Minnesota.

1970   "Requa" appears in *Iowa Review*.

1971   "Requa" reprinted as "Requa I" in *Best American Short Stories*. Gives talk at the Modern Language Association, "One Out of Twelve: Writers Who Are Women in Our Century."

1972–1973   Develops and publishes "Tillie Olsen's Reading List" in *Women's Studies Newsletter* on topics related especially to women's lives and social change. Spends five months at MacDowell Colony to work on rediscovered manuscript of *Yonnondio*; also writes "A Biographical Interpretation," which appears as afterword in Rebecca Harding Davis's *Life in the Iron Mills*, the first of the Feminist Press women's reprints; part of Olsen's extended work with the press to publish important and otherwise unavailable works by women.

1974   Publishes *Yonnondio: From the Thirties*. Father dies.

1975   Award for distinguished contribution to American literature from the American Academy and National Institute of Arts and Letters.

1975–1976   Receives John Guggenheim Fellowship.

1978   Publishes *Silences*.

1979   Receives honorary degree, Doctor of Arts and Letters, University of Nebraska. Subsequently receives five other honorary degrees.

1980   International Visiting Scholar to Norway.

1984   Publishes *Mother to Daughter: Daughter to Mother: A Feminist Press Daybook and Reader*, a collection of personally selected writings about mothers and daughters; includes "Dream-Vision," Olsen's essay about her own mother; "Dream-Vision" also appears in *Ms*.

1989   Jack Olsen dies.

1994 Receives Rea Award for advancing the art of short-story writing. Issues new editions of *Tell Me a Riddle* and *Yonnondio*, the latter including never-before-published material.

Selected Bibliography

Primary Sources

Short Fiction in Collection

Tell Me a Riddle. Philadelphia: Lippincott, 1961. Reprinted, with stories in order of writing: New York: Dell, 1962; New York: Delta/Seymour Lawrence, 1989. Reprinted, with a new introduction by John Leonard: New York: Delta/Seymour Lawrence, 1994. Includes "I Stand Here Ironing," originally published as "Help Her to Believe" in *Pacific Spectator* 10 (1956): 55–63; "Hey Sailor, What Ship?" originally published in *New Campus Writing No. 2*, edited by Nolan Miller (New York: Putnam's, 1957), 199–213; "O Yes," originally published as "Baptism" in *Prairie Schooner* 31 (1957): 70–80; and "Tell Me a Riddle," originally published in *New World Writing 16*, edited by Stewart Richardson and Corlies M. Smith (Philadelphia: Lippincott, 1960), 11–57.

Uncollected Short Stories

"Not You I Weep For." In *First Words: Earliest Writing from Favorite Contemporary Authors*, edited by Paul Mandelbaum, 380–405. Chapel Hill, N.C.: Algonquin Books, 1993.

"Requa." *Iowa Review* 1 (Summer 1970): 54–74. Reprinted as "Requa I" in *The Best American Short Stories 1971*, edited by Martha Foley and David Burnett, 237–65. Boston: Houghton Mifflin, 1971.

Novel

Yonnondio: From the Thirties. New York: Delacorte/Seymour Lawrence 1974. Republished with the addition of three never-before-published fragments: New York: Delta/Seymour Lawrence, 1994.

Poems

"I Want You Women Up North to Know" (Tillie Lerner). *Partisan* 1 (March 1934): 4. Reprinted in *Feminist Studies* 7 (Fall 1981): 367–69. Also reprinted [by Tillie Olsen] in *Writing Red: An Anthology of American Women Writers*,

1930–1940, edited by Charlotte Nekola and Paula Rabinowitz, 179–81. New York: Feminist Press, 1987.

"There Is a Lesson" (Tillie Lerner). *Partison* 1 (April 1934): 4. Reprinted in *San Jose Studies* 2 (1976): 70.

Nonfiction

"A Biographical Interpretation." Afterword to *Life in the Iron Mills* by Rebecca Harding Davis, 69–174. Old Westbury, N.Y.: Feminist Press, 1972. Reprinted in *Silences* as "Rebecca Harding Davis: Her Life and Times," 47–118.

"Dream-Vision." In *Mother to Daughter, Daughter to Mother: A Feminist Press Daybook and Reader*, selected and shaped by Tillie Olsen, 261–64. Old Westbury, N.Y.: Feminist Press, 1984. Reprinted in *Ms.*, December 1984, 136.

Foreword. In *Black Women Writers at Work*, edited by Claudia Tate, ix–xi. New York: Continuum, 1983.

Mother to Daughter, Daughter to Mother: A Feminist Press Daybook and Reader. Selected and shaped by Tillie Olsen. Old Westbury, N.Y.: Feminist Press, 1984.

"Mothers and Daughters." Prefatory essay with Julie Olsen Edwards. In *Mothers and Daughters: That Special Quality, an Exploration in Photography*, edited by Estelle Jussim. New York: Aperture Foundation, 1987.

"On the Writing of a Story: Tillie Olsen: Help Her to Believe." Appendix to *Stanford Short Stories: 1956*, edited by Wallace Stegner and Richard Scowcroft, 134–36. Stanford, Calif.: Stanford University Press, 1956.

Personal statement included in "Tillie Olsen." In *First Drafts, Last Drafts: Forty Years of the Creative Writing Program at Stanford University*, prepared by William McPheron with the assistance of Amor Towles, 63–65. Stanford: Stanford University Libraries, 1989.

Silences. 1978. Reprint. New York: Delta/Seymour Lawrence, 1979.

"The Strike" (Tillie Lerner). *Partisan Review* 1 (September–October 1934): 3–9. Reprinted in *Years of Protest: A Collection of American Writings of the 1930s*, edited by Jack Salzman, 138–44. New York: Pegasus, 1967. Also reprinted in *Writing Red*, 245–51.

"The '30s: A Vision of Fear and Hope." *Newsweek*, 3 January 1994, 26–27.

"Thousand-Dollar Vagrant" (Tillie Lerner). *New Republic*, 29 August 1934, 67–69. Reprinted in *Years of Protest: A Collection of American Writings of the 1930s*, edited by Jack Salzman, 67–69. New York: Pegasus, 1967.

"The Word Made Flesh." Prefatory essay to *Critical Thinking, Critical Writing*, 1–8. Iowa, 1984.

Secondary Sources (On The Short Fiction)

Banks, Joanne Troutman. "Death Labours." In *Fictive Ills: Literary Perspectives on Wounds and Diseases*. Vol. 9 of *Literature and Medicine*, edited by Peter W. Graham and Elizabeth Sewall, 162–71. Baltimore: Johns Hopkins University Press, 1990. Reprinted in *The Critical Response to Tillie Olsen*, 158–68.

Barr, Marleen. "Tillie Olsen." In *Dictionary of Literary Biography*, vol. 28, 196–203. Detroit: Gale Research Co., 1984.

Bauer, Helen Pike. " 'A Child of Anxious, Not Proud, Love': Mother and Daughter in Tillie Olsen's 'I Stand Here Ironing.' " In *Mother Puzzles: Daughters and Mothers in Contemporary American Literature*, edited by Mickey Pearlman, 35–40. Westport, Conn.: Greenwood Publishing, 1989.

Bonetti, Kay. Tillie Olsen, interviewed in San Francisco, Calif. March 1981. American Audio Prose Library, cassette tape.

Boucher, Sandy. "Tillie Olsen: The Weight of Things Unsaid." *Ms.*, September 1974, 26–30.

Burkom, Selma, and Margaret Williams. "De-Riddling Tillie Olsen's Writings." *San Jose Studies* 2 (February 1976): 64–83. Reprinted in *The Critical Response to Tillie Olsen*, 33–53.

Clayton, John. "Grace Paley and Tillie Olsen: Radical Jewish Humanists." *Response: A Contemporary Jewish Review* 46 (1984): 37–52.

Coiner, Constance. *Better Red: The Writing and Resistance of Tillie Olsen and Meridel Le Sueur*. New York: Oxford University Press, 1995.

———. " 'No One's Private Ground': A Bakhtinian Reading of Tillie Olsen's *Tell Me a Riddle*." *Feminist Studies* 18, No. 2 (Summer 1992): 257–81. Reprinted in *The Critical Response to Tillie Olsen*, 169–95. Also reprinted in *Listening to Silences: New Essays in Feminist Criticism*, 71–94.

Coles, Robert. *The Call of Stories: Teaching and the Moral Imagination*. Boston: Houghton Mifflin Company, 1989.

Connelly, Julia. "The Whole Story." In *Fictive Ills: Literary Perspectives on Wounds and Diseases*. Vol. 9 of *Literature and Medicine*, edited by Peter W. Graham and Elizabeth Sewall, 150–61. Baltimore: Johns Hopkins University Press, 1990.

Craft, Brigette Wilds. "Tillie Olsen: A Bibliography of Reviews and Criticism, 1931–1991." *Bulletin of Bibliography* 50, no.3 (September 1993): 189–205.

The Critical Response to Tillie Olsen. Edited by Kay Hoyle Nelson and Nancy Huse. New York: Greenwood Press, 1994.

Culver, Sara. "Extending the Boundaries of the Ego: Eva in 'Tell Me a Riddle.' " *Midwestern Miscellany* 10 (1982): 38–48.

Cunneen, Sally. "Tillie Olsen: Storyteller of Working America." *Christian Century*, 21 May 1980, 570–73.

DeShazer, Mary K. " 'Tell Me a Riddle.' " In *Tillie Olsen Week: The Writer and Society, 21–26 March 1983*, 20–32.

Duncan, Erika. "Coming of Age in the Thirties: A Portrait of Tillie Olsen." *Book Forum: An International Transdisciplinary Quarterly* 4 (1982): 207–22. Reprinted in Duncan's *Unless Soul Clap Its Hands: Portraits and Passages*, 31–57. New York: Schocken Books, 1984.

Faulkner, Mara. *Protest and Possibility in the Writing of Tillie Olsen.* Charlottesville: University Press of Virginia, 1993.

Frye, Joanne S. " 'I Stand Here Ironing': Motherhood as Experience and Metaphor." *Studies in Short Fiction* 18 (Summer 1981): 287–92. Reprinted in *The Critical Response to Tillie Olsen*, 128–33.

———. "Tillie Olsen: Probing the Boundaries between Text and Context." *Journal of Narrative and Life History* 3 (1993): 255–68.

Gardiner, Judith Kegan. "A Wake for Mother: The Maternal Deathbed in Women's Fiction." *Feminist Studies* 4 (June 1978): 146–65.

Gelfant, Blanche H. "After Long Silence: Tillie Olsen's 'Requa.' " *Studies in American Fiction* 12 (Spring 1984): 61–69. Reprinted in Gelfant's *Women Writing in America*, 59–70. Hanover, N.H.: University Press of New England, 1984. Also reprinted in *The Critical Response to Tillie Olsen*, 206–15.

Gottlieb, Annie. "Feminists Look at Motherhood." *Mother Jones*, November 1976, 51–53.

Huse, Nancy. "Re-Reading Tillie Olsen's 'O Yes.' " In *The Critical Response to Tillie Olsen*, 196–205.

Jacobs, Naomi M. "Earth, Air, Fire, and Water in 'Tell Me a Riddle.' " *Studies in Short Fiction* 23 (Fall 1986): 401–6.

———. "Olsen's 'O Yes': Alva's Vision as Childbirth Account." *Notes on Contemporary Literature* 16 (January 1986): 7–8. Reprinted in *The Critical Response to Tillie Olsen*, 134–35.

Johnson, Sally H. "Silence and Song: The Structure and Imagery of Tillie Olsen's 'Tell Me a Riddle.' " In *Tillie Olsen Week: The Writer and Society, 21–26 March 1983*, 33–45.

Jones, Beverly. "The Dynamics of Marriage and Motherhood." In *Sisterhood Is Powerful*, edited by Robin Morgan, 49–67. New York: Vintage Books, 1970.

Kamel, Rose Yalow. "Literary Foremothers and Writers' Silences: Tillie Olsen's Autobiographical Fiction." *Melus* 12, no. 3 (Fall 1985): 55–72. Reprinted in revised form as "Riddles and Silences: Tillie Olsen's Autobiographical Fiction." In Kamel's *Aggravating the Conscience: Jewish-American Literary Mothers in the Promised Land*, 81–114. New York: Peter Lang Publishing, 1988.

Kaplan, Cora. Introduction to *Tell Me a Riddle*. London: Virago, 1980.

Kirschner, Linda Heinlein. " 'I Stand Here Ironing.' " *English Journal* 65 (January 1976): 58–59.

Listening to Silences: New Essays in Feminist Criticism. Edited by Elaine Hedges and Shelley Fisher Fishkin. New York: Oxford University Press, 1994.

Lyons, Bonnie. "Tillie Olsen: The Writer as Jewish Woman." *Studies in American Jewish Literature* 5 (1986): 89–102. Reprinted in *The Critical Response to Tillie Olsen*, 144–57.

McAlpin, Sara. "Mothers in Tillie Olsen's Stories." In *Tillie Olsen Week: The Writer and Society, 21–26 March 1983*, 46–58.

McCormack, Kathleen. "Song as Transcendence in the Works of Tillie Olsen." In *Tillie Olsen Week: The Writer and Society, 21–26 March 1983*, 59–69.

McElhiney, Annette Bennington. "Alternative Responses to Life in Tillie Olsen's Work." *Frontiers* 2 (Spring 1977): 76–91.

Manning, Gerald F. "Fiction and Aging: 'Ripeness is All.' " *Canadian Journal on Aging/La Revue Canadienne de Vieillissement* 8, no. 2 (Summer 1989): 157–63.

Martin, Abigail. *Tillie Olsen*. No. 65 in Western Writers Series. Boise, Idaho: Boise State University Press, 1984.

Middlebrook, Diane. "Circle of Women Artists: Tillie Olsen and Anne Sexton at the Radcliffe Institute." In *Listening to Silences*, 17–22.

Mintz, Jacqueline A. "The Myth of the Jewish Mother in Three Jewish, American, Female Writers." *Centennial Review* 22 (1978): 346–55.

Niehus, Edward L., and Teresa Jackson. "Polar Stars, Pyramids, and 'Tell Me a Riddle.' " *American Notes and Queries* 24 (January–February 1986): 77–83. Reprinted in *The Critical Response to Tillie Olsen*, 136–43.

Nilsen, Helge Normann. "Tillie Olsen's 'Tell Me a Riddle': The Political Theme." *Etudes Anglaises: Grande-Bretagne, Etats-Unis* 37 (April–June 1984): 163–69.

O'Connor, William Van. "The Short Stories of Tillie Olsen." *Studies in Short Fiction* 1 (Fall 1963): 21–25.

Olsen, Violet. "The Writer and Society." In *Tillie Olsen Week: The Writer and Society, 21–26 March 1983*, 70–74.

Orr, Elaine Neil. "Rethinking the Father: Maternal Recursions in Tillie Olsen's 'Requa.' " In *The Critical Response to Tillie Olsen*, 216–28.

———. *Tillie Olsen and a Feminist Spiritual Vision*. Jackson: University Press of Mississippi, 1987.

Pace, Stephanie. "Lungfish; or, Acts of Survival in Contemporary Female Writing." *Frontiers* 10 (1988): 29–33.

Park-Fuller, Linda. "Voices: Bakhtin's Heteroglossia and Polyphony, and the Performance of Narrative Literature." *Literature in Performance* 12 (November 1986): 1–12. Reprinted in *The Critical Response to Tillie Olsen*, 90–103.

———. "An Interview with Tillie Olsen." *Literature in Performance* 4 (November 1983): 75–77.

Pearlman, Mickey and Abby H. P. Werlock. *Tillie Olsen*. Boston: Twayne, 1991.

Peterman, Michael. " 'All That Happens, One Must Try to Understand': The Kindredness of Tillie Olsen's 'Tell Me a Riddle' and Margaret Laurence's

The Stone Angel." In *Margaret Laurence: An Appreciation*, edited by Christl Verduyn, 70–81. Peterborough, Canada: Broadview Press, 1988.

Pratt, Linda Ray. "The Circumstances of Silence: Literary Representations and Tillie Olsen's Omaha Past." In *The Critical Response to Tillie Olsen*, 229–43.

Rhodes, Carolyn, and Ernest Rhodes. "Tillie Olsen." In *Dictionary of Literary Biography Yearbook, 1980*, edited by Karen L. Rood, Jean W. Ross, and Richard Ziegfield, 290–97. Detroit: Gale Research, 1981.

Rohrberger, Mary (revised by Louise M. Stone). "Tillie Olsen." In *Critical Survey of Short Fiction*, edited by Frank N. Magill, 1812–17. Englewood Cliffs, N.J.: Salem Press, 1993.

Rose, Ellen Cronan. "Limning: or, Why Tillie Writes." *Hollins Critic* 13 (April 1976): 1–13. Reprinted in *The Critical Response to Tillie Olsen*, 118–27.

Rosenfelt, Deborah. "Divided against Herself." *Moving On*, April–May 1980, 15–23.

———. "From the Thirties: Tillie Olsen and the Radical Tradition." *Feminist Studies* 7 (Fall 1981): 371–406. Reprinted in *Feminist Criticism and Social Change: Sex, Class, and Race in Literature and Culture*, edited by Rosenfelt and Judith Newton, 216–48. New York: Methuen, 1985. Also reprinted in *The Critical Response to Tillie Olsen*, 54–89.

———. Introduction to *"Tell Me a Riddle": Tillie Olsen*. Edited by Rosenfelt. In the series Women Writers: Texts and Contexts. New Brunswick, N.J.: Rutgers University Press, forthcoming.

———. "Rereading *Tell Me a Riddle* in the Age of Deconstruction." In *Listening to Silences*, 49–70.

Rubin, Naomi. "A Riddle of History for the Future." *Sojourner*, July 1983, 1, 4, 18.

Schwartz, Helen J. "Tillie Olsen." In *American Women Writers*, edited by Lina Mainiero and Langdon Lynne Faust, vol. 3, 303–5. New York: Ungar, 1981.

Sommer, Vicki L. "The Writings of Tillie Olsen: A Social Work Perspective." In *Tillie Olsen Week: The Writer and Society, 21–26 March 1983*, 75–87.

Stimpson, Catharine R. "Tillie Olsen: Witness as Servant." *Polit: A Journal for Literature and Politics* 1 (Fall 1977): 1–12. Reprinted in *Where the Meanings Are: Feminism and Cultural Spaces*, 67–76. New York: Methuen, 1988.

Tillie Olsen Week: The Writer and Society, 21–26 March 1983. Sponsored by Augustana College, Rock Island, Ill.; Marycrest College, Davenport, Iowa; St. Ambrose College, Davenport, Iowa; Scott Community College, Bettendorf, Iowa.

Trensky, Anne. "The Unnatural Silences of Tillie Olsen." *Studies in Short Fiction*, 27 (Fall 1990): 509–16.

Van Buren, Jane Silverman. *The Modernist Madonna: Semiotics of the Maternal Metaphor*. Bloomington: Indiana University Press, 1989.

Wolfe, Kathy. " 'Coming to Writing' through the Impressionistic Fiction of Tillie Olsen." *Midwestern Miscellany* 21 (1993): 57–67.

Yalom, Marilyn. "Tillie Olsen." In *Women Writers of the West Coast: Speaking of Their Lives and Careers*, edited by Yalom. Santa Barbara, Calif.: Capra, 1983.

Index

African Americans, 56–57;
community among, 61; friends of
Olsen's as source for "O Yes,"
158–60, 161–62; readers who are,
204–5; and religion, 61, 62,
64–70, 160–61. *See also* Civil
Rights movement; Race; Racism
Alcoholism, 152. *See also*
Drunkenness
Alva's dream vision (in "O Yes"),
61, 68, 69, 71, 122, 158
Amherst College, 178
Anticommunism, 82. *See also*
McCarthyism
Arcana, Judith, 187, 190
Atheism, 79, 161
Audience, for "I Stand Here
Ironing," 24–25, 147. *See also*
Readers
Aural quality of Olsen's language,
117, 120, 180
Author, concept of, 125n9
Autobiographical roots: for "Hey
Sailor, What Ship?" 151–52; for
"I Stand Here Ironing," 20–22,
159; for "O Yes," 64–65; for
Olsen's fiction, explored in
conversation, 141–83

Bakhtin, Mikhail, 13–15, 127n25, 207
Balzac, Honoré de, 15
Barthes, Roland: "The Death of the
Author," 125n9
Bauer, Helen Pike, 193
Belief: vs. cynicism in the fifties,
75–76, 167, 169–72; as Olsen's
heritage, 167, 169–72; persistence
of, in "Tell Me a Riddle,"
97–100

*Best American Short Stories of 1971,
The,* 101
Bonus march of 1932, 109, 178
Boucher, Sandy, 190–91
Bund, 76–77, 166, 173
Burkom, Selma, 194

Call-and-response, in "O Yes,"
69–70, 71
Calvary Baptist Church (Omaha,
Nebraska), 8, 61, 158
Cemeteries: in "Requa I," 107–8;
Yurok, 177
Chaffin, Roger, 202, 205, 206
Chaplin, Charlie, 38
Character: complexity of, 16, 31–32,
41–47; as compound 65, 78–79,
160; protagonist not single, 16,
89–91; readers' involvement in
constructing history of, 203–4
Children: differing perceptions of,
49–50, 150–51; knowledge of
through parenting, 27, 31, 43–44,
50; in relationships with men,
153. *See also* Parental insight
China, revolution in, 152
Circumstances: as central concept
for Olsen, 8, 194; of Olsen's
writing in general, 7–10, 15,
141–43; of writing "Hey Sailor,
What Ship?" 51–53; of writing
"Ironing," 143–46; of writing "O
Yes," 156–57; of writing "Requa
I," 104–5; of writing "Tell Me a
Riddle," 88–89
Civil Rights movement, 56, 57, 60,
61, 78, 152, 154, 157, 160–63
Class: in "Hey Sailor, What Ship?"
52; in "O Yes," 58–59; in "Requa

Index

Class (*cont.*)
  I," 110–11, 113–14, 180–81;
    shaping character of for Olsen,
    162–64; as source of writing, 4–6
Clayton, John, 194
Cobb, Jonathan, 113
Cognitive psychology and reading,
    126n23, 202–3
Coiner, Constance, 16, 195, 199
Cold War, 39, 57, 76, 148, 170
Coles, Robert, 192, 201, 204–5, 207
Collage technique, in "Tell Me a
    Riddle," 93–94
Communist party: addressed in
    literary criticism of Olsen's work,
    194; Olsen's membership in, 56,
    79; U.S. membership in, 78,
    133nn.67, 71, 169. *See also*
    McCarthyism; Young Communist
    League
Community, importance of: in "Hey
    Sailor, What Ship?" 46, 52,
    153–54; in "O Yes," 55–66,
    73–74, 154, 159–60
Connelly, Julia, 192
Crawford, Mary, 202, 205–206
"Crown 'n Deep," 46–47, 49, 51.
    See also El Ultimo Adiós
Culture: ideologies of, as source of
    interpretation, 12; as multiple, 13;
    readers as participants in, 17, 18
Cunneen, Sally, 191–92
Cynicism: as cultural context for
    writing "O Yes," 163; as cultural
    context for writing "Tell Me a
    Riddle," 78–82, 167, 169–72;
    rejected in "Tell Me a Riddle,"
    81, 97–98
Czarist Russia, 8, 76–77, 171

Davis, Rebecca Harding, *Life in the
    Iron Mills*, 4
Debs, Eugene, 4, 163
De Lauretis, Teresa, 16
Depression, the: in "I Stand Here
    Ironing," 19; in "Requa I," 102,
    109–10, 178

Dialogical form: of "Hey Sailor,
    What Ship?" 52; of "I Stand Here
    Ironing," 19, 26, 31–32. *See also*
    Dialogue; Narrative form;
    Polyphony
Dialogue: in "Hey Sailor, What
    Ship?" 48–49, 51–52; in "O Yes,"
    70–71; in "Tell Me a Riddle,"
    94–95. *See also* Dialogical form
Dickinson, Emily, 15, 123
Dinkin, Seevya. *See* Seevya
Donne, John, 153
Drabble, Margaret, 3
Drugs, 152
Drunkenness, in "Hey Sailor, What
    Ship?" 41, 43, 47. *See also*
    Alcoholism
DuBois, W. E. B.: *Souls of Black
    Folk*, 166
Duncan, Erika, 194

Education, public: increasingly
    available in the 1950s, 170; in "O
    Yes," 57–59
Eggan, Jack, 54, 154–55
El Ultimo Adiós, 44, 151. *See also*
    "Crown 'n Deep"
Ermath, Elizabeth, 12
Essentialism, motherhood and, 87–88
Experience: as basis for reading,
    197–208; inseparable from
    language, 10–14, 18, 63–64;
    understanding through reading
    fiction, 3

Family: importance of in Olsen's
    fiction, 18; in the 1950s, 35,
    38–39, 48; portrayal of in "Hey
    Sailor, What Ship?" 45, 150–51;
    portrayal of in "O Yes," 62–63; as
    source of narrative voice in "Hey
    Sailor, What Ship?" 47–54; as
    source of narrative voice in "O
    Yes," 70
Faribault, Minnesota, 104, 165
Father tongue, 118, 122
Faulkner, Mara, 25, 195, 201
FBI, 38, 60, 157

226

Index

The Author

Joanne S. Frye is professor of English at The College of Wooster, Wooster, Ohio, where she was instrumental in developing the women's studies program, which she chaired for seven years; she has also chaired the English Department. Her first book was *Living Stories, Telling Lives: Women and the Novel in Contemporary Experience* (1986), which won the Alice and Edith Hamilton Prize. She has written articles on such writers as Virginia Woolf, Gail Godwin, and Maxine Hong Kingston, and on issues in feminist literary criticism and cultural criticism.

The Editor

Gordon Weaver earned his Ph.D. in English and creative writing at the University of Denver and is a professor of English at Oklahoma State University. He is the author of several novels, including *Count a Lonely Cadence, Give Him a Stone, Circling Byzantium,* and most recently *The Eight Corners of the World.* His short stories are collected in *The Entombed Man of Thule, Such Waltzing Was Not Easy, Getting Serious, Morality Play,* and *A World Quite Round.* Recognition of his fiction includes the St. Lawrence Award for Fiction (1973), two National Endowment for the Arts fellowships (1974 and 1989), and the O. Henry First Prize (1979). He edited *The American Short Story, 1945–1980: A Critical History* and is currently editor of the *Cimarron Review.* Married and the father of three daughters, he lives in Stillwater, Oklahoma.